Other books by Michael D. Yapko

Trancework: An Introduction to the
Practice of Clinical Hypnosis

When Living Hurts: Directives for Treating Depression

Hypnosis and the Treatment of Depressions

Free Yourself from Depression

Brief Therapy Approaches to Treating
Anxiety and Depression (Ed.)

Suggestions of Abuse

True and False Memories
of Childhood Sexual Trauma

Michael D. Yapko, Ph.D.

Simon & Schuster
New York London Toronto Sydney Tokyo Singapore

SIMON & SCHUSTER
Rockefeller Center
1230 Avenue of the Americas
New York, New York 10020

Copyright © 1994 by Michael D. Yapko

SIMON & SCHUSTER and colophon are registered trademarks
of Simon & Schuster Inc.

Designed by Hyun Joo Kim
Manufactured in the United States of America

1   3   5   7   9   10   8   6   4   2

Library of Congress Cataloging-in-Publication Data
Yapko, Michael, D.
Suggestions of abuse : true and false memories of childhood sexual trauma /
Michael Yapko
p.   cm.
Includes bibliographical references and index.
1. Adult child sexual abuse victims. 2. False memory syndrome.
I. Title.
RC569.5.A28Y37   1994
616.85'83690651—dc20   94-333
                                                   CIP

ISBN 13: 978-1-4391-7099-1

ISBN 10: 1-4391-7099-1

With the deepest love to my wife, Diane, who is my partner in all I do, and the one person I would most like to be stranded on a tropical island with . . . and soon!

ACKNOWLEDGMENTS

A book doesn't just magically appear on a shelf one day. The final product is a result of many efforts by many people, some directly involved, some indirectly. I want to acknowledge those who helped bring this all-consuming project of mine to life. My heartfelt appreciation is extended to all of them.

My wife, Diane, has been and continues to be the light of my life, the apple of my eye, and all those other things that clearly define her as the very best. Her love, support, patience, playfulness, and overall unwavering approach to life is nothing short of inspirational.

As hectic and demanding as my professional life is, I am lucky to have the right person coordinate it all and still be fun to be around mid frenzy. Linda Griebel makes my job so much easier even though I tend to make hers difficult. She can work hard and still be soothed with a chocolate chip bagel, clearly a sign of higher consciousness.

I also share my professional life with my friends and office mates, MaryBeth Chruden, L.C.S.W., Doris Murphy, M.A., and Marian Richetta, M.A. Individually and collectively, they make going to work a lot more enjoyable.

I am especially indebted to my friends and colleagues who unselfishly lent their time and expertise to my work by reviewing my manuscript with a very critical eye. Pam Freyd, Ph.D., Miriam Iosupovici, M.S.W., Judith Johnston, Ph.D., Elizabeth Loftus, Ph.D., and Alan Scheflin, LL.M., all gave valuable feedback that had a marked influence on the content and structure of this book. I want to acknowledge Beth Loftus in particular as a source of inspiration for her vision and courage.

Acknowledgments

Throughout this project, I spoke with many different experts, including experts in memory, sexual abuse, hypnosis and suggestibility, psychotherapy, and research. Their ideas and challenges to my thinking led me to better clarify my perspectives and more deeply understand the complexity of the issues associated with the volatile subject of suggested memories. I extend my thanks to Brian Alman, Ph.D., Norma Barretta, Ph.D., Philip Barretta, M.A., Peter Bloom, M.D., David Calof, Yvonne Dolan, M.A., Dabney Ewin, M.D., Pamela Freyd, Ph.D., Stephen Gilligan, Ph.D., D. Corydon Hammond, Ph.D., Miriam Iosupovici, M.S.W, Judith Johnston, Ph.D., Richard Kluft, M.D., John Koriath, Ph.D., Stephen Lankton, A.C.S.W., Elizabeth Loftus, Ph.D., Steven Lynn, Ph.D., Bill O'Hanlon, M.S., Virginia Rutter, Alan Scheflin, LL.M., Robert Schwarz, Psy.D., Richard Simon, Ph.D., Diane Sollee, and William C. Wester II, Ed.D.

The research data were untangled with the help of two very competent people with great attitudes, Diane Bianchi and Neil Bechdel. Thank you for pulling it all together.

My literary agent, Audrey Wolf, immediately grasped the importance of this project and did a phenomenal job of making sure it would see the light of day. She has my deep and eternal gratitude.

My editor at Simon & Schuster, Becky Saletan, is a woman of remarkable clarity. She was able to patiently take "clunky" and whittle it into "clear." I appreciate all she did on behalf of this project.

I'd like to thank all those therapists who took the time to complete my questionnaires. Many went above and beyond and wrote quite a bit about their perspectives and experiences, and they helped add depth to my own.

On the personal side of it all are my family and friends. I am lucky to have a wonderfully supportive and loving family. The Yapkos and Harrises provide constant reminders that books are nice but are no substitute for a loving family. I appreciate that message very deeply.

Wendy and Richard Horowitz have been my closest friends

Acknowledgments

darn near forever. They have given their love and support in the best and worst of times—the mark of true friends. And Megan Leigh Horowitz, barely three years old at the time of this writing and the coolest little kid on the planet, is, for me, the greatest example of why childhood is *not* an expendable commodity.

Steve Roseberry and Steve Cooper were, without really realizing it, the taskmasters who kept my nose to the grindstone. They gave me the additional room to do what I needed to do. They are artists in their chosen field, and their many aesthetic contributions to my life are greatly appreciated.

Finally, I want to gratefully acknowledge the many people who shared with me their painful life stories. Individuals and families, accusers and the accused, all taught me a great deal about the responsibilities that go with my job. I appreciate their collective willingness to attempt to chart some very rough territory.

The case examples presented in this book are based on real patients and their experiences, but I have changed names and other details to protect the anonymity of the patients and their families.

It isn't so astonishing, the number of things that I can remember, as the number of things I can remember that aren't so.

—Mark Twain

CONTENTS

PREFACE

He told his wife that he simply couldn't deal with the scars remaining from Vietnam. In more than twenty years of marriage, there had been plenty of episodes that led her to believe him. One night, he went berserk, apparently in reaction to the sneakers she happened to be wearing. After he calmed down, he told her that he had been a prisoner for fifteen days after a carrier-based F-4 jet fighter on which he was navigator was shot down. His Vietcong captors wore similar sneakers when they came to the bamboo cage in which he was kept prisoner. They regularly beat and degraded him by urinating on him. He said he escaped after strangling a guard, who, incidentally, was wearing the same kind of sneakers.

He finally went to see a therapist for his problems, describing in detail his terrible experiences in Vietnam and his pervasive symptoms. He was diagnosed as suffering from "posttraumatic stress disorder" and was treated for severe depression, extreme guilt, and explosive anger. Treatment did not help quickly enough, however. Less than three years later, he ended his troubled life by inhaling carbon monoxide.

After his death, his wife attempted to get his name placed on the state's Vietnam memorial, declaring him a casualty of the war as surely as if he'd died overseas. His therapist wrote a letter in support of her petition. Only then was his background researched.

How could anyone have known that he had never been to Vietnam?

THIS IS A TRUE STORY. THE THERAPIST IN THE CASE IS ONE OF MY most highly esteemed colleagues. His perplexing client's severe symptoms were associated with such specific memories that he never questioned whether the events themselves had actually occurred. The client's wife believed him. (Wouldn't *you*?) Indeed, from all evidence, the client believed himself. How could this have happened?

Now, let's change the story a bit. Let's make the client a woman in her mid-thirties. She comes to therapy reporting terrifying nightmares, an eating disorder, and difficulties in her interpersonal relationships, especially with men. She claims to have no idea what causes her symptoms. But soon, with the therapist's help, she recovers some vague memories of sexual abuse occurring at a very early age. As her therapy progresses, the memories become much more graphic and detailed. She recalls that her parents had guests to their home, with whom they forced her to have sex. She further recalls being tortured and burned with cigarettes when she cried out for help. Her therapist encourages her to confront her parents with her newly recovered awareness. They respond with vehement—and convincing—denials.

Did the episodes of abuse actually happen? Who can say?

WHY I WROTE THIS BOOK

I am a clinical psychologist with nearly two decades' experience in working with individuals and families for whom issues of abuse are prominent. In the early 1980s, while I was writing the first edition of a textbook on clinical applications of hypnosis, every three months or so I would get a phone call from a therapist who would ask me to conduct a hypnosis session with a client in order to "find out" whether or not he or she had been molested as a child. I always declined. As I will explain, hypnosis is *not* truth serum, nor is it a lie detector—facts my colleagues seemed not to know. By the late 1980s, when I was revising *Trancework* for its second edition, I was getting such inquiries nearly *once a day!* It was apparent to me that therapists were more highly sensitized to the possibility of abuse in their clients' backgrounds than ever before. At the same time, the queries I received made it clear that they remained as underinformed and misinformed as ever about suggestion, memory, and the relationship between the two.

It seemed obvious to me that the momentum was building for therapists to rush in imprudently where they ought to tread with caution. The cultural climate was ripe for widespread accusations of abuse. Radio and TV talk shows, newspapers, magazines, lectures, workshops, and books deluged us with gut-wrenching stories of abuse.

I added to *Trancework* a section on the potential hazards of using hypnosis or other suggestive procedures to recover hidden memories. It triggered an avalanche of mail from all over the country. People stunned by wild accusations of abuse wrote to me, seeking a rational explanation for their devastation. Others wrote asking for advice on how to deal with a therapist who pressured them to accept the notion that they had been abused but had repressed the memories. Survivors of abuse contacted me to ask about the validity of the circumstances and methods in which they had recovered their repressed memories.

Over the last several years, I have had the opportunity to work with and learn from many people caught up in the phenomenon of repressed memories of sexual abuse. I have done therapy with accusers and the accused, spouses and siblings, friends and relatives. I have been deeply impressed with their strength as well as their grief. The stories people shared with me were intensely painful ones, of broken families, shattered lives, and overwhelming despair. They led me to write this book, one that I hope will provide both valuable information and support for people caught up in truly agonizing circumstances.

As a clinical psychologist, I am all too aware of the enormous pain suffered by incest and abuse survivors, and my concern for them is deep and genuine. It is a profoundly moving experience to share in a survivor's anguish and in the painfully slow rebuilding of a life. In my many years of clinical practice, I have participated in the rebuilding process many, many times. I am glad that we as a profession and we as a society have finally paved the way for survivors to come forward and confront abuse and their abusers without shame or self-blame. We have taken a huge step forward in taking seriously the sanctity of the family and in responding sensitively to the terrible suffering that ensues when that sanctity is violated.

But as deeply concerned as I am for abuse survivors, I am also deeply concerned about the trend in the mental health profession to treat so sensitive an issue in a sweeping, undiscriminating fashion. Their methods can easily ensnare innocent people and can lead therapists themselves to choose an approach that may be incorrect, even seriously harmful, in a particular case. The therapist who erroneously treated his client as a Vietnam vet suffering from posttraumatic stress disorder may have prevented him from getting proper treatment for whatever was really wrong with him. A therapist who hunts relentlessly for a hint of sexual abuse may miss or misinterpret signs of more salient disorders requiring treatment.

For a long time, the sexual abuse of children was considered so rare a phenomenon, and its perpetrators were thought to be so obviously deviant, that it seemed unnecessary to address it publicly. After all, Sigmund Freud and his disciples had informed us that while fantasies of sexual relations with our opposite sex parent were relatively normal, only the psychologically unsophisticated or seriously pathological would actually mistake them for reality. Finally the mental health profession caught on that incest and the sexual abuse of children aren't so uncommon after all, and that perpetrators can appear to be quite normal, responsible, high-functioning, and well-regarded people.

The floodgates opened, and before long clinicians and researchers were proclaiming that the incidence of abuse, already widespread, was growing daily. Abuse became a "hot topic" in the media, generating an unprecedented amount of attention. On September 4, 1992, television history was made when three major networks (PBS, CBS, and NBC) simultaneously ran *Scared Silent*, a special program on child abuse produced by Oprah Winfrey, herself a survivor of abuse. Other celebrities have since declared histories of abuse and more than a few people have *become* celebrities by doing so. In a short time, publicly acknowledging what had previously been a private shame had become not only acceptable but even admirable.

My point is that the epidemic of allegations of child sexual abuse does not exist independently of the culture in which the allegations are made. In the past, when therapists were convinced that abuse reports were sheer fantasy, there wasn't much of an abuse problem. Now that the media and the mental health profession have announced that it is widespread, we are beginning to see the phenomenon in more and more instances.

FAMILIES MAY BE HAZARDOUS TO YOUR HEALTH

Many therapists believe that families in the United States are not now, and for the past few decades have not been, environments in which children may safely grow up. In fact, they believe that huge numbers of families have been contexts of violence, emotional abandonment, incest, physical neglect, satanic worship, and even murder. One widely recognized expert suggested that a whopping 96 percent of Americans come from "dysfunctional families," where any or all of these abuses might have taken place. Can this really be true? What are the implications of someone in a position of authority promoting such a painful perspective of family life? What impact does it have on an individual who encounters it while seeking help or personal growth?

The therapeutic community can and does play a significant role in shaping people's perspectives. Beyond the consulting room, therapists generate research data, self-help books, media interest, and a plausible set of reasons to believe in their theories. As in any field, there are leaders and "gurus" who influence the work of other therapists and convince them to adopt particular perspectives. On multiple levels, therapists are in a position to hurt as well as to help with their beliefs.

In ever-increasing numbers, therapists all across the country are actively or passively encouraging clients to identify themselves as victims of abuse—or, to be "politically correct," as "abuse survivors." These clients may be told, "You seem to have the kind of symptoms that suggest you were abused as a child." They do not know that the symptom checklist, as we will see, is general enough that almost any of us could qualify as survivors of abuse. Perhaps even 96 percent of us. They may even be told, "If you have the feeling abuse occurred, then it did."

To me, the perpetration by professionals of such questionable, even dangerous, practices on the vulnerable and unsuspecting is a call to arms.

TAKING THERAPISTS TO TASK

Throughout 1992, I undertook the task of gathering data from more than 860 therapists all over the country about their ideas and practices in regard to the roles of suggestion and memory in therapy, especially as they relate to repressed memories of sexual abuse. I wanted to find out whether therapists were thinking critically and in an informed manner about this highly volatile issue. I was dismayed, to say the least, by what I found. (See Chapter 2 for a detailed discussion of the responses.) It is not an exaggeration to say that many therapists appear to practice their profession on the basis of sheer myth.

One result of this approach is that some therapists continue to encourage their clients to believe they are repressing memories of sexual abuse without any legitimate grounds for doing so. They require individuals to label themselves as more pathological than they may be. The label accepted, they encourage their clients to cut off contact with their alleged abusers, in the process destroying families and the avenues of communication that might make reconciliation possible. They demand full exploration of every gory detail of every episode of abuse. If the client comes up short, the therapist is all too willing to help fill in the blanks.

I want to state emphatically at the outset of this book that while it is clear to me that abuse is a widespread phenomenon, the exact role of repression in the recovery of accurate memories is unclear. Unquestionably, people can be influenced to believe things that are not true, but it is impossible to say to just what extent this is occurring in the epidemic of repressed memories of abuse. Certainly it is happening, though. At the moment, far too many unanswered, and perhaps unanswerable, questions remain about these sensitive and complex issues to say more than that with authority.

Some will no doubt misinterpret my views, simply because I question the practice of those therapists who use their influence unwittingly to create more victims. That they do so unwittingly is a key point of this book. The acknowledgment that therapy can unintentionally hurt people ought not to be dismissed as a "backlash against feminism," an "inability to face the harsh reality of abuse," or a symptom of "denial." *Abuse happens, but so do false accusations.*

The survey data I have gathered make it abundantly clear that too many therapists treat their clients on the basis of personal beliefs and philosophy, rather than according to an objective consideration of the facts. Too many therapists seem ignorant about the suggestibility inherent in the therapy process, and ignorant about the workings of human memory, *even though memory is central to the enterprise of identifying and treating survivors.*

I am deeply concerned that therapy clients will be led to believe destructive things that are untrue, to recall memories of terrible things that never actually happened, to jump to conclusions that are not warranted, and to destroy the lives of innocent people—including their own—in the process. I am all too aware that the abuse of children is a huge problem growing to ever more sickening proportions. I am also aware that people can be led to believe things that are not true. *Abuse happens, but so do false accusations.* The important task of mental health professionals is to sort out which is which with a considerably greater degree of responsibility than we have demonstrated thus far. I hope we are up to the challenge, because the integrity of families and individuals rests on the outcome.

CHAPTER 1

Into the Light

Frank went out to the mailbox with the same mixed feelings he seemed to always have lately—hoping there would be a letter from her and yet feeling anxious that one might actually come. He took a deep breath, opened the mailbox, and grabbed the bundle of letters and circulars within. As he walked back up the driveway, he saw his wife, Jean, watching him expectantly through the screen door. He did a quick flip through the letters and started to signal to her that there was nothing from Jennifer in the stack, when all of a sudden one letter seemed to jump out at him. He held his breath involuntarily while his stomach did a somersault and his eyes did a double take. It was from her. Now, despite the advance warnings from his other kids that this letter was coming, Frank felt he wasn't up to the task of opening it and reading with his own eyes the unbelievable things that Jennifer had said about him to her siblings. He gave the letter to Jean. "You read it. I just can't." She hesitated, then accepted the burden.

Jean opened the letter while Frank stared straight ahead, his fists clenched. His other kids had already told him in graphic detail the experiences Jennifer had recounted to them, apparently looking for their corroboration. They were every bit as shocked as Frank had been, maybe more so. Jennifer was the second oldest and certainly the black sheep of the bunch. She had always been more difficult than the others: headstrong, hypersensitive, argumentative. Her older sister and her brother, the youngest, were so outraged at her wild accusations that they refused to have anything more to do with her. Only her younger sister, Susan, was still talking to her, but even that relationship was now strained to the point of breaking. Frank hoped it didn't, because he felt he needed someone to keep a line of communication open. Besides, he knew that Susan didn't believe Jennifer, even for a second. It was all too crazy for any of them to understand. And the tension it had created was almost unbearable.

Jean pulled the handwritten note out of the envelope, and almost immediately her eyes began to tear. She drew in a sharp breath, and read aloud:

Dear Mother and Father,

It is very painful to have to write this letter to you. I don't know if I'll ever be able to talk to you or see you again. Time will tell. Right now, I am at the very beginning of coming to terms with what I have begun to remember about my childhood. After Peter broke up with me, I felt this dreadful feeling that something must be really wrong with me. Man after man in my life has abused me, mistreated me, and, eventually, left me. I went to therapy to get some answers. I got some, but not the ones I wanted. My therapist, a very caring woman, asked me if I had been abused by you, physically, emotionally, or sexually. I was sure I hadn't been, but then she did hypnosis with me a few times. In the fifth hypnosis session, I had a clear image of Dad penetrating me with his finger while changing my diapers. I couldn't have been more than six months old. Dad, how could you? What are you that you could do such a thing? You are a sick man whom I trusted and thought I felt close to throughout my life, and yet you betrayed my trust at the very start of my life. And you, Mother, must have known and chosen to protect that sick, perverted man, also betraying me. It's hard to know which of you is worse.

I am now starting to remember other episodes of abuse, some involving strange men who forced me to have sex with them while you watched with apparent satisfaction. And I remember some of them shoving things in me like broom handles and hurting me in unspeakable ways. Hypnosis has helped me remember, and now I know how sick you are and how damaged I am.

I will not talk to you or see you. Do not try to reach me. I am moving and leaving no forwarding address. Perhaps one day I will be able to see you again, but for now it is impossible. I have no forgiveness in me for what you did to me.

Jennifer

Dumbfounded, Frank and Jean sat in silence. What insanity was this? What evil would possess their daughter to make her believe such filthy delusions? Finally, Jean got up and went to her husband, who was shaking uncontrollably. They held each other for nearly an hour, until Frank gently pushed Jean away and said, mostly to himself, "I could not have loved and protected her more. I was a good father, wasn't I? Wasn't I?" Four days later, Frank still hadn't showered or shaved, much less gone back to work.

WHEN ACCUSATIONS OF SEXUAL ABUSE ARE MADE, IT IS A HORRENdous time for all involved. The survivor struggles for the strength and resolve to confront the horror of the past, which infects the present and sabotages the future. Meanwhile, the alleged abuser's world goes up in flames with the first hint of accusation. Devastating as this may be, though, no true child abuser deserves or gets much in the way of sympathy. But what if charges of abuse are made against someone who never did and could never do such a thing? Does this ever happen? If so, how often? And why?

We are witness to a remarkable shift in societal perspectives about the issue of child sexual abuse. What was only recently considered a relatively rare phenomenon is now thought to be epidemic. It is estimated (probably incorrectly, since exact figures are not possible to obtain) that one in four women and one in six men have been sexually abused as children. The fact that our society now seeks to better protect children and has created opportunities for abuse survivors to share their anguish is a sign that our consciousness of these delicate issues has evolved. In years past, public attitudes forced "victims" of abuse (now given the more empowering term "survivors") to keep their private hells private.

But in our heightened recognition that sexual abuse happens with shocking frequency, we have also created an environment that encourages a less than critical consideration of some of the most salient issues. Specifically, can we and should we believe every allegation of abuse? Is it as simple as "If she says it happened, it happened"? What about those cases in which the memories surfaced under the influence of another? In our zealous pursuit of perpetrators, is it possible that some innocent people are being falsely accused?

A PROFESSION DIVIDED

These difficult questions lie at the heart of one of the most heated controversies in the therapy field. The mental health profession is angrily and bitterly divided over the phenomenon of repressed memories of childhood sexual abuse. A repressed memory is one that has been buried in a person's unconscious, usually for decades, which may then surface, often in dramatic ways. Repression is a natural psychological defense mechanism that serves to keep painful and traumatic material out of your awareness. (Repression can't be studied directly, it can only be inferred. You can't ask someone, "Are you repressing memories of abuse?" If he or she knows about it, it isn't repressed.) Despite the past trauma being out of your awareness, though, its lingering effects on your thoughts, feelings, and behavior can be dramatic. Some very severe symptoms can be a direct consequence of repressed traumas.

Why is the mental health profession so bitterly divided about repressed memories? On one side are clinicians and researchers who believe that the existence of repressed traumas due to sexual abuse can and should be readily identified from a set profile, in the form of a symptom checklist. They believe that treatment should involve first lifting the veil of repression with a variety of memory recovery techniques, then working with the newly discovered traumatic material. They believe that memories recovered in therapy are essentially true, and need to be acknowledged as such in order for treatment to succeed. They are also concerned that perpetrators of sexual abuse not be given a new basis, legitimized by professionals, for evading responsibility for their actions.

On the other side of the issue are those clinicians and researchers who are skeptical of anyone's professed ability to diagnose repressed memories of trauma on the basis of symptoms that might be just as readily explained by other means. These clinicians and researchers further believe that by forming a conclusion that an individual has been abused and is repressing memories to that effect, a therapist can intentionally or unintentionally influence that person to reach that same conclusion, when it may not be true. They recognize that people can be influenced, especially in vulnerable situations like therapy, to believe damaging things that may have no basis in fact. They are concerned that innocent people will be falsely accused, and that many peoples' lives will be all but destroyed in the process.

What makes the controversy so intensely emotional is that clinicians and researchers on both sides are genuinely concerned for the well being of the clients and their families who are caught in the cross fire. Those who are confident that memories of trauma are inevitably accurate do not want their abused clients to face doubt or outright accusations of deception (or worse) from others. They know that abuse survivors need to be able to come forward openly and without shame, to be believed, and to be treated sensitively and skillfully. But those who are confident that untrue memories can be implanted or false beliefs created through poor clinical techniques or misinformation presented by a credible authority are equally earnest in their desire to protect vulnerable clients—and their families—from getting absorbed into a potentially destructive belief system.

It is my general assumption that professionals on both sides of the issue want to serve their clients and colleagues well. In preparing this book, I have had the opportunity to interview many of the most well known and respected clinicians and researchers in the field. I was impressed, even when I disagreed, with the good intentions of each. It is unfortunate that this controversy has created rifts among professional friends, made enemies among professional rivals, and further confused an already uncertain public about just what is going on with all those people discovering they were abused after years and years of never suspecting it at all. The confusion and despair of those who have been directly caught up in the melee is heartbreaking. I hate to think of the pain of all the families I have seen who have been devastated by this phenomenon. The issues associated with child abuse are, understandably, very powerful and emotionally charged. For that reason, it is especially important to step outside a purely emotional framework and to seek a more distant and objective vantage point.

THE GOALS OF THIS BOOK

In nearly two decades of clinical work, I have been greatly affected by the many survivors of incest and sexual abuse I have worked with, for they represent both the best (hopefulness, resilience, endurance, forgiveness) and the worst (despair, giving up, withdrawal, revenge) of human experience. I have tremendous sympathy and empathy for them, and little or none for perpetrators of abuse. But I am also concerned for those who may have been falsely accused of abuse on the basis of questionable clinical practices by therapists and others in positions of influence.

This book is concerned primarily with those cases in which allegations of abuse are made on the basis of memories that were recovered through the suggestions of a therapist. My goal is to serve as a voice of dissuasion from jumping to the conclusion that abuse "must have" occurred. How can we distinguish fact from myth, or truth from belief, if we prohibit careful examination? Millions of lives are on the line—survivors, perpetrators, the falsely accused, the falsely accusing, their families, spouses, and friends. In no way do I wish to contradict or invalidate the anguish of genuine survivors. My intention is to show that there is a well-considered basis for concluding that not every allegation of abuse can be believed, and to offer some hope and guidance to those who have already been touched by the epidemic.

WHEN I CAME TO MY WAITING ROOM TO GREET FRANK AND JEAN, I was struck by the urgency in their faces. We exchanged polite introductions, then they followed me into my office. New clients usually look around, curiously noticing the arrangement of the furniture and my personal effects. Frank and Jean never took their eyes off me; it was hard to tell whether they were sizing me up or were so preoccupied with their concerns that they were looking right through me. Perhaps they were doing both.

Frank prefaced his remarks by telling me how much he cared for all his children, how great an effort he had made to be a good father, and how strongly he had hoped and expected that his four kids would learn his values of hard work and family. He confessed that he "wasn't the perfect father," and that sometimes he worked too hard and paid too little attention to the kids. But he said he always had the goal of making their lives better—by giving them good educations, providing them with nice things, and so on.

Frank paused, and Jean jumped in. She described herself as a full-time mother who had always been very proud of their four children. She looked down and her eyes became moist. She deferred to Frank.

Frank described how Jennifer, aged twenty-eight, had in recent years become more difficult than ever. She had gone through considerable emotional upheaval when she left home to go to school, and was so angry all the time, seemingly about everything in her life. She didn't contact them much that first year, and they decided to give her room to "find herself." Eventually, she seemed to. She lived with a boyfriend her junior year, did pretty well in school, and seemed, for the first time in her adult life, happy. Her happiness came to an abrupt end, however, under tragic circumstances. Her boyfriend was killed in an accident with a drunk driver. Eventually, she seemed to "get it together" again, and even began dating. Two more live-in relationships, two more unhappy endings. Each man, in turn, proved selfish and insensitive, and treated Jennifer badly. When she met Peter, her most recent boyfriend, Frank and Jean both hoped she'd found someone more loving and attentive. For a while it seemed she had. She was in good spirits, was productive at her job, and regularly wrote to and visited with the family. Frank and Jean hoped she had cleared the hurdles of her painful past, but again it was not to be. Jennifer came home unexpectedly one day and found Peter in bed with someone else. She went wild, smashing things and screaming. A frightened neighbor called the police.

Jennifer ended up in therapy, where she reported terrible dreams of men hurting her in disgusting ways. She described all men as animals, hateful and manipulative. Her therapist asked if that included her dad. Well, she had resentments toward him that she carried from as far back as grade school, of times he treated her, at least to her mind, unfairly. So, yes, she'd include her dad. The therapist told Jennifer that her checkered history with men and her strong feelings that they are all abusive indicated she must have been physically or sexually abused. It was important that she admit it openly if she was ever going to get better.

Jean reached into her purse and gave me the wrinkled letter Jennifer had written them. As I read it, I could feel their intense gaze on me, watching for my reactions.

I WANT TO REMIND YOU OF A VERY IMPORTANT DISTINCTION I MADE earlier. It is necessary to distinguish (1) those cases in which someone knows *and has known all along* that he or she was abused from (2) those cases in which someone independently remembers repressed memories from (3) those cases in which a therapist facilitates recall of repressed memories from (4) those cases in which a therapist *suggests* memories of abuse. I am concerned with this latter phenomenon exclusively. How often does it happen? No one can know for certain, but both anecdotal evidence and data gathered directly from therapists suggest that stories like Jennifer's happen far more frequently than we might like to believe.

Recently, a woman called me and asked if I would hypnotize her in order to determine whether she had been molested as a child. I asked where she got the idea that she might have been.

She told me she had called another therapist about her poor self-esteem, and the therapist—*never having met her*—told her that she must have been abused and should be hypnotized to find out when and how. It was *not* great insight born of experience that led the therapist to offer such suggestions. It was foolishness of the worst sort, and I consider it tantamount to professional malpractice. Worse, this tendency toward knee-jerk diagnosis has permeated the culture.

Consider the following letter published on July 20, 1993, which was written to advice columnist Ann Landers, and Landers's response.

DEAR ANN: This is in response to "Housemates in the Northwest," whose wife rejected him sexually.

I am one of those wives who rejected her husband. We've been married only two years. I'm in counseling now, and my husband appreciates my efforts to overcome my aversion to sex. When I read the letter from "Housemates," I felt terrible, because I saw myself doing the same thing.

I was active sexually as a teenager, but when my husband and I married, intimacy came to a screeching halt. I love him dearly and enjoy the hugs and kisses and cuddling at night, but sex is terrifying.

In this world of wife beaters, divorce and cheating husbands, I realize that my husband is a prince. I am sick at heart that I am not able to be as generous and loving as he is. We also want children, but I've already suffered two miscarriages and an ectopic pregnancy.

Although I feel sorry for "Housemates," I wanted to let someone know that not all wives who are unable to be sexually active hate their husbands. I adore mine and pray that my condition is not permanent.

—LOVING BUT NOT ABLE IN TEXAS

DEAR TEXAS: I'm glad you are getting counseling because you need it. There is a strong possibility that your miscarriages and ectopic pregnancy have a lot to do with your aversion to sex. *Or can it be that you were sexually abused as a child?*

I'm sure your counselor will pick up on all of the above. Good luck, dear, and here's a gardenia for your husband's lapel. He sounds wonderful.

While the woman who wrote the letter may actually be an abuse survivor, just how casual will we come to be in tossing around the sexual trauma hypothesis?

If the client noncritically accepts the over-the-phone or newspaper diagnosis of abuse from the "abuse expert," the prescription is that he or she now recover and "work through" specific memories. If the client rejects the diagnosis, he or she is "in denial" and unwilling to deal "realistically" with his or her history of abuse. The client has been caught in a classic double bind (either you're an abuse survivor or you're in denial) and loses either way. As a guest on the *Oprah Winfrey* show, Roseanne Arnold put it this way when she discussed recovering her own repressed memories of sexual abuse from early childhood:

> When someone asks you, "Were you sexually abused as a child?" there are only two answers: One of them is "Yes," and one of them is "I don't know." You can't say "No."

Arnold's stated belief that the possibility of repressed memories must always be left open for consideration is one heavily promoted by the recovery branch of the mental health profession. The associated popular belief is that when abuse is suspected for whatever reason, the memories are always there to be found. If they are not readily remembered, they are assumed to be repressed, i.e., kept from conscious awareness, presumably because they are too painful to deal with directly. The widespread belief is that these repressed memories *must* surface in conscious awareness in order to be acknowledged, addressed, and resolved.

How do we recover repressed memories? What are the techniques therapists employ to bring forth apparently repressed memories that are *assumed* to be present? Are these methods valid; that is, do they bring forth actual repressed memories, or can they involve suggesting memories of events that never actually occurred yet the client comes to accept as genuine?

What about the not uncommon scenario in which someone is encouraged to recover a memory in a therapy session, and the individual has a single image, ostensibly from the age of six months, that involves some kind of abuse? Should it be considered real? Should the client go home and allege abuse and tear apart the family on the basis of such an image? Those who already believe such early "memories" are valid will say yes, and those who don't will say no. And that's one of the problems I will address in this book, namely that an individual's fate is placed in the hands of a therapist's seemingly arbitrary belief system about the nature of memory.

As an authority on patterns of suggestion and hypnosis, I am keenly aware of the power of suggestion in influencing perceptions, including perceptions of memory. Formal hypnosis, in other words, a hypnotic procedure openly identified as such, does *not* need to be employed in order for an individual to respond to suggestions that are either directly stated or merely implied. How easily can this be done? Consider the abuse guru John Bradshaw, who, through a series of television programs and books, persuaded a large number of Americans to believe they have an "inner child." People now literally talk to their inner child, comfort it, give it a name and personality, defend its right to exist, and find ways to get to know it better. *There is no inner child—it is simply a metaphor!* But to millions its existence is now a "fact" and dictates their way of life. That is *very* effective use of suggestion.

• • •

IN THE FIRST OF THE HYPNOSIS SESSIONS, WHICH OCCURRED IN HER fourth meeting with her therapist, Jennifer was anxious and afraid. She didn't know what to expect, and most of what she'd heard still wasn't very reassuring. Her therapist told her hypnosis was the best tool for recovering repressed memories and finding out "what really happened" to her. She trusted her therapist, and her therapist convinced her she would only get better if she faced her past. Jennifer couldn't understand why her therapist was so sure she'd been sexually abused, but she reluctantly agreed that it provided an explanation for her low self-esteem, her poor relationships with men, her anxiety and anger.

Jennifer closed her eyes and listened to the soft, soothing voice of her therapist. She was very conscious of listening to what her therapist was saying, and at first she felt anything but relaxed. A little at a time, though, she began to feel less of a need to be so attentive, and soon she found her thoughts drifting off to no place in particular. Occasionally, she heard her therapist say something about safe places to visit and important memories from childhood, but nothing she was saying seemed to be having much impact. She heard that soft voice saying other things, too, about having lots of different experiences, both good and bad.

Jennifer had an image of her brother, Jeff, playing in the backyard with some toys she'd long forgotten having given him for his birthday. A moment later, she remembered her older sister, Sandy, helping her play dress-up one day, and she couldn't help but smile. She was probably only four or five years old, and loved how she looked wearing lipstick. In the next moment, she saw an image of a baby, a girl, having her diapers changed, but the image was unclear. Her therapist noticed that Jennifer's brow was raised and her forehead wrinkled, and asked what she was seeing. Jennifer told her about the baby girl being diapered, and reported truthfully that she didn't know the baby's identity. The therapist asked how old the baby girl was, and Jennifer guessed that she was about six months old. Who was changing the diapers? The blurred face sharpened, and to her mild surprise, it was Dad! The therapist encouraged her to see whose room it was, but she couldn't tell. Was it her own room? Jennifer heard herself say yes. "Well, then, the baby must have been you," the therapist said. It only made sense for Jennifer to believe it. Then, a flurry of questions: "Where is he touching you?" "Can you see his hands?" "Can you see his fingers?" "What are his fingers doing?" "What are they doing to you?"

All at once Jennifer saw her father's hands on her, in her, around her, and through her. She bolted upright, panting, frightened. My God, she thought, what was that terrible image? She breathlessly asked her therapist what had happened and was told that she had just taken the first step on the road to her eventual recovery.

CULTURAL INFLUENCES ON INDIVIDUAL PERSPECTIVE

For at least two decades, the very important question has been asked, "Do television and the media *reflect* societal trends, or do they *cause* them?" Researchers have gathered enormous amounts of data that indicate the correct answer is "Both." Television, in particular, has come to so dominate our culture that we have increasingly come to rely on it as a reference point for making decisions and interpreting the meaning of our experiences. An endorsement from Oprah sells a lot of liquid diet powder. A mention from Phil Donahue can sell a lot of books. Their expert guests define for us what life experiences mean, and we tend to believe them. As television violence grows, so does violence in America. As television tolerates more blatant sexual expression in its programs, so does sexuality become more permissive. Does television simply show these things or does it cause them? The evidence overwhelmingly suggests that the relationship between cause and effect is circular: The media and our culture influence each other.

Therapists play a similar peculiar role in society. Like television, they both influence and are influenced by the society in which they live. In the same ways that television can guide your perceptions and tell you what should matter to you, therapists can play a significant role in shaping perspectives about yourself and your life.

Consider the trends in therapy and self-awareness. As I write this, one book is leading countless men into the forest to beat drums and find the meaning of masculinity. Of course, many men didn't know they had lost their masculinity until they read it. Another book leads us to believe that if your sense of responsibility toward those people you are deeply committed to is too well developed, you may be suffering from "co-dependency." Meanwhile, the drug companies are selling and psychiatrists are prescribing increasingly large doses of Valium and Prozac for our "anxiety disease" and "depressive illness." The "disease model" is in, and support and recovery groups abound for every "disease" from eating too much ("food addiction") to wanting lots of sex ("sex addiction").

Right now, our culture is encouraging us in many ways to identify ourselves as victims. When John Bradshaw proclaims that 96 percent of Americans grew up in dysfunctional families, nearly everyone gets to share the identity of "abuse victim." If we broaden the criteria for defining an abuse victim widely enough, as Bradshaw obviously has, then nearly everyone can fit the mold. But why would we want people to fit such a pathological mold? How are people empowered by identifying themselves as abused? What about all those who get *worse* as a result of such approaches?

I wonder how wide the criteria should be for defining yourself as an abuse victim. I know of a case in which a woman claimed, "I was abused by my father's secret attraction to me. I could tell that he *thought* about having sex with me, which is a form of sexual exploitation almost as bad as if he'd actually done so." And then she joined a support group to help her cope with her abuse! That she is accepted noncritically into a recovery group where she is reinforced for her "mind-reading" abilities certainly suggests a need to be more strict in differentiating true from imagined abuse.

Many therapists now accept such reports uncritically, and some will even suggest such notions to clients themselves if the reports are not forthcoming. Some experts would have us believe that not only has the great majority of people been abused, but organized satanic ritualistic abuse involving sacrifice and torture is a common phenomenon. And, if you don't readily believe it—which I don't—then you are in denial and are thought to be too psychologically fragile to face "reality."

THE BUCK STOPS
SOMEWHERE OVER THERE

Once a trend in beliefs is established, it gathers a momentum all its own. It attracts followers, but it also creates a backlash. In the case of sexual abuse, at one extreme there are alarmists who seem to see evidence of abuse almost everywhere they look. At the other extreme, are those who hide their heads in the sand because they believe that abuse is only a nasty figment of someone's perverse imagination. Such radical positions rarely represent reality.

Our society encourages us to believe that our individual desire for contentment supersedes all else. Such self-indulgent perspectives lead to a diminished awareness of and respect for others. When a friend doesn't do as we wish, we may be quick to end the relationship. We may regard family as an expendable commodity, thereby precluding the continuity necessary for true intimacy. Loyalty to employers or employees is a thing of the past; one indication of this trend is that the average recent college graduate will change jobs nearly eight times in his or her career. Socially, people are more disconnected from one another than ever before. Dating through classified ads? In the absence of fundamental relationship skills, people become objects to manipulate, things to exploit for personal satisfaction. In this atmosphere, it is sadly predictable that child abuse will continue to increase in prevalence.

It is also a prime climate for accusations of abuse and victimization. Blaming, accusing, or alleging that others have done things to hurt us is the rallying cry for every minority, even for those in the majority. By the time this perspective trickles down to the life of an individual, it has considerable momentum and a force substantial enough to bend that person's perceptions—including perceptions of memory—to conform to the overriding cultural belief.

MORE IMAGES CAME UP FOR JENNIFER IN SUBSEQUENT THERAPY sessions. Her therapist praised her lavishly for her willingness to confront these terrible memories, and encouraged her to continue to remember more and more. Her therapist remarked that sometimes the sexual abuse of children seems to be part of a ritual of some sort. Did Jennifer have any memories that involved rituals? In the very next session, Jennifer had images of being someplace entirely dark except for lots and lots of candles around her. She saw herself on a table, strapped down and terrified. A procession of people came into the room. More candles were lit, and the participants began to chant in some strange tongue. She saw the leader stand over her and chant something unintelligible about Satan. A knife appeared in his hand, and he pricked her finger and drew blood. Suddenly a number of the men threw off their robes, revealing both their nudity and their sexual arousal, and proceeded to rape her one by one. Off in the corner, she saw the unmistakable faces of her mother and father. They both looked unusually peaceful.

At that image, Jennifer literally jumped out of her chair. She was so obviously terrified that all her therapist could do was hold her and comfort her. After a while, Jennifer asked what had happened. She was told that some particularly powerful memories had surfaced. The therapist explained to her just how pervasive the practice of satanic ritualistic abuse really is, and how lucky she was that she was still alive to be able to come to terms with what had happened to her.

Jennifer was more confused and scared than ever. Could these images be true memories? If not, where did they come from and why? How could they be so graphic and detailed if they didn't really happen?

In the following session, Jennifer and her therapist discussed her therapist's suggestion that she write a letter to her parents to tell them what was going on. Once the letter was sent, Jennifer was told, she should prepare to cut off all contact with them. When she asked why, she was told that naturally they would deny any wrongdoing, undermining her own belief in the truth of what had happened. Her therapist said she must be absolutely confident in her knowledge of her abuse before she could confront her abusers, who were obviously still in denial. Any doubts she had not only were a sign of weakness in her resolve to get better, but helped her parents to stay in denial as well.

Together, they wrote the letter. Her therapist offered to mail it for her. Jennifer wondered how her parents and brother and sisters would react, but only for a moment.

KEY POINTS TO REMEMBER

- Abuse survivors can now get valuable help in overcoming their problems, help that simply wasn't available until a few years ago.
- Therapists may be so sensitive to abuse issues that they see evidence of abuse where none has actually occurred.
- Suggestive therapy procedures can instill false beliefs in clients, including beliefs of having been abused.
- Repression clouds our understanding regarding memories of abuse, because little is known about its effects on the accuracy of memory.
- The belief of some therapists that the mere existence of certain symptoms marks people as abuse survivors is a potential source of untoward influence on their clients.
- Therapists' subjective beliefs about memory inevitably influence the manner in which they treat their clients' memories.
- Like television, therapy both reflects and causes shifts in public awareness and popular beliefs.
- Because sexual abuse is not a well-defined phenomenon, conflicting ideas of what constitutes such abuse abound.
- A black-and-white categorization of professionals as "believers" or "nonbelievers" with respect to repressed memories of abuse has been damaging to the quest for a deeper consideration of the issues.
- Our culture plays a significant role in shaping our beliefs about abuse and victimhood.

CHAPTER 2

Therapists Reveal Their

Attitudes about Memories

and Suggestions of Abuse

*T*his ad appeared in a professional newsletter available only to therapists:

Regression Therapy Using the Higher Self: A unique workshop for therapists. Learn a procedure which is very simple yet extremely effective in retrieving memories very accurately. Saturday, November 7th, 9–12 p.m. Fee: $45.00. Call. . . .

A THERAPIST WHO PROFESSES TO BE AN ABUSE EXPERT APPEARED on the CNBC program *Real Personal* on April 27, 1992. Inter-

viewed by host Bob Berkowitz, the therapist confidently discussed her uncanny ability to identify individuals with sexual
abuse in their backgrounds, even if they don't know it themselves.

> It's so common that I'll tell you, I can within ten
> minutes, I can spot it as a person walks in the door, of-
> ten before they even realize it. There's a trust, a lack
> of trust, that's the most common issue. There's a way
> that a person presents themselves. There's a certain
> body language that says, "I'm afraid to expose myself.
> I'm afraid you're going to hurt me."

The general public seems to believe that mental health professionals serve their clients on the basis of objective diagnosis and
well-established, reliable methods of treatment. Unfortunately,
this is not the case. Psychotherapy involves a unique blend of art
and science, but it is mostly art. Consequently, skill levels vary
quite dramatically, as do perspectives about treatment. During
the time I have been in practice, I have seen many diagnostic and
treatment fads come and go. At any given time, there is an "in"
diagnosis and a "revolutionary new approach" to therapy, which
are often greeted enthusiastically by the profession but with little
of the objectivity necessary to evaluate accuracy and effective-
ness. Half a century ago, orthodox psychoanalysis was the mainstream approach. Techniques like "free association" and "dream
analysis" were typical in treatment. Then came behaviorism and
its more mechanistic approaches. The 1960s gave rise to human-
ism, and on the wave of the drug craze came "LSD therapy" and
encounter groups. More recently, the "adult children of alco-
holics" have been in the limelight, and there has been an enormous surge of recovery groups for these and other "adult
children" harmed by parents. Diagnoses and treatments are often
products of the era in which they arise.

In the age of entrepreneurial approaches to clinical practice, "flash" often counts considerably more than "substance." A therapist who doesn't attend the latest trendy workshop or learn the newest methods and jargon may be seen as failing to evolve, as too rigid or too narrow in method at clients' expense. Yet if therapists get drawn into each new promise to make their clients get better faster, they risk lapsing into noncritical thinking and adopting potentially dangerous practices. The consequences with respect to the diagnosis and treatment of abuse are particularly serious. Do we know enough about abuse to infer its presence accurately in the absence of specific memories of its occurrence? Is it a successful therapeutic intervention when the family splinters as a result of speculative allegations? Wanting to find out directly from my colleagues how they viewed this and related issues, I undertook a survey.

In 1992, I devised two questionnaires. The first was called the *Memory Attitude Questionnaire* (MAQ); it listed a series of statements regarding various aspects of memory, to each of which respondents were given the option of agreeing strongly or slightly, or disagreeing strongly or slightly. The second questionnaire was called the *Hypnosis Attitude Questionnaire* (HAQ); it listed a series of statements regarding suggestibility and hypnosis with which, again, respondents could agree or disagree, either strongly or slightly.

The MAQ was created to assess the range and depth of therapists' understanding of the workings of human memory, especially in relation to clinical issues and treatment. Memory is an inevitable core component of *any* therapy approach, since it is the client's recollections about his or her history that serve as the basis for creating and understanding his or her current predicament. Even the most "here and now" therapy approaches, such as the newer "brief therapy" approaches (strategic therapy, solution-oriented therapy, directive therapy), which de-emphasize the value of insight in treatment, still rely on a client's memory to a large extent. Therapy approaches that demand a detailed review and analysis of past experiences rely even more heavily on the workings of memory.

When a therapist first suspects and then looks intently for a history of abuse that may have been repressed in a particular client, his or her beliefs about memory are directly involved in the "search and rescue" mission. Believing, for example, that one can accurately store and later remember memories of conversations from the very first moments of one's life leads to some very different therapy techniques than if you held no such belief.

The HAQ was created to assess how therapists view hypnosis as a method for retrieving memories and about the role of suggestibility in the therapy process. The chief advantage the use of clinical hypnosis affords to a competent clinician is that it allows the client to be absorbed in "a different reality"—one more helpful and therapeutic than the "reality" he or she lives in and finds distressing. Hypnosis is, to quote one of the pioneer hypnosis researchers, Dr. Ernest Hilgard, "believed-in imagination." The things we believe—our "everyday trance states," so to speak—can either help or harm us. Believing, for example, you are worthwhile as a person and can enjoy good relationships with others feels a lot better than believing you're no good and no one will ever like you. Both beliefs are arbitrary, but they sure don't feel the same! Getting absorbed in a different and more adaptive way of thinking and feeling about life experiences can diminish symptoms or even make them disappear.

Most therapists, as the survey shows, have a positive attitude about hypnosis as a clinical tool. As one who teaches hypnosis courses to therapists on a regular basis, I am aware that most therapists get their only formal training in hypnosis through brief workshops, usually only several days in length. The quality of the various trainings varies dramatically, and the range of skills of therapists who learn and use hypnosis is quite broad. It bears mentioning that there are no laws about who may practice hypnosis—not even a high school diploma is required—and many people are practicing hypnosis at levels well beyond their actual skills.

Hypnosis, in one form or another, is commonly used as a tool for "uncovering" memories of abuse. But some therapists employ

MEMORY ATTITUDE QUESTIONNAIRE

Demographics

Age _____ Degree _____
Years in clinical practice _____
Setting in which you work _____
Is your knowledge of the workings of memory:
Below Average _____ Average _____ Above Average _____
Do you use hypnosis in your work?
Yes _____ No _____
Do you work hypnotically to recover memories?
Often _____ Sometimes _____ Rarely _____ Never _____

Below are 10 statements which you are asked to state your relative agreement or disagreement with. Please place a check mark in the appropriate place by each item.

Items	Agree Strongly	Agree Slightly	Disagree Slightly	Disagree Strongly
1. The mind is like a computer, accurately recording events as they actually occurred.	_____	_____	_____	_____
2. Events that we know occurred but can't remember are repressed memories—i.e., memories that are psychologically defended against.	_____	_____	_____	_____
3. Memory is a reliable mechanism when the self-defensive need for repression is lifted.	_____	_____	_____	_____
4. If someone doesn't remember much about his				

Items	Agree Strongly	Agree Slightly	Disagree Slightly	Disagree Strongly
or her childhood, it is most likely because it was somehow traumatic.	___	___	___	___
5. It is necessary to recover detailed memories of traumatic events if someone is to improve in therapy.	___	___	___	___
6. Memory is not significantly influenced by suggestion.	___	___	___	___
7. One's level of certainty about a memory is strongly positively correlated with that memory's accuracy.	___	___	___	___
8. I trust my client such that if he or she says something happened, it must have happened, regardless of the age or context in which the event occurred.	___	___	___	___
9. I believe that early memories, even from the first year of life, are accurately stored and retrievable.	___	___	___	___
10. If a client believes a memory is true, I must also believe it to be true if I am to help him or her.	___	___	___	___

Do you attempt to distinguish between what appear to you to be true memories and false memories?

Yes _____   No _____

If yes, how do you do so? Please write your response on the back of this form. Thank you. Include your name, address, and telephone number if you are willing to discuss your response.

HYPNOSIS ATTITUDE QUESTIONNAIRE

Demographics

Age _____ Degree _____
Years in clinical practice _____
Setting in which you work _____
Do you use hypnosis in your work? Yes _____ No _____
Do you work hypnotically to recover memories?
Often _____ Sometimes _____ Rarely _____ Never _____

Below are 15 statements which you are asked to state your relative agreement or disagreement with. Please place a check mark in the appropriate place by each item.

Items	Agree Strongly	Agree Slightly	Disagree Slightly	Disagree Strongly
1. Hypnosis is a worthwhile therapy tool.	_____	_____	_____	_____
2. Hypnosis enables people to accurately remember things they otherwise could not.	_____	_____	_____	_____
3. Hypnosis seems to counteract the defense mechanism of repression, lifting repressed material into conscious awareness.	_____	_____	_____	_____
4. People cannot lie when in hypnosis.	_____	_____	_____	_____
5. Therapists can have greater faith in details of a traumatic event when obtained hypnotically than otherwise.	_____	_____	_____	_____
6. When someone has a memory of a trauma while in hypnosis, it objectively must actually have occurred.	_____	_____	_____	_____

Items	Agree Strongly	Agree Slightly	Disagree Slightly	Disagree Strongly
7. Hypnosis can be used to recover memories of actual events as far back as birth.	___	___	___	___
8. Hypnosis can be used to recover accurate memories of past lives.	___	___	___	___
9. It is possible to suggest false memories to someone who then incorporates them as true memories.	___	___	___	___
10. Hypnotic age regression has positive value as a therapeutic tool.	___	___	___	___
11. Someone could be hypnotically age regressed and get "stuck" at a prior age.	___	___	___	___
12. Hypnotically obtained memories are more accurate than simply just remembering.	___	___	___	___
13. Hypnosis increases one's level of certainty about the accuracy of one's memories.	___	___	___	___
14. There is legitimate basis for believing that hypnosis can be used in such a way as to create false memories.	___	___	___	___
15. The hypnotized individual can easily tell the difference between a true memory and a pseudomemory.	___	___	___	___

Do you know of any cases where it seemed highly likely that a trauma victim's trauma was somehow suggested by a therapist rather than a genuine experience?

Yes _____   No _____

If yes, could you briefly describe such a case scenario on the other side of this form? Thank you. Include your name, address, and telephone number if you are willing to be contacted about your scenario.

methods like hypnosis to do memory work without recognizing that they may contaminate the investigative process through suggestive questioning, creating the very problems they must then treat.

The MAQ and HAQ were presented to more than 1,000 therapists all across the country during 1992, mostly (about 90 percent) at national and international psychotherapy conventions they were attending. (These included meetings held by the American Association for Marriage and Family Therapy (AAMFT), the Family Therapy Network, the American Society of Clinical Hypnosis (ASCH), and the Milton H. Erickson Foundation. All meetings were attended only by qualified professionals with advanced degrees.) The other 10 percent were attendees at therapy training courses I taught, none of which involved the subject matter of these questionnaires. Eight hundred sixty-four usable MAQs and 869 usable HAQs were returned by respondents. This is objectively considered a significant data base, one large enough from which to make a realistic assessment of therapists' attitudes and practices, although no questionnaire is entirely accurate in the relationship it suggests between thought and practice.

The "average" respondent was forty-four years old, had formal education slightly beyond a master's degree, had been in professional practice for more than eleven years, and was most likely in private clinical practice. Keep in mind, this sketch is a composite of *all* respondents and does not represent any one individual. The specific demographic data are reported in Appendix A.

Of 869 respondents to the HAQ, only 43 percent said they had received formal training in hypnosis, yet 53 percent said they use hypnosis in their work. Eight percent said they frequently use hypnosis to recover memories, while an additional 28 percent said they do so occasionally. Twenty percent said they rarely employ hypnosis to recover memories, and 40 percent said they never engage in the practice.

More than one in six therapists surveyed—17 percent—admitted that their knowledge of how memory works was below average. Sixty-six percent described their level of knowledge as average, while a paltry 12 percent thought of their knowledge as above average.

RESPONSES TO KEY ASPECTS OF THE *MEMORY ATTITUDE QUESTIONNAIRE* (MAQ)

Data frequencies and averages for all the MAQ items are reported in Appendix B. The ten main items of the MAQ can be divided into three categories for the purpose of general discussion:

1. Therapists' attitudes regarding the nature of memory, specifically its relative degree of both accuracy and reliability
2. Therapists' attitudes regarding the degree to which memory is affected by the defense mechanism of repression
3. Therapists' attitudes regarding the role memory plays in the therapy process

These three categories together form the underlying philosophical framework for the therapeutic practices derived from them, although the correlation between the two is not exact, as I have mentioned.

Therapists' Attitudes Regarding the Nature of Memory
How a therapist views memory naturally plays a key role in determining his or her responses both to clients' memories and to methods for retrieving and working with them. The single greatest issue in this category is whether or not a therapist views memory as objective and infallible—whether, as the questionnaire states, he or she believes that "the mind is like a computer, accurately recording events as they actually occurred." Approximately

one third of all respondents agreed with this statement, and about one in eight (12 percent) agreed strongly.

About one in ten therapists surveyed believed that "memory is not significantly influenced by suggestion," in direct contradiction to one of the most basic and well-known facts about memory. The statement "One's level of certainty about a memory is strongly positively correlated with that memory's accuracy" was designed to get at beliefs about the relationship between *feeling* right and *being* right. Feeling certain you are correct has no more to do with actually being right—as you will see in the next chapter—than shouting louder in an argument does, but nearly one in four respondents believed that feeling certain about a memory means the memory is more likely to be correct. And 41 percent believed that ". . . early memories, even from the first year of life, are accurately stored and retrievable."

Therapists' Attitudes Regarding Repression and Memory

Nearly six in ten respondents agreed that "events that we know occurred but can't remember are repressed memories—i.e., memories that are psychologically defended against."

Conflicting notions about the classic defense mechanism of repression is the complicating factor in the phenomenon of suggested abuse. The notion that any time you forget something there must be some deep psychological motivation for doing so is widely held, particularly among more traditional psychodynamically oriented and insight-oriented therapists. A therapeutic goal, then, is to discover the source of the forgotten material and resolve any associated emotional conflicts.

Does repression, or defensively motivated forgetting, exist? Despite some extreme views to the contrary, the wealth of cumulative clinical experience suggests that it does. However, repression is not the only reason why people forget. The ability to forget is, in some ways, as biologically necessary as the ability to remember, and there is a variety of mechanisms for forgetting that have nothing to do with trauma or repression. But a therapist who believes that if someone forgets, it automatically means there is something negative associated with the memory, will likely initiate a search for the source of the presumed repression. This is a major reason why therapists unintentionally ask leading or suggestive questions of their clients.

A related set of questions includes whether memories are reliable once repression is lifted, and whether a generalized lack of childhood memory is to be interpreted as likely evidence of trauma. The underlying assumption of those who believe that "memory is a reliable mechanism when the self-defensive need for repression is lifted"—as nearly half the respondents did—is that when emotions are dealt with effectively, as they would be in therapy (theoretically, anyway), then recollection can be assumed to be accurate. Therapists who believe this do not consider the possibility that memories may be inaccurate or the product of confabulation.

Forty-three percent of the respondents believed that "if someone doesn't remember much about his or her childhood, it is most likely because it was somehow traumatic." In other words, they believed that so-called "childhood amnesia" (the lack of memory for early life) is a "functional amnesia," meaning it is psychologically motivated. Most people's memory for early childhood experiences is nearly nonexistent before around ages two to three, and is quite sparse and only episodic until around ages six to eight. To assume, however, that the reasons for this *must* be emotional (rather than due to other, less sensational, reasons such as the biology of the brain's development) again leads therapists to conduct a search for "the reason."

Therapists' Attitudes Regarding Memories in Therapy
The way a therapist perceives the nature of memory and the effects of repression on memory naturally influences clinical demeanor and methods of treatment. A therapist who believes that memories are fundamentally accurate and true will not be inclined to doubt a client's narratives or to consider whether they have been influenced by other factors.

If a client reports a memory from the age of three months,

should it be considered accurate? What about memories in utero? Both age and context are significant influences on the accuracy of memory. More than a quarter of the respondents agreed with the statement "I trust my client such that if he or she says something happened, it must have happened, regardless of the age or context in which the event occurred."

I took this issue a step further with the statement "If a client believes a memory is true, I must also believe it to be true if I am to help him or her." More than one third of the respondents (36 percent) said they agreed.

Nearly a fifth (19 percent) of respondents felt that "it is necessary to recover detailed memories of traumatic events if someone is to improve in therapy." Many therapists hold a "no pain, no gain" philosophy regarding treatment. In their view, unless you are willing to bring forth *all* your hurtful memories and openly release your feelings associated with those painful experiences, you are in denial and will be viewed as emotionally restricted. Their assumption is that your symptoms cannot improve unless you follow the prescribed steps to acknowledge and "work through" your feelings.

Therapists' Attitudes about Distinguishing
False from True Memories

In the final MAQ item, "Do you attempt to distinguish between what appear to you to be true memories and false memories?" many therapists would simply like to believe that if a client believes something to be true, it may as well be true. But such a "narrative truth" viewpoint evades the real issues of therapy. If a therapist treats fiction as if it were true, then what happens to the real issues in the client's life? (Remember the supposed Vietnam vet who killed himself?) Can therapy succeed reliably when it is aimed in the wrong direction?

More than half of the therapists who completed the questionnaire (57 percent) openly admitted that they do nothing at all to differentiate truth from fiction. This question also yielded the highest rate—6 percent—of "no response" answers of all the survey items apart from the demographic ones (evidence of denial, perhaps?) and provoked a number of indignant written comments. A typical one was, "As a therapist and *not* an investigator, it is *not my responsibility* to verify the accuracy of my client's reports." To my mind, this attitude evades the crucial issues surrounding therapies that are built on the foundation of what might very well be suggested memories or beliefs, benevolent intentions notwithstanding.

RESPONSES TO KEY ASPECTS OF THE *HYPNOSIS ATTITUDE QUESTIONNAIRE* (HAQ)

The fifteen main items of the HAQ cover four general topics:

1. Therapists' attitudes about the relative value of hypnosis as a therapeutic tool
2. Therapists' attitudes about the value of hypnosis as a memory enhancer or memory recovery tool
3. Therapists' erroneous beliefs about hypnosis
4. Therapists' attitudes about the relationship between hypnosis and false memories

Data frequencies and averages for all the HAQ items are reported in Appendix C.

Therapists' Attitudes about the Value of Hypnosis

Hypnosis and hypnosis-related techniques (imagery, visualization, guided meditations, guided dreams) are widely employed in therapies that attempt to uncover memories of abuse. A belief in the intrinsic value of hypnosis may predispose therapists to accept its use less critically, even where it has been misapplied. Indeed, the overwhelming majority, 97 percent, of respondents viewed hypnosis in a very positive light. As a strong proponent of responsible uses of clinical hypnosis, I was pleased to discover that it is held in such high regard by my colleagues. But I also know that my field is filled with misconceptions about and indefensible applications of the technique (such as so-called "past-lives regression"), and so it is a source of considerable concern to me that hypnosis and all its subtle aspects be carefully and sensitively applied.

"Age regression" is a hypnotic procedure in which the client is immersed in the experience of memory. The client may be encouraged to *remember* events in vivid detail, a procedure called "hypermnesia." Or, the client may be encouraged to *relive* the events of the past as if they were going on right now, a procedure called "revivification." Either or both of these procedures are commonly used in memory recovery–oriented therapies. A great majority, 84 percent, of respondents viewed age regression in a positive light, suggesting a greater likelihood that they would use it themselves or encourage others to use it as a component of treatment—and also increasing the risk of its misuse if they are not well informed about it.

Therapists' Attitudes about Hypnosis and Memory Enhancement
Considerable research has been done on hypnosis as an investigative tool, and it generally yields conflicting conclusions about hypnosis as a reliable memory retriever. Some studies suggest that hypnosis can be used to enhance recall, while others demonstrate that it only increases the tendency to accept suggested memories or create confabulations and incorporate them into firmly held beliefs as if they were true. Despite the conflicting evidence, 75 percent of respondents thought of hypnosis as a tool for facilitating accurate recall whenever memories are otherwise not forthcoming.

Few therapists, or their clients, seem to know that the use of hypnosis will disqualify the client from testifying in court in the majority of states and may subject the therapist to a potential liability if hypnosis is performed without informing the client that it may preclude his or her testifying in court later, and the client sues the therapist for withholding this information.

Responses to the statement "Hypnosis seems to counteract the defense mechanism of repression, lifting repressed material into conscious awareness" indicate that 83 percent of respondents agreed. So if a therapist is motivated to find a repressed trauma in the client's background, he or she will likely think that hypnosis (or hypnotically based methods) is the way to do so.

Nearly half the respondents (47 percent) agreed with the statement "Therapists can have greater faith in details of a traumatic event when obtained hypnotically than otherwise." Attributing greater accuracy to a memory recovered hypnotically is a distortion of fact with potentially hazardous consequences for the client. Conducting investigative (uncovering) sessions is an art requiring considerable skill, and without a keen awareness for all the ways hypnosis can be misapplied, it is too easy to be gullible about information obtained. Nearly as many (43 percent) believed that "hypnotically obtained memories are more accurate than simply just remembering." This is a significantly smaller number of positive responses than in other items that make the same point but less forcefully. It seems that the more explicitly therapists must commit to a specific view of the effects of hypnosis on memory, the less certain they show themselves to be.

Does the mere fact of being hypnotized indicate that the memory is authentic? Nearly one in three respondents agreed that "when someone has a memory of a trauma while in hypnosis, it objectively must actually have occurred."

The majority (54 percent) also agreed that "hypnosis can be used to recover memories of actual events as far back as birth." Associated with this belief is the notion that a memory can be stored in infancy at a physical (nonverbal, noncognitive) level that can be interpreted and understood years later when awareness and understanding develop. This is what is known as a "body memory," a memory stored at a physical level as a result of powerful emotional experiences of a physical nature, like abuse, rape, or extreme physical danger, as in wartime experiences. The presence of body memories stored in childhood from presumed sexual traumas is a leading basis for the diagnosis of repressed memories of abuse. Physical symptoms such as nausea or headaches are often viewed as body memories of repressed trauma, even from as far back as birth.

Many people hold the belief that this life is *not* all there is. They believe in reincarnation, the notion that a person's essence lives many lives over time—dying and being reborn later in the form of another. Some therapists who believe in reincarnation practice "past-lives regression therapy." They do imagery or other hypnotic procedures and encourage people to discover memories of having lived before in other incarnations. The client predisposed to participate in such sessions may "discover" that he or she lived as other individuals in other centuries. A basic premise of the therapy is that current issues faced in this lifetime are a consequence of events that took place in a past life. By "reliving" that past life and resolving whatever issues existed then, the person is empowered to improve his or her current circumstances. More than one in four survey respondents (28 percent) thought that "hypnosis can be used to recover accurate memories of past lives."

Sixty-one percent of respondents were aware that "hypnosis increases one's level of certainty about the accuracy of one's memories." This item asks about how one's level of certainty about a memory influences perceptions of its accuracy. Whatever the memory, the more certain you are in reporting it, the more likely it is to engender in your audience belief in its accuracy. Likewise, the more certain you *feel* a memory is accurate, the more likely you will believe it is accurate, even though greater certainty does *not* mean greater accuracy.

Therapists' Beliefs in Myths about Hypnosis

Whether or not therapists use hypnosis in their own clinical practices, their preconceived ideas and subscription to common myths about it can influence how they respond to other clinical situations.

A commonly held misconception is that "people cannot lie when in hypnosis." Nothing could be further from the truth.

Hypnosis is *not* a lie detector, nor does it prevent either intentional or unintentional deception on the part of the hypnotized person. Yet, nearly one in five respondents (18 percent) actually believed this myth. Even if they do not conduct the hypnosis sessions themselves, they will likely believe those clients who tell them, "During a hypnosis session, I discovered I was sexually abused."

A similar percentage (19 percent) subscribed to the myth that "someone could be hypnotically age regressed and get 'stuck' at a prior age." It is a virtual impossibility to get "stuck" in age regression in particular, or in *any* hypnotic experience in general. Hypnosis involves being absorbed in some important experience (a memory, an image, a fantasy, a feeling) to the exclusion of other peripheral goings-on. A common experience of hypnosis is being absorbed in a good book, a movie, a conversation, daydreams, television, a hobby, or anything else that engages your full attention and gives you a sense of detachment from all else. Can you get "stuck" reading a book? Obviously not, nor can you get stuck in *any* frame of mind. Conscious awareness jumps from place to place, noticing whatever happens to capture our attention at the moment, and belief in this myth reflects a basic ignorance of the characteristics and capabilities of the mind.

It was interesting to find that in comparing therapists who were and were not formally trained in hypnosis, those who were formally trained were also prone to misconception, though a little less so. Personal bias can overwhelm facts.

Therapists' Attitudes about Hypnosis and False Memories

It is somewhat heartening to note that 79 percent of respondents believed "it is possible to suggest false memories to someone who then incorporates them as true memories." Yet, 16 percent, nearly one in six respondents, did not seem to recognize this possibility.

A related item states "There is legitimate basis for believing that hypnosis can be used in such a way as to create false memories." Nearly two thirds of respondents (64 percent) agreed. But more than a quarter (27 percent) of those surveyed did *not* think of hypnosis as capable of generating false memories. Thus, it would not be likely to occur to them that a client who had undergone hypnosis for the purpose of recovering apparently repressed memories might be confabulating or otherwise in error. Treatment would then proceed along different lines than if the prospect of false memories being present was considered.

The line between what is "true" versus what is "believed" can blur significantly under *any* circumstance. Contrary to popular belief, in hypnosis the line can blur to an even greater extent, making it difficult, sometimes impossible, to distinguish fantasy from reality. Yet a fifth of those surveyed felt that "the hypnotized individual can easily tell the difference between a true memory and a pseudomemory," while 71 percent were aware that hypnosis assures neither greater nor lesser accuracy of recall. Only objective evidence can prove matters one way or the other.

Therapists' Beliefs that Traumas May Be Suggested

The final item on the HAQ asks, "Do you know of any cases where it seemed highly likely that a trauma victim's trauma was somehow suggested by a therapist rather than a genuine experience?" Almost one in five respondents (19 percent) said they could point to such cases.

The responses to this last item, along with the response patterns overall, indicate grave cause for concern. While the great majority of therapists are well-intentioned people who genuinely want to help their clients, the survey data make it abundantly clear that too many therapists hold beliefs that are sometimes arbitrary, sometimes sheer myth, and sometimes outright dangerous to their clients' well-being.

It is clearly time for us to give some attention to what we do know about memory, its suggestibility, and the implications for therapy when peoples' lives and the lives of their families rest on the way these volatile issues are handled. That is what the rest of this book is about.

KEY POINTS TO REMEMBER

- Therapy typically involves more art than science, and how it is practiced is largely a product of a therapist's subjective beliefs.
- Most therapists surveyed claimed their knowledge of memory was average to below average.
- Therapists often hold erroneous views on the workings of memory, repression, and hypnosis.
- Most therapists surveyed admitted they do nothing to differentiate truth from fiction in their clients' narratives.
- Nearly one in five therapists surveyed claimed they know of cases where a trauma victim's trauma was more likely suggested by a therapist than a genuine experience.
- Therapists are deeply divided among themselves on the key issues of memory and suggestibility.

CHAPTER 3

Memory in Perspective

Allison came to therapy reluctantly at the insistence of her sister, Terry, who lives in another state. Terry had always gone in for "New Age" therapy gimmicks, and recently had gone through a therapy process called "rebirthing and reparenting." The process involved guiding the individual back in time in order to relive the process of being born. Supposedly you could even feel the mother's labor contractions and remember delivery room conversation. The therapy stressed the moment of the first "bonding" with the mother, considering it to be crucial to development, especially with regard to the quality of one's self-esteem and familial relationships. Terry's rebirthing experiences had brought back "memories" of a traumatic birth and an ambivalent mother who verbalized during delivery that the child was unplanned and unwanted. Worst of all, Terry remembered her mother abandoning her in her first days of life, precluding any bonding between them. Terry retrieved "body memories" of having been sexually abused during this time, but no specific memories as to when or by whom.

Terry believed Allison was likely to have been treated similarly, and that she, too, should be in therapy "to learn the truth" about these earliest days of her life. Allison believed Terry's intentions were entirely honorable, and that discovering such early abandonment would explain a great deal about her own conflicted feelings about their mother. So Allison asked me, "Can you help me remember when I was emotionally abandoned—and maybe abused—as a baby?"

THE POPULAR SCIENCE-FICTION THRILLER TOTAL RECALL FEATURED intense and fast-paced intrigue surrounding its lead character, Douglas Quaid, played by Arnold Schwarzenegger. Set in a futuristic context where interplanetary travel is a fact of life, the movie opens with Quaid bored with life on Earth. His unusual interest in the planet Mars prompts him to have an artificial memory of having taken an exciting trip there implanted in his brain. As it turns out, he eventually discovers he has already lived on Mars, where he worked as a strongman for its highly corrupt governor. To keep the governor's devious schemes a secret, Quaid agreed to have his memory of his life on Mars removed. As bits and pieces of his memory begin to return, Quaid struggles to regain his sense of what is real and what isn't, where he has and hasn't been, and which of his memories are authentic and which have been artificially either implanted or removed.

Total Recall was a fascinating movie on many levels, particularly for its main vehicle of intrigue, namely the technological capability to implant artificial memories in someone who experiences them fully and completely, as if they were bona fide recollections of real experiences. The ability to remove specific memories or erase entire categories of memory selectively was an equally fascinating premise.

Total Recall was just a movie, of course, the product of some writer's vivid imagination. Consider the implications, though. You could implant lots of memories of happy childhood family experiences in someone who was abandoned or abused by his or her real family. You could implant wonderful memories of loving interactions with a parent who died in someone's early childhood. You could remove memories of any serious trauma like war or rape, or you could remove memories of ever having failed at anything very important. How might mental health professionals use such technology if it actually existed? What would the ethics of the day be—a value placed on "truth" or a value placed on "feeling good"?

The possibility of implanting or removing memories at will may seem like science fiction. And, of course, it *is* way beyond our current technological scope to create or remove specific memories with some sort of gadget. Yet, in a gross sense, the creation and removal of memories goes on all the time in peoples' lives, even though it doesn't happen by walking into a "memory shop" like the one in *Total Recall.*

Can memories, or even just the belief that such memories exist, be created for events that never actually occurred? The answer is yes. How easily can this be accomplished? I'll answer this question with another question: How easy is it to absorb people into a particular belief system? Consider all the unusual and even wild beliefs people have, and you realize that some people can be led to believe nearly *anything.* This point will be elaborated in detail in the next chapter.

In this chapter, I intend to describe and discuss the issues surrounding the workings of human memory. Greater insight into how memory works allows us to appreciate how the current epidemic of accusations of abuse arising from apparently repressed memories has reached such incredible proportions.

IS THE MIND A COMPUTER?

Since its initial rise decades ago, the computer has provided the most common metaphor for the workings of memory. Our brains carry out countless functions at remarkable speeds, just like the computer. The analogy holds that the brain represents the hardware of the computer, while our life experiences, which are programmed into it, represent the software. If you're suffering from psychological problems, then the computer analogy suggests that you need a new "program" for improving your life after you "erase the old tapes" from your earlier (dysfunctional) "programming." The analogy further holds that "the mind is like a computer, accurately recording and storing bits of information and experiences exactly as they were learned and experienced." The analogy further suggests that everything you experience, no matter how briefly, peripherally, or early in your life, is recorded and available to be remembered under proper conditions. Thus you need only to "push the right button" and the data will surface on the "computer screen of your consciousness" in the exact form in which it was originally programmed into your memory.

Unfortunately, the computer as a metaphor for mental functions has only limited usefulness when it comes to the workings of memory. In fact, the metaphor is so inaccurate that, at least as far as memory is concerned, it would probably be best if we simply discontinued its use altogether. Remembering is *not* just a simple process of retrieving what has been stored. The process of forming a memory is *not* simply the recording and storing of events in their entirety as they actually occurred. The phrase to remember is that "memory is reconstructive, not reproductive." Memories are often formed from multiple sources of information and may be modified over time.

Despite the popular misconceptions regarding memory (even among the professionals I surveyed, as discussed in the previous chapter), the fact is that memory can be, and often is, an unreliable mechanism prone to a variety of errors.

However, for the one third of respondents who incorrectly believed in the accuracy and completeness of the mind's recording of events, it then follows that whatever someone remembers is inherently true. Furthermore, it leads to the erroneous belief that all experiences can be remembered if only the right conditions can be created. This belief provides a ripe climate for the suggestion of memories in the attempt to facilitate remembering.

HOW DOES MEMORY WORK?

So much of the controversy about repressed memories of abuse revolves around the true nature of memory. Is memory a reliable process, one that is efficient in its operation? As with the issue of repression, our limited understanding of memory precludes forming absolute conclusions about its nature. Although memory has been studied for over a century, the best, most solid research on the subject has only been undertaken in the last couple of decades. So far, a number of different models have been proposed to describe the workings of memory.

First, what is memory? One useful definition given by attorney and psychologist Alan Scheflin is that "memory is a capacity and faculty to retain information, thoughts, feelings, and other experience in the mind and to recall what is past."

It is important to appreciate that there are many different kinds of memory, or, perhaps more accurately, many different contexts for memory. For example, memory may be visual, verbal, spatial, sensory, incidental, deliberate, state bound, conscious, unconscious, and so forth. The contexts in which a memory is both formed and remembered play a significant role in the overall quality of the memory.

Consider, for example, the differences in the quality of recalled memories that are either incidental or deliberate. Incidental recall involves the attempt to retrieve memories of information or events that were experienced without advance knowledge that they would later be examined. Deliberate memories are made when you know you are learning or observing something that you will be tested on later. The attempt to recover repressed memories of abuse starts out as incidental recall but turns into a test of deliberate memory. Yet, predictably, the quality of information is simply not as great as would be obtained if deliberate strategies to remember had originally been employed. Why is this so?

The primary reason is because memory is a process, not an event. There are multiple steps involved not only in the sequence of forming a memory, but in remembering it later. Simplistically, these steps are (1) sensory registration of a stimulus; (2) organizing the information into meaningful units; (3) storing the information; and (4) retrieving the information. This multiple-step model of the workings of memory is a simple composite of several of the most widely accepted perspectives about memory, and is meant to highlight the fact that memory is complex and multidimensional. No one understands all of it.

Nothing gets into our memories from the outside that does not begin with perception through one or more of our physical senses of sight, hearing, touch, smell, and taste. In other words, every potentially memorable experience has to pass through at least one of our senses first. Thus, there automatically and inevitably are differences between what happens "out there" and what our senses can perceive, since we are limited even at a neurological level. (Light and sound exist at wavelengths we don't perceive, for example.) If there is too much sensory data to attend to, overload can prevent attaining clear sensory impressions. Likewise, if your sensory acuity (the sharpness of your senses) was too poor to pick up the sensory impressions of whatever was going on out there in the first place, it will be impossible to remember accurately what you never or only partially experienced in the first place.

Other factors operate at this first stage of memory as well. Can a sensation register that is not consciously attended to? Yes. It is known as a subliminal perception, a response to a stimulus that is sensed but not consciously perceived. If a stimulus is perceived but not in conscious awareness, will it necessarily be remembered? No. Can a subliminal experience be recorded unconsciously and later be remembered consciously? Research is inconclusive, but it generally appears to be quite unlikely.

The first level of memory is known as "sensory memory." It is memory of an extremely short duration—only about one-half second. For example, if you were to visit my home, and you share my interest in music, you might scan my collection of compact discs. Your eyes would move over the various titles, but you would not be storing these bits of information for long-term recall.

The next step, organization, refers to the necessity of making meaning out of sensations we experience, a process known as "perception." Sensory experiences remain simply transient neurological impressions unless they are organized into something with meaning. It is simply not true that "you can remember everything that ever happened to you if conditions are right." Memory research shows definitively that what makes a stimulus memorable is the meaning it is given as it is interpreted at the time. For example, you are far more likely to remember a phrase on a billboard in your own native language than if you happen to see one in a language you don't speak. Organizing sensory impressions by giving them meaning and making an appraisal of their significance helps determine whether the information will likely be remembered.

For example, as you peruse my music collection, the titles and artists that you share an interest in will stand out in your awareness and likely get organized according to a perception that our tastes in music are similar. As we talk about our mutual interest in and appreciation of a particular artist, our focus is narrowly on that specific artist and none of the others represented in my collection. All those other titles and artists are now gone, a routine example of forgetting that demonstrates its value in preventing mental clutter.

Short-term memory follows sensory memory in the process of

transferring information to long-term memory. When some bit of information or an event is perceived in sensory memory as noteworthy, it may pass into short-term memory, where it will be held for anywhere from several seconds to several minutes. Since our attention is selective, noticing only what we deem worthy, much of what we are actually exposed to never even gets as far as short-term memory. Without rehearsal and establishing meaningful associations to the information or event, the material is quickly forgotten.

In the third stage, storage, the memory is "coded." Is the information to be stored as a visual image? A physical sensation? Whether the information is deemed significant and is "anchored" (through repetition or by carrying an intense emotional charge) dictates whether the information will pass into long-term memory and thus be eligible for later retrieval, or whether the information will stay in short-term memory just long enough to use it (like a phone number you just looked up) and then be discarded. Also, situational associations are important in coding, for memory is powerfully affected by the context in which it is acquired.

Long-term memory is the dimension of memory that allows us to retain information over time. Long-term memory is the largest component of human memory, holding information ranging from a minute ago to decades ago. Long-term memory is fundamental to life, allowing us the continuity of our experience. You don't have to relearn your name and address every day, or how to do the routine things you do. Continuity of information allows for evolution, progression, mastery. Information must be rehearsed and given meaningful associations in order to be available in long-term memory.

A key point to note here is that *not everything is stored in long-term memory*. The brain has an established protocol for remembering and forgetting, and not all experiences are memorable. Forgetting is, in many ways, as important a capability as remembering, and it is not necessarily psychologically induced. There is a difference between forgetting and repressing, despite the belief held by many therapists (43 percent of my survey respondents) that a lack of memory suggests a psychologically motivated repression and not just simple forgetting. In fact, forgetting can occur for many reasons that have little to do with psychological defenses, including the interference of subsequent events that block access to a memory, the lack of a retrieval strategy, and the possibility that the experience was never rehearsed long enough to pass from short-term to long-term memory.

The final stage of memory is retrieval, the actual recovery of the information that has been sensed, interpreted, and stored. Memory retrieval is a process vulnerable to many influences. The common experience of "going blank" at exam time when asked to recall material you know that you know gives an indication of how your level of emotional distress and your mood can affect memory retrieval. High levels of emotionalism can distort and block memories, decreasing their accuracy and availability.

Another factor affecting memory retrieval is the length of time that has elapsed since the memory's formation. A memory doesn't just sit passively in the recesses of your mind waiting to be pulled out in pristine form at just the right moment. As time passes, new information and new experiences add to and take away from our interpretations of memories of past experiences. The "good old days" can seem better and better, or, conversely, the "bad old days" can seem worse and worse, as your life continues and new perceptions mingle with old ones. In general, the passage of time leads us to embellish or diminish memories, distorting them in one way or another. Remember: Memory is a representation of an experience; it is not the experience itself.

Other factors have been identified that influence the accuracy of memory, including (1) the person's motivation to notice, interpret, and remember; (2) the expectations that lead one to "see only what one expects to see," and not what is really there; (3) the methods used to retrieve memory, which can suggest additions or deletions to a remembered experience that alter its face completely (a point especially relevant to the process of recovering repressed memories); (4) the relationship with an outside memory investigator, which may increase or decrease responsiveness to prompts; and (5) the person's personality and reactions to memory gaps that may exist (one person may accept them as gaps, while another may have a need to fill them in, even with misinformation, as in a process called "confabulation."

In sum, memory is a process that involves many variables, each of which has the potential to enhance or disrupt the storage and retrieval of accurate memories.

MEMORY IS SELECTIVE

I am aware that people generally do not care for the notion that memory is not always reliable. After all, aren't we the sum of all our history? Aren't we who we are because of who we have been and what we have experienced? No—who we are is *greater* than the mere sum of our parts. We are more than who we've been or what we have experienced because there is an interactive effect that takes place between all of our individual parts. How you read this book, for example, will not only be a function of what I have objectively written on these pages, but will be amplified or diminished by the range and quality of your own experiences. Thus, what you will remember from having read this book will be determined not only by what was actually written here by me, but also by how it related to and interacted with your own beliefs and experiences. It is a safe and easy bet that if both you and your friend read this book, each of you will remember quite selectively—and differently—what I had to say. You'll only find that out by discussing it and reminding each other of significant points and examples that one or the other of you forgot or never even noticed to begin with.

How unreliable is memory? Scores of studies, many by leading memory researcher Elizabeth Loftus, Ph.D., at the University of

Washington, have been done in recent years, particularly in response to the great need for clarity on this issue in the forensic, or legal, arena. Law enforcement personnel have to know whether an eyewitness to a crime can be trusted to have accurate recall. They need to know whether someone can be picked out of a lineup with absolute certainty that he was the actual offender. After all, we have all heard stories of innocent people going to prison for crimes they did not commit. How does this happen?

In experiments conducted by Dr. Loftus and many others in the United States, Canada, Great Britain, Germany, Australia, and the Netherlands, a phenomenon known as the "misinformation effect" was identified. In a typical experiment, misleading information was credibly presented to witnesses, who accepted the suggested information as accurate and incorporated it into their narratives as genuine. In one informal field experiment filmed for television, for example, Dr. Loftus staged a theft of a woman's purse in her university classroom before the entire class. A man grabbed a woman's purse and quickly left the room amid the victim's cries that she had been robbed. Dr. Loftus quickly took charge and told everyone to stay seated and not go after the thief because "he might be dangerous." She then asked for descriptions of the suspect. One student immediately volunteered her observation of the man's checkered shirt. Dr. Loftus quickly confirmed that she saw the checkered shirt, too, and added, in her voice of authority, that the man had a beard. Nearly every additional eyewitness description of the suspect now included his beard.

Dr. Loftus then informed the class the theft was staged, and presented four men to the group for eyewitness identification. They were dressed similarly, but not identically, as in a real police lineup. Two were bearded and two were not. Students quickly formed opinions as to which one of the four men in the lineup was "the bad guy." Most chose one of the bearded men. After giving everyone enough time to convince themselves (and the others, too, I suppose) which of the four was guilty, Dr. Loftus dropped the bombshell: It was *none* of the four! When she brought in the real culprit, most were shocked to see that he was clean-shaven. Dr. Loftus had *suggested* that he had a beard, a suggestion that people accepted as true, unconsciously revising their own memories. This informal experiment and many more controlled laboratory studies show clearly that misleading information that is credibly presented after an event can lead people to create and believe erroneous memories. Can misinformation credibly presented in therapy about experiences in the distant past lead to similar revisions?

The objective accuracy of the memory is one crucial aspect of its overall value, while another is the degree of confidence the individual has in the memory's accuracy. When someone points at an individual in a lineup and says, "I'm *sure* it's him," that individual is more likely to be believed than if he or she had said, "I *think* it's him." The person's level of certainty helps determine his or her believability. Can someone be very certain about the accuracy of a memory and yet be wrong? Yes. Consider a very interesting piece of research conducted by Ulric Neisser at Emory University addressing, in part, this very issue.

The day after the space shuttle *Challenger* exploded, Neisser had his students (aged eighteen to twenty-two) write out exactly where they were and what they were doing at the time they first learned of the *Challenger's* explosion. He had them do this within twenty-four hours of the shuttle's explosion, so these could be regarded as highly reliable reports.

Three years later, Neisser contacted students who had participated and again asked them, "Where were you when the space shuttle *Challenger* exploded?" *A full one third of them gave answers that were so far off as to be almost totally unrelated to what actually happened!* What struck Neisser, though, was how *certain* of their answers the students were, and what plausible details they gave. Despite their certainty, a full third of them were way off from their original descriptions. (Bear in mind, this research did not involve trauma of a personal nature to the respondents. Would such trauma increase or decrease the accuracy of their reports? The answer is not yet fully known.) Especially significant is how detailed and plausible the wrong accounts were. It is very trouble-some that people could be *so sure* and *so wrong*. Despite this tenu-ous relationship between certainty and accuracy, about one in four of the therapists I surveyed believed that a higher level of certainty suggests a higher level of accuracy.

Now, consider some of your own memories. How do you know the things that you believe happened to you really did? We all have direct and clear memories for many significant events, but pick one to recall now that isn't quite so clear. Did people tell you what happened enough times that now you simply remember it that way? Are the details "sort of fuzzy"? What about really early memories from childhood? Are they real memories, or did they evolve from stories that you've heard or old photos that you've seen? Are they remembered from a child's perspective in your adult years, or are they remembered with an adult perspective about childhood experiences? You may have had the perplexing experience of a parent or some other relative telling you about a significant-sounding experience you had that you have no recol-lection of. Such a story may eventually become a part of your memory of your distant past, even though it was merely suggested to you by someone you love and trust to tell you the truth.

THE BEGINNINGS OF MEMORY

In a therapeutic process commonly called "rebirthing," a woman named Gloria is encouraged to reexperience what her therapist tells her must have been a traumatic birth. The thera-pist leads Gloria to believe that her symptoms are directly derived from the way her birth occurred, deducing that her problem in creating or maintaining intimate relationships arose from inade-quate bonding with her mother in the earliest moments of life.

Gloria accepts the therapist's invitation to close her eyes and relax, and soon she is comfortably detached from the rest of the world and deeply absorbed in her own internal experiences. The therapist suggests she go back, way back in time, all the way to the darkness, warmth, and weightlessness of being in her mother's womb. Soon Gloria gradually shifts into a fetal position, and there is a look of blissful comfort on her face, though she says nothing.

The therapist prepares her for the shock to come—squeezing painfully through her mother's birth canal, the bright lights of the delivery room, the cold air against her sensitive skin, the feel of cool air rushing into her lungs, and the slap on her behind. Soon Gloria is crying. She begins to scream, "I don't want to go. I'm not ready to go!" The therapist encourages her to express her rage at being born, which Gloria forcefully does. She is told to listen to the conversation in the delivery room, and for a moment she is quiet, straining to hear. She says she hears someone saying to her mother, "Congratulations, you have a beautiful baby girl." Her eyes fill with tears and she whispers her mother's answer: "She was an accident. How can I be a mother?" Gloria cries intensely, and the therapist gently asks, "You were an accident?" Gloria says, "I never knew that before. My mother never wanted me. I was never meant to be." The therapist touches her lightly in a kind and supportive way and says, "Now you know why you have never been able to feel connected to anyone."

MEMORIES FROM WITHIN THE WOMB? REMEMBERING CONVERSA-tions and feelings from the first moments of life? Let's complicate matters a bit. Let's say Gloria then asks her mother if she was a planned, wanted baby and her mother truthfully tells her she was not. Does that prove she "remembered" accurately? Or did she merely bring to life in the rebirthing process something that she had long sensed but simply could not face before? That is what a good therapy can often do—help people face what a part of them has known all along but couldn't deal with. But that is not to be confused with remembering actual events or conversations from so far back.

When does memory begin? What is the youngest age from

which an adult may have a clear and direct recollection of an event? What is *your* earliest memory, and how old were you when the event occurred? Your earliest memory is most probably very much like a snapshot—an image without continuity.

A great deal of research has been done on this topic, which is of obvious importance to our view of reports of abuse from infancy. For example, can a single memory ostensibly occurring at the age of six months be considered reliable? The research indicates overwhelmingly that the answer is no. Study after study indicates that memories occurring before the age of two or three are most uncommon, and must be considered questionable—that is, they are likely to be the products of suggestion (arising from seeing old photographs and hearing family stories), confabulation, or simple misremembering. You must bear in mind that this is not an absolute phenomenon. Parts of an early childhood memory may be wrong while other parts may be reasonably accurate.

Further studies show that the majority of people have little in the way of detailed memory for as much as the first five to seven years of life. How much do *you* remember of your day-to-day life as a four-year-old? Whatever you do remember of your childhood is likely to be vague and impressionistic images of significant but disconnected events. And, just as described earlier, they can be laced with inaccurate information.

Why do most people lose their early memories to what Freud termed "childhood amnesia"? Is there necessarily some psychological motivation to repress childhood memory? Nearly 60 percent of survey respondents assumed that motivated forgetting is the basis for things we can't remember. This assumption is based on an outdated theoretical formulation carried over from Freud's era, yet the majority of therapists surveyed still believed it. Nearly half believed that childhood amnesia necessarily indicates childhood trauma.

If it isn't necessarily repression, meaning a psychologically motivated forgetting, that causes childhood amnesia, what else could it be? The answer has far more to do with the development

of thinking and awareness (cognition) and the biological matura-
tion of the brain than it does with psychological defenses. In very
early childhood, the brain simply has not acquired the necessary
abilities to establish meaningful long-term memories that will last
into adulthood. It does not yet have the relevant mechanisms for
understanding and sorting out what is meaningful, nor does it
have a means for organizing and storing experiences in ways that
are necessary for retrieving memories in later life. The assimila-
tion of ongoing experiences into long-term memory that are retrievable in later life with a high level of accuracy does not occur
until later childhood. Yet, despite all the research indicating otherwise, nearly half of those responding to the survey believed that
as an adult you can recover accurate memories even from the first
year of life. How do therapists justify maintaining such an unfounded belief?

BODY MEMORIES AND
INFANTILE PERCEPTIONS

Therapists are just as likely as any other group to twist facts to
fit beliefs. They have devised a plausible means for maintaining
the belief that memories from the earliest hours and days of life
are recoverable with enough accuracy to justify believing them—
the so-called "body memory." Since most therapists are agreed
the infant mind is not yet sufficiently developed to organize and
store memories, they postulate that memories are stored in the
body. Years later, when cognitive development permits an understanding of what these body memories mean, particularly when a
"helpful" therapist is there to interpret them, the individual can
now translate his or her body memories into direct knowledge of
having been abused. What exactly is a body memory? Can someone store sensory impressions on a purely physical level for later
recall and accurate interpretation? As in the rebirthing process

described earlier, can an infant or even a fetus "record" conversations as sound sequences that later, when language has been learned, can be understood as meaningful conversation?

These are unprovable and not entirely plausible hypotheses set forth by therapists who want or need to believe in the innate wisdom of the infant mind and body. The facts about memory are twisted to fit the theory that all experiences are memorable and retrievable. Such ideas are hardly objective, and may be potentially dangerous when they are offered as "evidence" that abuse occurred.

REPRESSED MEMORIES OF PAST LIVES

As if dealing with memories from just this life isn't enough, some therapists are willing to go even further in seeking causal explanations for their clients' problems. These therapists believe that unconscious memories from past lives are creating the symptoms the client is reporting! Unbelievably, more than a quarter of survey respondents reported a belief in past lives that could be "accurately recalled under hypnosis." Such peculiar beliefs further confuse an already confused picture of the workings of memory, in which it is clear that beliefs are far more influential than facts.

Those who believe in them swear to the authenticity of memories of past lives. They get indignant, even enraged, when their beliefs are questioned. "How do *you* know these memories *aren't* real?" they ask. (In truth, I don't. As with all such utterly arbitrary, unprovable beliefs, it is simply a question of faith. And mere faith is something I don't rely on when peoples' lives are on the line.) Believers argue that the unconscious mind is a storehouse of accumulated information, and not from this lifetime alone. As evidence, they point to the dramatic "memories" that surface in techniques like so-called "past-lives regression therapy." In the course of sessions utilizing hypnosis or other suggestive procedures, a client is instructed to go back in time and recall past incarnations in vivid detail. The underlying "therapeutic framework" or assumption is that some unresolved issue from a past life is the unconscious cause of current symptoms. Thus, it is believed that someone with an inexplicable water phobia is likely to have drowned in a previous life. The client is guided by the therapist to recall details of the past life, and by uncovering the past life's experience and "releasing" the associated traumatic feelings, a "cure" is accomplished.

I have seen dozens of such sessions, and they are invariably dramatic. The amount of detail provided by clients of their past life experiences is extraordinary. Remarkably clear descriptions of the era, the locale, the dress, the customs, the people, the life-style, even the use of accents and phrases, seemingly from that past life lend an air of authority to the account. Such narratives may be very convincing, but usually only to those already open to such beliefs, some of whom may even participate in them.

THE SAN DIEGO UNION REPORTED IN JANUARY OF 1992 THAT A California woman named Maureen Williamson went to a hypnotherapist for help in resolving a nagging childhood trauma. During her hypnosis sessions, a name popped into her head, a name unfamiliar to her. In a later trance session, she "recognized" the name as that of her husband in a past life, with whom she lived in Millboro, Virginia, during the Civil War era. In later trances, she "recognized" many of her current friends and neighbors as friends and neighbors back in Millboro over a century ago. The therapist hypnotized them as well, and guess what? At least thirty-five members of Ms. Williamson's (current) community now "know" who they were and where they lived during the Civil War!

Should we conclude from this story that past lives are real because nearly three dozen people attest to their certainty about who they were in a previous incarnation? How could such clear and specific memories in so many people be false? Where do all the details come from if they're not true memories of past lives? The same questions arise, with far more serious consequences, when we consider early childhood, even infantile, memories of abuse. Does clarity and volume of detail mean greater accuracy? If such memories of abuse are not true, why would they arise in therapy?

Clarity of memories and volume of detail are not enough for judging truthfulness. Believing something to be true isn't the same as its being true. That is why lie detector tests used with accusers are often useless. Lie detectors measure the degree of conviction you have about what you are saying, and not whether it is really true. In other words, if I genuinely believe that Martians in the next room are controlling my blood pressure (because I'm suffering from a delusion that this is truly the case), I will pass a lie detector test on the subject.

But when very early childhood memories are assumed to be retrievable, pressure tactics ranging from very subtle to very blatant may be applied in order to recover them. To what extent are memories obtained under such pressured conditions authentic? Couldn't they be created as a product of imagination, out of a desire to please the therapist, or simply as a convenient way of explaining puzzling symptoms?

SEPARATING TRUTH FROM FICTION

Unfortunately, many therapists believe in past lives, the accuracy of infantile memories, and body memories. Many continue to maintain the rigid but unfounded belief that memories of all experiences *must* be in there somewhere in one form or another. If such therapists didn't believe the things that they believe, they would have to admit that a lot of the therapy they practice is based on mere speculation, even utter nonsense. This thought is much too threatening and so leads many therapists into the very "denial" they accuse those with a healthy skepticism of being in. Denial is just as likely to occur in therapists as in their clients.

The need to authenticate their clients' memories is simply not a priority for most therapists, as they clearly indicated in their responses to my survey. The majority make no attempt at all to distinguish true memories from false ones. Even the minority who do make an attempt to distinguish objective facts from subjective beliefs admit that their methods are crude. The methods they offered included how well the memory explained the person's symptoms, how detailed the memory was, how consistent the account remained over several tellings, and how convinced the client was of the memory's authenticity. These are the very methods cited earlier as unreliable means for determining a memory's accuracy! In fact, more than a third of all survey respondents gave up any attempts at critical thinking by adopting the crippling belief that in order to help clients, you must believe as they do.

How can you distinguish a real memory from a confabulation? The answer is, I'm afraid, discouraging: Without external corroboration, you can't. Virtually all of the experts I have interviewed agreed that there is no reliable means for distinguishing truth from fiction. Continued questioning only yields more details, plausible but unverifiable. Lie detectors measure only the degree of believing, not truthfulness. We can only speculate about motives. Finding out that the parts of the person's memory that *can* be verified (like what grade school he or she went to) are accurate doesn't mean the whole memory is accurate. Likewise, finding out that part of the memory is wrong doesn't mean the whole memory is wrong.

It is precisely because it is often nearly impossible to prove or disprove someone's memory that the role of therapists is so critical. Their suggestions of past lives, birth traumas, primal screams, body memories, infantile images, and so forth, are all potentially powerful influences on the quality of clients' memories. The relationship between suggestibility and memory will be considered in depth later, but it bears repeating here that memory is a process of reconstruction, assimilating information from multiple sources ranging from old movies to our own self-deceptions and illusions. It is imperative that caution and good judgment be exercised by therapists and clients alike in doing any work involving distant or presumably repressed memories.

WHERE DO THE DETAILS OF UNTRUE MEMORIES COME FROM?

Memory necessarily involves processes of perception. You simply cannot remember life events that did not first pass through your senses, singly or in combination. In the same way that you can be fooled by visual illusions (seen any good magicians lately?), or illusions in *any* of your sensory modalities, for that matter, you can be fooled by illusions of memory. Think of times you argued with your spouse or a sibling about some memory you were absolutely certain of that turned out to be absolutely wrong. Or, consider my recent experience of paying a visit to the place in Wisconsin where I lived as a boy. I remembered clearly, or so I thought, the school I went to, the neighborhood I lived in, the houses of friends of mine, and the places I used to hang out. I was shocked to discover that very little was as I remembered it! The huge school I went to was about a tenth of the size I remembered it to be. The great auditorium that could hold the whole student body at assemblies was just a gymnasium, and not a very large one at that. I didn't remember my neighborhood being tree-lined or so close to the shopping district. I didn't remember the nearby lake being so far from my house. A lot of my memories were quite distorted. Why? Because I'm an adult remembering experiences that took place and were stored in the perceptions of a child. A child's perceptions and understandings are inevitably limited by the range of resources a child has.

Memory is a process of reconstruction, not simply of remembering. Missing details are slowly filled in with plausible guesses that often aren't even recognized by us as guesses. This is the process of "confabulation" I have referred to previously. It is most apparent in older people suffering senility, as when you ask your grandfather if he's had breakfast and he says, "Yes, they took us to Paris for crepes." He really can't remember otherwise, so he says it quite sincerely. If you want the truth, you'll need to ask someone else who was at breakfast who isn't as prone to confabulation.

I must make it clear that unconscious confabulation, though deceptive, is *not* the same as consciously lying. It is merely a way of filling in the gaps in your memory. The false memories that arise in response to suggestions of reliving past lives, a birth trauma, or a repressed memory of abuse are genuinely believed by the rememberer. That is what makes accusers so convincing. And just as they typically cannot prove the truth of their memories, typically no one else can disprove them, either. This is the basis of faith, not science. As soon as someone asks me, "Well, isn't reincarnation possible? Couldn't these memories be true?" I have to concede that, yes, it's theoretically possible. And it's theoretically possible that Martians are in the next room controlling my blood pressure. Theoretical possibilities are not evidence.

IMAGINATION IS THE KEY

Detailed memories of experiences you have never actually had can come from countless sources, with your imagination being the primary one. Any imaginative writer creates characters, their backgrounds, and challenging situations for them to live through. For example, when Gene Roddenberry created *Star Trek*, he created characters, personalities, preferences, histories, goals, problems to solve, and experiences, all in tremendous detail. Some people—so-called "Trekkers"—have become so involved with se characters, they may even feel more strongly about them than they do about members of their own families! People can and do develop a "believed-in imagination" that serves as an endless supplier of "facts" and details that can sound remarkably plausible, yet have no truth to them. If you watch enough television, see enough movies, read enough books, and talk to enough people, you end up with plenty of details for whatever stories you wish to create.

People typically do not intentionally lie about a newfound belief that they have been abused, and the terms "false memories" and "suggested memories" do not in any way imply deliberate deception. People confabulate for all sorts of innocent reasons, most commonly: (1) out of a need to define an identity, (2) out of hostility toward the accused for perceived injustices unrelated to abuse, (3) out of delusional beliefs created for entirely idiosyncratic reasons, or (4) as a result of outside influences that lead the individual to misinterpret or misunderstand his or her past experiences. Therapy is perhaps the most common of these outside influences in ways that will be explored in detail later.

THE PARADOX OF REPRESSED MEMORY

Despite the lack of intention, at their most devastating, accusations of abuse can tear families apart and ruin individual lives, all on the basis of presumably repressed memories. Repression is a highly controversial concept within the mental health profession. At one end of the repression continuum is David Holmes, a University of Kansas psychologist who reviewed six decades' worth of research and concluded that there was no evidence to support the notion of repression at all. At the other end of the continuum is Renee Fredrickson, a psychologist and the author of *Repressed Memories*. Fredrickson makes no distinction between repression and forgetting, apparently considering all absence of memory to be psychologically motivated or repressed. Regarding repression and trauma, she writes:

> The traumatic and the trivial are the two kinds of information your mind represses. . . . Trauma is any shock, wound, or bodily injury that may either be remembered or repressed, depending on your needs, your age, and the nature of the trauma. Some of your childhood traumas may be remembered with incredible clarity, while others are so frightening or incomprehensible that your conscious mind buries the memory in your unconscious. . . . Although all forms of abuse can result in repressed memories, sexual abuse is particularly susceptible to memory repression.

The assumption is that traumatized individuals go through a process called "dissociation," a defensive splitting off of awareness for the horrific aspects of the trauma. It is as if they removed themselves psychologically from the traumatic experience as it occurred, retaining no conscious memory for what took place. Dissociation, repression, suppression, and denial are all ways for an individual to avoid consciously dealing with painful realities, but the questions about these mechanisms are many and to date they have gone largely unanswered.

Fredrickson's assumption that repression is a product of need, age, and the nature of the trauma is too simplistic to be entirely true. All sorts of traumas happen to all kinds of people at all ages, and everyone has the same need to avoid pain. Why some people repress memories and others do not, and even how often repression occurs, is still largely unknown. To assume, as Fredrickson does, that repression and forgetting are the same, and that a memory gap is most likely associated with a sexual trauma, is an arbitrary belief system that would be highly suspect in a therapist for its potential to unduly influence clients.

There is no scientific evidence whether memories which surface after years of being repressed are authentic or inauthentic. It is a legitimate concern to wonder how we can objectively tell when repression is in force in a client's life. Symptoms alone are not evidence.

There is a well-known phenomenon operating both in research and clinical contexts called a "confirmation bias," which is a tendency to look selectively for evidence that supports what you already believe. For example, if you believe your friend is angry with you for some unspoken reason, you may look for evidence in what he or she says or does to support your belief he or she is angry with you. Comments you would normally let go by without even noticing may now be interpreted as veiled anger. Or, as another example, a therapist who theorizes that a particular client smokes cigarettes as a product of some unconscious suicidal wish may ask the client, "Have you ever thought about dying?" Naturally, the client says, "Sure." The therapist concludes, "I'm right—this client thinks about death and so must have a death wish." It is a hazard for the mental health profession that a single problem can be interpreted plausibly in literally hundreds of ways, none provable or disprovable. The repression of memories is just one more plausible but subjective interpretation, albeit a potentially explosive one.

Repression, because it is poorly understood and subject to conflicting interpretations, muddies our understanding of trauma and its effects on survivors. If a therapist sees repression as inevitable where trauma is concerned, then there is no need to seek truly objective evidence that confirms or disproves the belief. The confirmation bias can be so great that therapists literally believe that the "evidence" for repression is greatest from the person who least suspects it. In other words, if you were directly asked whether or not you were abused, and you said, "No," the therapist with a confirmation bias would feel justified in saying, "Well, you have the symptoms of someone who has been abused, and since you don't think you were, you must be repressing the memories of abuse."

Do you see the bind in which the client is placed? How can you remember what you are repressing, or know what you don't know? And if you must always leave open the possibility you were abused, then how do you ever safely conclude you weren't?

REDEFINING YOUR MEMORIES

Some abuse experts suggest that the great majority of adult Americans come from "dysfunctional families" where some level of abuse, however mild or severe, was present. Where this idea comes from is not clear, but there is no question that whenever you broaden criteria for membership, more people join the club. Some go so far as to rank the petty disappointments, humiliations and rejections of life as abuse right alongside serious cases of violence or incest. Such superficial examples trivialize the depth of pain that survivors of serious abuse suffer. They also illustrate the point that old memories can be redefined in light of new perspectives.

Why do so many people inappropriately jump on the recovery movement bandwagon? Quite frankly, I think that when you appeal to the lowest common denominator in people, you will always get a big response. Television programs that are crude and vulgar are big hits. Movies that are sexually explicit or graphically violent are instant box office successes. Many recovery experts shine their spotlights on people's emotional needs, weaknesses, and vulnerabilities. They soothe people with acceptance and cajole them with permission to "let it all hang out." Any time you offer to free people from personal responsibility and let them loosen their restraints, you'll have lots of followers.

Some leaders of the abuse recovery movement give powerful emotional validation to those who already feel justified in identifying themselves as victims—abused by their parents' insensitivity, neglect, or rejection. Who *wasn't* painfully disciplined at times? Who wasn't told "no" when he or she wanted to be told "yes"? Who has never been hurt, humiliated, or ignored, and who hasn't suffered all the rest of what happens that is painful in human relationships? Such leaders provide definitions of abuse that will cover these instances, too, even if you were not violently or sexually assaulted. They offer sympathy in these generally unsympathetic times, and they promise eventual salvation if only you believe. Their widespread acceptance is one indicator of how poor many people's self-esteem really is.

REWRITING HISTORY

Adding new perspective to old experiences can literally rewrite them. "Modest upbringings" may become redefined as "poverty," a "hard-working father" may be redefined as "detached and unavailable," and a "loving and protective mother" may become a "co-dependent." (They used to just be "Mom and Dad.") Once the new labels stick, it's hard to lose sight of them, and they tend to create new issues that justify lots of therapy by standing out suddenly as if in neon. Many therapists argue smugly that this is what achieving mental health is all about. Meanwhile, though, research shows that people are more anxious, depressed, and substance-dependent than ever. While the number of therapists in the country has roughly doubled in the last decade, the mental health of the country has not improved accordingly. All sorts of issues can get stirred up in you as you learn to rewrite your own personal history with new perspectives obtained in therapy. Therapy can be especially powerful in this rewriting process when it involves the questionable premise of unquestioningly bringing to light and believing repressed memories.

WHAT DO WE REALLY KNOW ABOUT REPRESSION?

The truth is, we don't know very much about the repression of memories of trauma. We don't know how common repression really is. We don't know how authentic seemingly distant memories are that suddenly and dramatically surface in response to a lecture, a self-help book, or a therapy session. We don't know whether repressed memories always exist where troubling symptoms are present, the source waiting to be uncovered, or whether the same kind of symptoms can exist independently of negative experiences that have been repressed. We don't know how to characterize the differences between repression and simple forgetting. We don't know from what age repression is even possible. We don't know if trauma makes a repressed memory less or more accurate in a given individual. We don't know which techniques for recovering repressed memories will alter them in significant ways merely by using them. We don't know why some people repress a particular type of trauma and others don't. We don't know why in some people memories of traumatic events, known to exist in their backgrounds, never surface at all, while in others these memories eventually return. When there is so much we don't know, how can so many therapists be so assured in their belief that what they are doing is legitimate and therapeutic?

It is unknown just what percentage of people are repressing memories of abuse, since you cannot directly ask, "Are you repressing memories of abuse?" Repression is associated with trauma in a statistically significant number of cases, but it is not possible to obtain exact figures. Consider one example, reported in *The New York Times* in July 1992. A Rhode Island man who had been sexually abused as a child by a priest repressed the memories until he was well into adulthood. Aware of an underlying feeling of "mental pain" despite a successful life, he lay on a bed and tried to understand why. First came an idea he'd been betrayed, and later came the memory of the priest who abused him at the age of twelve. He then confronted the priest who, thankfully, admitted that the molestations did, in fact, occur. Subsequently, no fewer than fifty others then came forward to accuse the same priest of abusing them similarly. Only the accuser and two others claimed to have repressed memories of the abuse; the others remembered and simply had not discussed it with anyone.

In one study involving a twenty-year follow-up of 100 children who had been treated in a hospital setting for sexual abuse, Linda Meyer Williams, of the Family Violence Research Laboratory at the University of New Hampshire, found that one in three did not spontaneously remember the abusive experiences that had been documented in their hospital records. In another study, researchers reported that 60 percent of their sample of 468 clients with a reported history of sexual abuse in childhood had been unable to remember the abuse at some point in their lives.

In still another study, one not involving sexual abuse, 14 percent of people hospitalized after an accident had forgotten their hospitalization only six months later. Is this evidence of repression?

Since what constitutes abuse is ambiguously defined, and the boundaries separating repression from simple forgetting are not clearly drawn, it is apparent that the range of reports of repression is currently too broad to be meaningful. Furthermore, it is clear that not all traumas lead to repression, for some people remember quite clearly and have never forgotten what happened to them. In fact, the majority of abuse survivors are like Oprah Winfrey, who always knew she was abused but apparently never spoke to anyone about it.

What causes repression and who represses memories of trauma? Clearly, it is not the nature of the trauma that determines the repression, since one can find some people who repress every kind of trauma and others who live in distress with the constant memory of it. Is it a particular personality type prone to repression? This is one of the very important questions that is as yet unanswered.

KEY POINTS TO REMEMBER

- The comparison of the mind to a computer is an inaccurate one.
- Memory is reconstructive, not reproductive.
- Memory is a process, not an event. It involves the stages of sensory registration, organizing the sensory impressions into meaningful information, storage, and retrieval.
- Many factors influence the accuracy of memory, including level of emotional arousal, expectations, motivations, the methods used to retrieve it, and the time elapsed since its formation.
- Memory, like perception, is selective.
- Certainty that a memory is true does not mean it actually is. Nor does the amount of detail provided or the degree of emotionality accompanying its telling.
- Accurate memory for very early childhood experiences (before the age of two or three) is generally unavailable primarily for biological/developmental reasons.
- There is no evidence that "body memories" can be considered accurate or reliable.
- Therapists and researchers have no reliable means to distinguish authentic from false memories.
- "Confirmation bias" leads therapists to look selectively for information that confirms their preexisting beliefs.
- Memories can be rewritten retroactively with newly acquired information.
- Little is known about repression, including how frequently it occurs and why some do and others don't repress memories of trauma.

CHAPTER 4

Suggested Realities

A while ago I received the following letter:

Dr. Yapko:

As bizarre as the following question seems, please take the time to read further and give serious consideration to the subject discussed.

During a hypnosis session, have you ever had a client that believes that he/she has had an alien (extraterrestrial) abduction or encounter? Has this person experienced missing time or repetitive dreams about unusual night visitors? In the last four years there has been a 65 percent increase in reported abduction cases. Many of these reports have surfaced during hypnosis sessions.

What would you do if information similar to this was revealed by one of your clients during a hypnotic session? How do you help this person?

. . . Some of the people have had conscious recall of the event. However, the majority of them recalled the encounter while under hypnosis—which many had sought out to help them with other problems. . . .

WHAT IS YOUR REACTION TO THIS LETTER? MY REACTION IS IRRITA-tion and disbelief. Let's look at the serious implications of this letter, especially as they relate to the practice of psychotherapy.

One fact the letter doesn't mention is that a popular book called *Communion*, by Whitley Strieber, came out a few years ago. The book is an intelligent and articulate description of the author's belief that he has been repeatedly abducted by extraterrestrials. Until he became aware of the abductions, all Strieber had were periods of amnesia, and unusual dreams of abduction in which he served as a human guinea pig for extraterrestrials' experiments. Is it coincidence that "there is a 65 percent increase in reported abduction cases" following the release of Strieber's book? Obviously not. Consider the example of so-called "trance channelers," people who go into trance and become the mediums through which other entities, as old as 35,000 years, according to one, can share their "wisdom." If so many people can be convinced so easily of "trance channelers," thanks to popular books like Shirley MacLaine's *Out on a Limb,* then you can convince a percentage of the population of *anything.*

A key point of the previous chapter was that memory is a malleable, fluid process rather than a rigid, fixed one. Because of this, memory, like all other mental processes involving perception, is highly responsive to suggestive influences. In this chapter, we will consider the phenomenon of human suggestibility in a broad sense, before we go on to focus specifically on how suggestions of abuse can lead to "recovered memories" with the capacity to re-define—and destroy—entire lives.

Consider the power of suggestion to reshape perception: I've mentioned the claims of some leaders of the so-called "recovery movement" that most of us were raised in dysfunctional families headed by dysfunctional parents—people who were so out of touch with themselves, their own parents, or their children that they could not provide emotionally supportive or nurturing environments in which their children could develop. Proponents describe in elaborate, excruciating detail abuses that range from the trivial to the profound. They stress the need to discover and heal "the wounded child within" each of us. They encourage each of us through powerful suggestions to find—or create—and then develop our sensitivity to our "inner child." We are encouraged to visualize it in detail, to bring it to life, to give it a name and personality, to soothe it and do for it all the things our parents never did for us, so that we may become "whole." (Some therapists encourage us to hold stuffed animals as we do so.)

As a result of its relentless promotion through books, lectures, and tapes, the "inner child" is now a fact of life to countless Americans. They talk to it, write about it, interpret its dreams, indulge it in carefully constructed fantasies, and most of all, they try to fix it. "Healing the inner child within" has become the goal of therapists across the country, and a handy, highly publicized framework from which to launch their clinical practices and workshops. In the past month alone, I have received brochures advertising workshops entitled "Healing the Child Within," "Learning to Nurture Your Inner Child," and "A Healing Workshop for Adult Children of Affluent Parents." The trauma of wealth?

So, what's the problem? *There is no inner child!* It is a metaphor, a representation, a suggested way of thinking about your experience; *it is not the experience itself.* But, for some people, the suggestion has transcended mere metaphor and become a reality. When

I have publicly discussed it as an illusion, I've seen these people become angry and defensive, as if I've just called into question the legitimacy of one of their most precious beliefs. To be truthful, I have. Isn't it interesting, though, how so arbitrary a perspective can assume such personal importance and intensity?

The therapy trade has always relied upon metaphor to make a point. Freud's id, ego, and superego; Jung's archetypes; Berne's ego states; Bly's *Iron John*; Erroneous Zones; Peter Pan syndromes; Cinderella complexes; and on and on. The key question is, "Does this perspective empower you in some way?" Invariably, the answer is yes for some, no for others. But if the former adopt the metaphor as real, they can all too easily see the world in terms of "us" and "them." Their message is clear: Believe or you are sick. Believe and you will be healed.

Therapists may have spent a few more years in school than other people, but we can never shake the fact that we are people first, therapists second. Thus, there are countless "us versus them" conflicts deeply embedded within the mental health profession itself. Psychoanalysts typically dislike behaviorists, long-term therapists generally dislike short-term therapists, cognitive therapists usually don't approve of "touchy-feely" therapists, psychiatrists don't often like psychologists, family therapists look down on practitioners of individual psychotherapy. Does the average person know that the therapy business is so internally divided? That a given therapist's views and methods are a product of almost arbitrary personal preference?

Therapists generally offer their suggestions benevolently, in the genuine belief that they will truly help a client. From a clinical standpoint, suggestion is a necessary, inevitable, and valuable means of convincing people to adopt viewpoints and behaviors that can help them to feel better. The great majority of people's problems are a direct consequence of false and self-limiting beliefs. For example, if you believe that terrible things will happen to you if you don't wear your lucky socks, you will go into full-blown panic if you misplace them. This is not a personally empowering belief. A therapist who suggests powerfully that good or bad events occur independently of which socks you happen to be wearing can help free you from panic and a life ruled by superstition.

People can and routinely do accept others' suggestions, and then build their lives around them. Their responsiveness to others' beliefs, perceptions, ideas, behaviors, feelings, attitudes, and values is known as suggestibility. It is an inherent human trait that can predispose us to accept suggestions of all sorts, including suggestions of abuse.

SUGGESTIBILITY, HYPNOSIS, AND FALSE MEMORIES

Researchers in the field of hypnosis have known for well over a century that false memories can be implanted in individuals through the use of formal hypnotic procedures or even through simple suggestion, without formal hypnosis. As early as 1889, hypnotist Albert Moll wrote of his experiences with instilling false memories of specific scenes—even crimes—under hypnosis, and urged the legal system to exercise caution. Alan Scheflin, a legal expert and author of the important book *Trance on Trial*, has documented the long history of hypnosis in creating false memories and unreliable testimony in the contexts of courtroom proceedings and police investigations.

In the British television documentary *Hypnosis on Trial*, Dr. Martin Orne, an expert on hypnosis and memory, demonstrated the ease with which false memories can be hypnotically implanted in an experimental subject. In an initial interview, the subject reported to Orne an excellent night's sleep on a particular night of the previous week. After hypnotizing her, Orne suggested to her that she had not slept well at all because her sleep was interrupted by loud noises that sounded like gunshots, at a time of night he specified. When the woman came out of hypnosis shortly afterward, she reported that the night's sleep had been disturbed at the time Orne had suggested by loud noises that sounded like gunshots.

Orne then played back to her a tape recording of her earlier account, in which she reported a sound night's sleep. The woman seemed confused, but was surprisingly insistent that she had, in fact, been awakened by loud noises. It was evident that she was more confident of the truth of the memories suggested to her than of the real memories she had described previously. Other researchers have replicated Orne's findings.

Dr. Herbert Spiegel, another hypnosis expert, conducted an equally dramatic demonstration in May 1968, which was filmed for American television. He hypnotized a man and told him that radio and television stations across the United States were being targeted for takeover by Communists. He provided no details, but suggested to the man that he would remember specific details associated with the plot. When the man came out of hypnosis, he began describing the Communists' plans, providing a very elaborate set of details right down to the furnishings of the room he was in when he first learned of the intended takeover. Spiegel then rehypnotized the man and removed the original suggestions. The man was shocked to see himself on film elaborately and sincerely describing the Communist plot. Spiegel called this phenomenon the "honest liar" syndrome; such individuals are saying what they genuinely believe to be true, despite the fact that they are responding to implanted memories. Such individuals make exceptionally good witnesses; they are sincere, believable, and detailed in their accounts. But they are *entirely wrong*. Spiegel concluded that "it is quite possible to so contaminate the memory of the subject that he confuses the hypnotic implantations with his own knowledge. Then, by so fusing them, he cannot tell one from the other." Many researchers are finding that once the general premise of an implanted memory is accepted, the subject elaborates even further, adding plausible but equally untrue deils. This highlights a key point that will be of great interest to us later—that general beliefs precede specific memories.

Further research is showing that formal hypnosis is not necessary for false memories to be accepted as true. Research subjects who are "task-motivated," meaning that they are earnest in their desire to fulfill the demands of the researcher, are every bit as likely to accept an implanted memory as hypnotized subjects are. It is fairly obvious that most people who have bothered to seek therapy are *highly* task-motivated. They want answers, they want symptom relief, and they generally want to cooperate with whatever a therapist deems is necessary for them to recover.

In many studies of hypnotically implanted false memories, subjects have remained confident of the accuracy of their new memories despite graphic evidence that the memories were suggested. The need to believe and the need for internal harmony apparently allow for a dissociation to take place—a parallel existence of real and suggested memories that make it possible for suggested memories to coexist with or even supersede real ones.

Critics of this type of false memory research typically claim that getting people to believe loud noises occurred in the night or other such suggested experiences have little or no relevance beyond the laboratory and that such findings should not be extrapolated into the context of therapy or the issue of sexual abuse. But while their exact relevance has yet to be established, clearly some of the findings above appear to have particular relevance for the therapeutic situation, and they cannot simply be dismissed out of hand.

WHAT IS REAL?

Most people seem to understand and to accept, in varying degrees, the notion that "reality is what you think it is." Consider the many diverse cultures on this planet, ranging from the most primitive to the most technologically advanced. Clearly, perceptions of reality differ dramatically among them.

"Socialization" is the psychological term for learning the rules of a society and becoming a member. From the first moments of your life, you were exposed to concepts of social roles and relationships, language, politics, art, history, goals, and countless other matters, via your particular family and the larger society of which it was a small part. You learned to view the world from an acquired perspective unique to your culture, your family, and your personal history. Your entire view of life has been, in other words, *suggested* to you. Socialization is inevitable, and the quality of our lives is, in large part, the product of how the things we have learned about ourselves and about life either enhance or diminish us. From this standpoint, "healing the wounded child within" is simply a well-intentioned idea for overcoming the limitations of one's socialization. And, for many people, it does exactly that. Unfortunately, for others, it does the reverse.

Reality is pretty hard to pin down. While some things in life can be identified, measured, or manipulated with a clear understanding of cause and effect, much is as unclear as those inkblots some therapists ask their clients to interpret. In many ways, life is an experiential inkblot: It has no clear, objective meaning, just whatever you happen to believe. Consider the fact that I have spent the last twenty years of my life studying psychology, learning and developing principles of human experience, writing books, traveling the world, and teaching. I do all of this as if what I do is very important. But, others don't share my "reality." They don't like psychologists, and they don't even like people who like psychologists! They don't and won't read this kind of book. And you know what? Many of those people get married, have kids, take vacations, work at their jobs, and in general, live life just fine. And yet they live by entirely different versions of reality than I do. Likewise, there are lots of things they believe in that I don't, and I manage to have a satisfying life anyway.

Your version of reality may be no more true than anyone else's, but clearly there *are* differences in the way various versions of reality affect one's mental and physical health. Believing that your parents were terribly abusive generates very different feelings in you than does believing your parents just weren't very skilled at parenting. It is often difficult to be objective about what is real, and the consequences on *all* levels must be considered in determining the value of a particular belief. If a client comes to therapy with beliefs that are hurtful and arbitrary, it is a legitimate and important goal of therapy to attempt to examine and alter them. It seems obvious that therapy should not *provide* such beliefs. Unfortunately, all too frequently it does.

WHY DO PEOPLE BELIEVE IN FALSE REALITIES?

People do not knowingly or deliberately adopt false realities. Deluded as they may appear to you, they are convinced of the truth of their beliefs—and would undoubtedly view you as oblivious. Someone who believes that we are all reincarnated and have lived countless previous lives really believes it. Someone who believes that his or her religion is the "right" religion really believes it. Someone who believes that the alignment of the stars controls his or her destiny really believes it. When someone gets really crazy and believes that the dishwasher in the kitchen is stealing his or her thoughts, that person really believes it. People can be and routinely are convinced of beliefs that they hold as objectively true that have no real basis in "truth." Mental health professionals and their clients are no exception. Clients believe in arbitrary things that hurt them, such as that they can never be happy without feeling guilty. Therapists believe in things that they think will help, like the necessity of lying on a couch and talking endlessly about your mother. These things are not true in an objective sense, yet people firmly believe them.

The reasons why people get absorbed into belief systems and life-style practices that appear bizarre to outsiders are complex, but they have two main components: the need to believe and the need to understand. And the underlying hope is that with understanding will come control over what has seemed uncontrollable. Nowhere is this more true than in therapy: People come for professional help when some aspect of their lives is not working, or when their symptoms have become too painful to endure.

UNCERTAINTY AND THE NEED TO BE SURE

Social psychology and common sense have taught us that when people are uncertain, they tend to rely on others to guide them. The old saying, "When in Rome, do as the Romans do," reflects our reliance on other people's judgment and behavior as models of what to do in situations where we are faced with uncertainty about what is appropriate. I'm sure you can recall a situation that was new to you and how uncomfortable you felt because you weren't sure whether you were doing things in the right way. Did you watch and rely on others around you to guide your behavior? Almost everyone has had experiences like that. When we are confused or uncertain, we are more responsive to the influence of others.

With this principle in mind, it's easy to see what importance a troubled client might assign to a therapist's views. The client's own attempts to manage some portion of his or her life have failed, so help is sought from someone who is apparently more knowledgeable.

People want to alleviate confusion and contradictions within themselves, and they usually do so by omitting contradictory bits of information, or by twisting bits of seemingly contradictory information around until they all fit together comfortably. There is a well-known psychological principle called "cognitive disso-nance" that arises when people are given information or feedback that contradicts what they already believe. To reduce the discor-dant (dissonant) feelings associated with apparent contradic-tions, they will rationalize, ignore, or otherwise find ways to dismiss the new information and continue believing as they al-ways have. For example, if I view myself as an unlovable guy and then you tell me you love me, your statement contradicts my view of myself. So I might conclude that you're just saying that because you feel sorry for me or because you have some ulterior motive to manipulate me. I reject your professed love as insincere and thereby continue to see myself as unlovable.

People have a strong desire to feel certain, and when we are in an uncertain frame of mind, we will usually turn to others to find out what is proper, expected, or "true." The more the explana-tions we are given fit our personal needs, the more easily we will accept them as true. This is how conformity happens. In a very telling study, researchers injected some subjects with epineph-rine, which is a synthetic form of adrenaline that causes all the physiological symptoms of excitement, and others with a placebo (an inactive substance). All were told the injected drug was a vit-amin supplement. Some of those given epinephrine were told they would experience an increased heart rate as a side effect of the drug, but others were not told of the side effects of the "vita-min supplement." What were the uninformed subjects to con-clude when their hearts started to pound in their chests and their hands began to shake?

Accomplices to the experimenter were then introduced into the experiment by placing each alone in the room with a research subject. The subject was told that this other participant was also given an injection of the "vitamin supplement." The accomplice had been given specific instructions on how to behave—in some instances as if euphoric, in others, angry. Experimental subjects who were uncertain as to the cause of their own physical reac-tions typically ended up acting in the same way as the experimenter's accomplices! Here is just one example of how the ambiguity of your own feelings can lead you to adopt others' perspectives. Because they did not know what to make of the physical excitation they were experiencing, they incorporated within themselves the reactions of those around them.

AUTHORITY AND COMPLIANCE

When a person comes to therapy for help in dealing with a distressing problem, he or she is making an emotional investment in the therapist as a person of authority and, hopefully, a source of help. Power is not typically something the therapist inherently *has*; rather, it is primarily acquired from the client's expectations and reactions. Researcher Stanley Milgram conducted a highly controversial experiment a couple of decades ago that illustrated quite dramatically how much power people will grant to someone they perceive as being in a position of authority. Today it seems every bit as relevant, perhaps even more so.

Milgram's experiment involved leading subjects to believe that they were involved in an experiment on learning. They were informed that the purpose of the study was to discover whether the use of punishment in the form of electrical shocks would increase a subject's ability to learn word pairs. They watched as Milgram's "subjects"—who were actually his accomplices—were strapped into chairs and hooked up to the shock-delivering electrodes. They were then placed in a nearby room and positioned in front of a "shock generator." They were instructed to deliver a shock of increasing intensity with each incorrect response. As the shock levels escalated, they could hear the learners' shrieks and pounding on the adjacent wall.

In reality, the accomplice-learners were not being shocked at all, but the "teachers" clearly believed they were delivering painful shocks. Most were visibly anxious about what they were doing and were often reluctant to continue on with the experiment, especially when a learner became silent. But when they turned to the experimenter for guidance, he simply said, "You must go on. The experiment must continue." In the end, more than 50 percent of the "teachers" delivered the highest shock level on the generator, past the point labeled "DANGER: SEVERE SHOCK," past the point where the learner went silent. Believing they had no alternative, they followed orders that were obviously destructive. Some subjects, when told, "You have no choice. You must continue with the experiment," folded their arms firmly across their chests and said, "I have a lot of choice and I refuse to continue." But they were in the minority.

The phenomenon of obedience to authority is observable in many contexts. You yourself may have followed orders (from a parent or boss, perhaps) that you knew were wrong but felt you had to obey or face some terrible consequence. Business relationships and even some intimate relationships are built on a markedly disproportionate balance of power. The same can generally be said of the therapist-client relationship, where the fear of not getting well or being rejected by the therapist reinforces the therapist's authority.

The client must divulge personal and sensitive information to a person about whom he or she knows very little, usually only the therapist's professional status and, for the more inquisitive, his or her professional training and experience. The client is in the vulnerable position of revealing his or her problems, inadequacies, symptoms, and fears to a person who, based on what the client knows, seems to be going through life entirely successfully. A person in such a position of power can give unusual interpretations of a problem (as long as they are plausible) and prescribe unlikely treatments without damaging his or her credibility. A client is likely to require little beyond that the explanation fit his or her need to understand.

SUGGESTIBILITY AND SUGGESTIONS

Given the suggestible nature of the therapy client—by definition—the therapist's use of suggestion (which is inevitable) must be especially skillful and exact. As I have said, anything that has the ability to influence for the better has an equal capacity to influence for the worse.

One of the most potent forms of suggestion available to therapists is the "process suggestion," which purposely offers general or even ambiguous ideas to the client, who is invited to "fill in the blanks" with his or her own details. I might say to you, "Pause now and think of someone important from your past who had a positive influence on you." Note that I do not specify whether it should be someone from long ago or more recently, whether it should be someone male or female, or what kind of positive influence I mean. Rather than offering specifics, I let you respond in your own way according to your own projection of what you thought I meant. I can make statements so general that you will inevitably find a way to make the suggestion fit you, and it will then seem very personal to you.

If you read your horoscope in the newspaper, you see examples of process suggestions daily. You may have noticed that the observations and predictions it offers are so vague that they could apply to virtually anyone:

> You are a person who generally likes to be with those people you care about, but sometimes you prefer to just be left alone. Sometimes you get very frustrated with events in your life and even lose your temper on occasion. You would like more people to appreciate you and you think you deserve to make more money than you do. Sometimes you fantasize about having the perfect body so that others will be instantly attracted to you. Other times, you fantasize about having endless wealth so that you can spend

money on whatever particular whim happens to strike your fancy. Sometimes you get angry with yourself for not using your time as well as you could.

I think the above description represents just about everyone on this planet, but if I offered it in a therapy context or even at a cocktail party, you might find yourself silently agreeing and wondering, "How did he know that about me?"

THERAPISTS PROJECT, TOO

In the same way that clients supply the details that flesh out therapists' vague or ambiguous suggestions, therapists often engage in projection to assign "meaning" to clients' symptoms, which can be equally ambiguous. What confounds the issue is that therapists' projections about "the reason" for their clients' problems typically tend to sound plausible. For example, a physician might interpret your difficulty in losing weight as "metabolic." A Freudian analyst would likely interpret the same problem as evidence that you are "fixated at the oral stage of development." A behavioral therapist would probably want to identify the "reward" (i.e., positive reinforcement) you obtain from overeating. A Gestalt therapist might want you to "identify your polarities and establish a dialogue between your fat and thin selves." A cognitive therapist would likely tell you that you are attributing characteristics to food that food does not objectively have. An abuse specialist would perhaps tell you that you eat to distract yourself from the pain of your repressed abuse trauma.

In each case, the problem—overweight—is the same, but the perspectives about how to interpret and then to treat it differ markedly. Yet, each of these widely divergent interpretations is plausible. And even after decades of research on therapy practices, we often cannot distinguish with certainty between what is merely plausible and what is true.

Therapists typically want to identify the "root cause" of a problem. Sometimes, they may even succeed in doing so. More often, however, the "root cause" is inferred (i.e., projected) and not known directly. When the inferred cause of the problem is not serious or damaging to the person's self-esteem or close relationships, it may provide a new perspective that actually makes the client's problems easier to solve. However, when the inference is likely to scar the client's self-esteem and to destroy his or her closest relationships, the therapist's need to obtain clarity is achieved at the client's expense.

Often, therapists will identify a number of symptoms as evidence of a particular diagnosis. This is normal diagnostic procedure and is necessary for both accurate diagnosis and treatment. However, sometimes symptom "checklists" are reduced to such simple dimensions that they lose their accuracy and, hence, their value. Superficial lists that suggest "if you have three of the following symptoms, then you suffer from [fill in the blank]" make for good sound bites on radio or television, but they tend to simplify complex issues to the point of inaccuracy while maintaining an air of authority. It is a good idea to approach such checklists with caution.

THE NEED FOR ACCEPTANCE

Our need for other people is a cornerstone of society. Combined with our personal feelings of inadequacy, it creates a powerful need for acceptance. One of the biggest fears in the minds of clients coming in for therapy is, "If I disclose my real self to you, with all my fears, doubts, and imperfections, will you be able to like me and accept me? Or will you find me weak, repulsive, and somehow less than human?" How far will people go to obtain acceptance from others? Think of all the things you have done in your life in order to win approval.

One of the more interesting pieces of research in the literature of social psychology is the work of Solomon Asch on conformity. Asch grouped each subject with three trained accomplices, for what he said was an experiment on perception. In reality, he intended to study the dynamics of conformity. Asch presented a series of cards featuring four lines of different sizes. Each group member was to identify which of the first three lines was closest in size to the last. The task was a pretty easy one because the lines were generally of distinctly different sizes, and indeed, on the first few rounds, all four group members quickly agreed. In later rounds, though, the three accomplices agreed upon an obviously incorrect answer, generating a great deal of confusion and uncertainty in the research subject. Nearly one in three subjects typically conformed and agreed to the incorrect answer! Why? Through the early trials, a group identity had formed. A sense of belonging and feeling accepted by others fills a very basic need of people. To disagree openly means separating yourself from those whose acceptance you seek. This was apparently too uncomfortable a prospect for many of Asch's subjects to bear.

A basic principle that guides relationships, as you can verify from your own experience, is that similarity is rewarded, and dissimilarity is punished. We tend to like those who are like us, and dislike those who are different. The need to belong and to be accepted is also a powerful factor in the therapeutic relationship. Clients seek acceptance by avoiding confrontations with therapists, doing things to please them (ranging from generating therapeutic results to knitting them sweaters) and conforming to their language style, values, and theoretical ideas. This conformity is a well-documented phenomenon in the clinical literature, and often it is quite helpful. In some cases, however, such conformity can be downright dangerous.

Here's a positive example: A colleague of mine was treating a woman we'll call Mary for depression. Mary was a very emotional woman who made many of her most important life decisions impulsively, with little regard for eventual consequences. As a result, Mary often made poor decisions that would later backfire on her. She had poor self-esteem, and was convinced that her judgment was terrible and her life was destined for disaster. My colleague practices a form of therapy called cognitive therapy, which focuses on identifying distortions of thought and teaching clear and rational thinking as a way of managing life more skillfully. He taught Mary how to monitor her thoughts and feelings, how to project likely consequences and make decisions accordingly, how to gather and weigh evidence to support her decisions, and other such skills. Mary learned to think rationally and experiment with her perceptions much as my colleague who treated her does when he is treating such individuals. She benefited greatly from getting absorbed in his therapy framework, a credit to both of them.

In marked contrast was the case of a client I'll call Marie, who had initially gone to a therapist because she felt stressed with her many responsibilities. She was married and the mother of two small children, worked full-time, was active in several community groups, took care of her ailing elderly mother, and helped coach her young son's soccer team.

The therapist told her she was obviously overcommitting herself to avoid the emptiness she must feel inside. Marie had never thought of herself as empty inside, but now she wondered whether she might be fooling herself. The therapist pressed her to disclose details of her childhood. Marie described being raised by strict parents along with five siblings. The therapist focused on Marie's sadness and anger over not getting enough attention from her parents, even though Marie had never thought of them as anything but good parents who worked hard to raise their kids as well as possible. Session after session, Marie's awareness of despair and feelings of inadequacy grew. She dutifully followed her therapist's prescription to beat on chairs and express her anger, to write angry letters to her parents expressing her rage and then burn them, and so forth. Eventually, she was told that since she wasn't improving, the anxiety and depression that were now clearly evident (her therapist said they must have been "masked" before) must be biologically based. Medication and perhaps hospitalization were suggested as the proper course of treatment.

To make a long story short, the deeper Marie got absorbed into her therapist's framework for understanding her, the worse she became. She hated the side effects of the medications, and they did not relieve her symptoms. Finally she decided that maybe it wasn't she at all, but her therapist's view of her, that was the problem. She was referred to me through another therapist she consulted, who thought we would work well together. She responded well to my treatment, which emphasized specific goals and amplified her strengths rather than dwelling on hypothetical issues from childhood.

We have seen how perfectly innocent, "normal" people get to be "believers"—in religious cults, in radical political parties, in therapy as a way of life, in what someone else thinks happened in the past. We have seen how vulnerable the need to "know" and the need to "belong" make us. They open us up to interpretations and demands from those we view as credible, precisely because we are uncertain and in distress. That is just when we are most vulnerable to suggested realities, which can detach us from whatever beliefs we used to hold, no matter how strongly.

In the next chapter, we will see how potent the capacity of such influence to help or hurt is in scenarios of abuse.

KEY POINTS TO REMEMBER

- Reality is, by and large, a subjectively conceived phenomenon.
- Those who share a given set of beliefs tend to pressure others to believe similarly with an "us versus them" rhetoric that suggests "you're either with us or against us."
- The mental health profession is divided within itself about theories and techniques of clinical practice.
- Suggestibility is inherent in human nature.
- Viewpoints about life are often better judged by whether they enhance life experience rather than whether they are "true."
- People do not knowingly or deliberately adopt false beliefs. They believe they are right to believe as they do.
- The main reasons why people get absorbed in arbitrary views are the need to believe and the need to understand.
- Uncertainty generally increases responsiveness to others' influence.
- When people feel personally powerless, they will obey those they view as credible authorities; credibility is in the eye of the beholder.
- Therapists use ambiguous "process suggestions" to encourage clients to project personal details, often to give them a sense of "connectedness" to the therapist and the therapeutic process.
- Therapists project meanings onto ambiguous symptoms; these may be plausible without necessarily being accurate.
- Clients' need for acceptance is a powerful factor that leads them to conform with therapists' perceptions.

CHAPTER 5

Suggested Memories of Abuse

*T*he following letter appeared in Dear Abby's nationally syndicated column on September 14, 1992.

> DEAR ABBY: My wife and I have been married for 36 years. Our only child, "Ellie," is 34 years old. She was having some emotional problems, so she started to see a therapist, and she is now convinced that I—her father—raped her when she was an infant! She said that she had repressed the memory of this rape, and her therapist helped her to remember it.
>
> Abby, there can be no such memory as I would never do such a terrible thing! This is the greatest tragedy of my life, and I can't convince Ellie that this

"memory" of hers never happened. Thank God my wife believes me; in fact, this crisis has brought us closer together. We have bitter tears over this.

Can you please help us?

—A GRIEVING FATHER

Abby replied:

DEAR FATHER: Whatever did (or did not) happen to Ellie must be ascertained.

How this "memory" from your daughter's infancy was recalled, and the effect it has had on her, is very important.

Perhaps Ellie was sexually abused by someone else—or it is possible that she never experienced the rape at all.

Try to resolve this by collaborating with her, if possible. Family sessions with a therapist can be therapeutic for every member of your family. For Ellie's sake as well as your own, do not let this charge go unexplored.

I HAVE DESCRIBED SUGGESTIBILITY AS A TRAIT ALL HUMAN BEINGS share to some degree. I have discussed the power clients ascribe to their therapists and why. Even if you have never been in therapy, it should be clear by now that the entire process is almost always intensely emotional, carrying as it inevitably does powerful messages of hope, caring, and urgency. In this context, it is difficult to underestimate the impact of a suggestion of abuse. It is also difficult to underestimate how devastating such a suggestion can be if it is made erroneously.

But as we have seen, some therapists are working from checklists of symptoms, and in the case of abuse the checklists are often general enough to fit almost anyone. For example, symptoms such as poor self-esteem, phobias, depression, and fearing abandonment may relate to abuse in some cases, but they may have nothing at all to do with abuse in others. If a therapist projects or interprets that such common symptoms necessarily mean repressed memories of abuse, he or she will likely suggest that interpretation to the client. If the client rejects that interpretation, the therapist may accuse him or her of being in denial, and may even tell the client that his inability to accept "the truth" ruins any hope of recovery.

Many admitted in their responses to my survey that they make little or no attempt to establish what is objectively true in a given case. In fact, some therapists consider a *lack* of evidence proof! No specific memories? Repression. No specific images? Denial. No clear recall? Avoidance. It is a very strange notion that the less you know, the more certain you should be, and particularly strange to find it wholeheartedly endorsed by professed "experts."

THE REPRESSION BACKLASH

Partly we have Sigmund Freud to thank. For most of this century, psychotherapists have practiced their trade from a position that was bound to his elaborate theories. Freud was a figure of extraordinary power in shaping theoretical perspectives and clinical practices, although in recent years his influence in the world of clinical practice has declined considerably. Freud taught, and apparently believed, that sexual fantasies involving the opposite sex parent were developmentally normal. On that basis, he dismissed almost all reports of sexual contact between adults and children as fantasy, the product of wish, and not fact. Freud believed incest and child sexual abuse to be exceedingly rare, and undoubtedly his views led to "confirmation bias"—he and his followers saw only what they expected to see.

As a result, for roughly the first seven decades of this century, the sexual abuse of children was rarely discussed even among practicing professionals, nor was it addressed in clinical training. It was simply "not a problem." Fortunately, some "radical" thinkers began to question the Freudian perspective and, in so doing, they allowed for the possibility that perhaps incest and childhood sexual abuse were not so exceedingly rare after all. Once the floodgates were opened, reports of abuse began to pour in. The mental health profession was caught off guard by staggering numbers of people—mostly women, but men, too—who reported having been sexually abused as children.

Every movement creates a countermovement, or backlash. After decades of pressure not to come forward with or not to believe reports of abuse, we are in grave danger of leaping to the conclusion of abuse on the basis of mere whispers. The urgent task for mental health professionals is to find better ways of determining what is real and to stop relying on either personal bias or professionally sanctioned belief systems like Freud's.

The mental health profession is quite correct to want to protect the rights and integrity of children. It is correct to want to create avenues for people to get help in coping with the aftermath of sexual abuse. It is right to want to alert the general public to the fact that sexual abuse is sickeningly common and needs to be addressed responsibly and sensitively by *all* of us.

But what the mental health profession has not yet faced is the responsibility of finding and clarifying what constitutes genuine help in a climate of hypersensitivity and hypervigilance. More than one client has confessed to feeling anxious about even changing a baby's diapers, wondering what will be remembered later in some therapist's office as a sexually tainted experience. Surely such fears exceed the necessary cost of sensitizing the public to an important problem.

Report Abuse, Prevent a Lawsuit

Therapists are now obliged to take seriously direct revelations of a history of abuse, which is indisputably a mark of progress. We also must take seriously the potential for abuse. By law, there are few conditions under which a therapist *must* break the confidentiality of the therapist-client relationship: One is when the client threatens harm to him- or herself or another person, and the therapist can prevent such harm. Another is when the therapist knows or even *suspects* a client is abusing a child. If abuse occurred that a therapist knew about—or perhaps should have known about—and he or she did not report it to the proper authorities, the therapist could lose the license to practice and could also be sued for malpractice. If you had *your* entire career on the line, don't you think you might be more inclined to report even slight suspicions of abuse, just in case they turned out to be true?

Given the stakes, it's easy for therapists to get immersed in the abuse framework. They must be alert to signs of abuse, open to direct disclosures of abuse, and ready to ask about a history of abuse. When this sensitivity to abuse is coupled with subjective beliefs such as that dreams involving abuse are probable indications of actual abuse, the momentum to see abuse everywhere becomes powerful.

WHY DO THERAPISTS OFFER SUGGESTIONS OF ABUSE?

Therapists are, by and large, a benevolent bunch. They typically do not relish the idea of confronting abuse issues and they generally do not suggest abuse only for financial gain (despite the increase in insurance coverage that a diagnosis of sexual abuse or satanic ritual abuse generally carries), as has been cynically suggested. They typically do not suggest abuse for prestige ("I see more abuse survivors than you do!"), and they do not suggest it out of boredom. They suggest it to a particular client because they have genuinely come to believe that the signs of abuse are present and that a history of abuse is the only explanation that accounts for that client's symptoms. What they may not be aware of is that along with the conscious conviction that abuse occurred and that the client will not be able to have a satisfactory life until he or she accepts it and comes to terms with it, other powerful motives may be operating: (1) pressure from the legal system, (2) a powerful backlash against former times, when abuse could not be talked about at all, (3) peer pressure to conform and to recognize abuse as widespread so as not to be "in denial," (4) the comfort provided by having a concrete explanation for abstract and confusing symptoms.

HOW DO THERAPISTS OFFER SUGGESTIONS OF ABUSE?

Once the motivations are in place to convince a client that he or she has been sexually abused (even though the client has had no such revelation or belief), any or all of a variety of methods can be used to drive the point home. The artistry of therapy lies in a therapist's ability to use communication skills to get a particular message across to the client in ways that will effect changes on intellectual, emotional, and behavioral levels. Therapists are trained to take into account a client's psychological defenses and personality traits in determining how to get their ideas or philosophies across successfully.

To better understand how suggestions of abuse occur, let's look at them in context. A client seeks therapy and presents some troublesome symptoms. A checklist of symptoms, like those described by E. Sue Blume in *Secret Survivors*, are general enough to fit nearly everyone: headaches, arthritis, poor self-esteem, a preference for baggy clothes, difficulty in relationships with the opposite sex, drug or alcohol abuse, overweight, anxiety, depression, avoidance of mirrors, even a desire to change one's name. In fact, abuse survivors often do have some of these symptoms, but the error is in thinking that these symptoms reliably indicate sexual abuse. They can, but they don't necessarily.

It is a process suggestion even to suggest that there is a common profile of abuse survivors. In fact, to date there really is none. Survivors of abuse are male and female, young and old, well educated and poorly educated, married and single, gay and straight, religious and not religious. Some were abused in early childhood, some in later childhood; some in early adolescence, some in middle adolescence; some remember all of it, some remember very little of it; some feel guilty and blame themselves, and some feel angry and blame the perpetrator. Personally and professionally, I find it offensive to talk about "typical survivors," given the uniqueness of each person's situation and background, and I think it encourages therapists to respond to labels and categories, rather than individuals.

When a therapist has concluded that a client must have been sexually abused, in one way or another he or she communicates the message to the client. The most common approach is direct: "Your symptoms seem to fit the profile of someone who was sexually abused as a child. Were you?" Even if the client has never had such an idea before, he or she must now consider the possibility. Another common approach is, "I have reason to believe you were sexually abused as a child. Can you think of any experiences you might have had that would be considered evidence of abuse?" From within that suggested perceptual frame, memories are now reviewed from a whole different perspective. Can previously neutral or even positive memories now be tainted negatively with a sexual connotation? Of course.

One prominent therapist was featured in a segment on satanic ritual abuse on the program *PrimeTime Live* in January 1993. He was lecturing to a roomful of several hundred therapists on his "expert" approaches to uncovering a history of ritual abuse when general symptoms such as those described earlier are present. Describing his "mind reading" approach, he told his audience that he will introduce his impressions to the client by saying, "You know, I know a secret about you." The implication is clear that it is something the client doesn't know. Extraordinary! He professes to know someone's background, like some mystic or clairvoyant, and then he holds the person's earnest desire to know what he claims to know hostage.

"PRESUPPOSITION" IS AN INDIRECT SUGGESTION TECHNIQUE THAT typically bypasses critical thinking. It involves presupposing that abuse did, in fact, happen, and now we just want to know when, how, and by whom. So the suggestion given might be something like, "The pain you had to endure is obvious from your symptoms. It seems clear to me that you were sexually abused and have repressed it. Try and remember what was done to you and by whom."

A therapist might also say something like, "I saw another client with the same symptoms that you have, and it turns out that she was sexually abused as a child and repressed it." This is a more covert form of suggestion—the client is indirectly encouraged to identify with another person on the basis of analogous symptoms, and on that basis, to become aware of a shared history as well. This is a particularly powerful technique because it bypasses the emotional threat of directly talking about the client. After all, since I'm only talking about someone else, what is there for *you* to defend against?

Another suggestive approach is to redefine the client's resistance as cooperation. When the client says, "No, I wasn't abused," the therapist might smile knowingly and say something like, "Good, good. Denial is the first step on the road to acceptance and recovery." The client's certainty that abuse did not happen is now redefined as evidence that it did, and the result for the client is confusion. As we saw in the last chapter, confusion motivates a desire for clarity, which can be met by accepting the therapist's suggestions even if they are incorrect.

Or the therapist might say, "I wonder what terrible things must have happened in your childhood—things you probably can't even remember—that would cause these problems you have now." The implication of there being "terrible things" invites the client's projections. And what could be so terrible that it could not be remembered easily, if not the ultimate violation of a child? The therapist builds the trap and leads the client right to it without the client even realizing it.

Indeed, the therapist's unwavering belief in repressed memories of abuse is itself a powerful influence. The need for acceptance, support, empathy, and direction places the client in a vulnerable position. To confront the therapist directly, or even to disagree passively, may seem too risky.

The need to align oneself with the therapist's beliefs can seem "necessary" for all sorts of therapeutic reasons. But all these methods of suggestion are potent ways to encourage compliance. There are many others as well, including confrontation and threats ("If you won't face facts about your past, then I can no longer work with you"), praise ("I know you have the strength to come to terms with what I know must have happened to you"), bribery ("You're so bright and sensitive, I'd sure like to have you help me work with others like you once you have worked through your issues"), and guilt ("How can you be a good mother if you haven't fully explored your relationship with your own mother and father?"). All of these devices are generally used with the best of intentions, but by now their potentially abusive and manipulative nature is self-evident.

Misinformation and Interpreting the Ambiguous

As potent as all these techniques are in suggesting abuse and encouraging projection and conjecture, perhaps the most common and effective technique of all involves first encouraging uncertainty and then providing biased information as though it were objectively true. Consider, for example, the ambiguous pieces of "evidence," such as dreams and so-called "body memories," that (too) many therapists accept as valid purely on the basis of personal bias. Consider this common scenario: A client is told, "I think you were abused as a child." He or she denies it. The therapist smiles knowingly, like a parent patiently waiting for the child to come to his or her senses. The therapist then offers, quite matter-of-factly, a set of process suggestions: "When you're ready to get well, you may have dreams about the abuse at first. Then, when you're ready to progress, you'll have images and daydreams. When you're ready to work through your problems once and for all, you'll have full-blown, vivid memories when you're awake." There is, apparently, a correct order: denial, then dreams, then images, then memories. To a confused client, it can sound as if this sequence were well-known, documented science and not just some therapist's subjective beliefs. And not to accept the facts would mean you really *are* crazy.

So, the suggestion is accepted to have dreams. The client has a dream featuring inappropriate sexuality, or abstract symbols interpreted as inappropriate sexuality, and the therapist now has "confirmation" of repressed memories of abuse, no matter how vague or ambiguous the dream. The more vague the dream, in fact, the more justified the therapist feels in saying, "There's a lot here to deal with. As you get stronger and more ready to face your past, your dreams will get clearer."

The client's dream (or series of dreams) is then taken as "evidence" of repressed memories of abuse. Dreams as evidence? But the client's confusion gives way to noncritical acceptance of confidently presented misinformation. The client has been masterfully manipulated into forming hard conclusions out of thin air, all at the therapist's direction.

The next step is to do hypnosis, guided imagery, guided meditations, or visualization exercises (or an equivalent process that may go under a different name). The therapist asks suggestive questions, such as: "Who are you with? What is he doing to you? Do you sense he has an erection? Where is he touching you? Don't you feel dirty and used? What is that look on his face telling you?" Up come images of abuse—surprise!—right in line with the theories the therapist has presented as fact. The client emerges from these imagery sessions armed with more and more suggested or confabulated details that seem to further "prove" that abuse must have occurred. The power to misinform and to establish a chain of subsequent reactions is potentially the most dangerous part of any therapy process.

Dream interpretation involves making projections about someone else's projections. Who says a dream of falling down means this, while a dream of flying means that? This area is the astrology of psychotherapy. Body memories are another vagary that defy reasonable analysis. In the absence of clear memories of abuse, how can we know that an occasional tightness in one's chest or an inexplicable anxiety attack are signs that it occurred?

A woman in her late twenties whom I will call Andrea came for therapy. Andrea told me she had previously seen another therapist because she was suffering from bulimia, an eating disorder characterized by binge eating followed by deliberate purging (i.e., self-induced vomiting, inappropriate use of laxatives). Andrea was intensely preoccupied with the idea of maintaining a specific body weight, and went to the extremes of binging and purging in order to satisfy her desire to eat without gaining weight. Bulimia is a very extreme and destructive pattern, with many long-term health risks.

It has been frequently stated in the recovery literature that bulimia is associated with repressed memories of sexual abuse, despite some recent evidence that that is not necessarily the case at all. In any event, Andrea's previous therapist diagnosed and treated her from an abuse framework. Even though she did not believe she had been abused, her therapist told her that her body was clearly manifesting its memories of having been abused. Her feelings of disgust and shame when eating were symbolic of her reaction to being penetrated, and her need to purge was symbolic of her struggle to get out her terrible feelings of self-loathing for what had happened to her. Pressured to accept these interpretations as body memories, in this case the feeling of emptiness leading to binging and the bloated feeling of a too-full stomach compelling her to purge, Andrea continued in the therapy with the goal of trying to recover memories of the episodes of abuse assumed to have occurred.

Andrea described her experience to me in this way: "She [the therapist] was so sure that I was abused and that's why my body is all screwed up. She told me that that's what bodies do—they hold on to the crummy feelings even when your mind forgets. . . . My problems with food made sense all of a sudden, but I still can't find any memories like the ones she said must be somewhere in my mind. Even after we did a lot of imagery, I didn't have any memories, but my stomach really does some pretty big flip-flops. . . . She said my body memories are getting ready to become real memories. . . ."

Believers in the validity of body memories as firm evidence often know they are walking on thin ice, and many rationalize further by saying, "The memory of abuse is stored as a sensory impression as an infant or young child and is then interpreted later when the person learns language and can understand the meaning of those sensory impressions." It's an interesting hypothesis, but how do we prove it *or* disprove it? And in the meantime, how can we justify talking to clients about body memories as though they were objective evidence of abuse?

MEMORIES ARE NEGOTIABLE

The memory research to date has firmly established that memory is prone to error, for the many reasons described in Chapter 3. The recognition that memory is responsive to suggestion is a key point underlying all the issues surrounding repressed memories of abuse. As described in Chapter 4, a number of studies over the years have demonstrated that false memories can be implanted. Critics of these experiments, however, invariably claim they are not "ecologically valid," meaning that they may be interesting laboratory findings, but don't necessarily apply to the "real" world.

What happens in the "real" world? A trusted person—the therapist—creates a context of exploration and discussion of the client's inner experiences, including all his or her arbitrary beliefs and gaps in understanding. How can laboratory experiments approximate such conditions? One way is to make use of what is known as the field experiment—a study conducted in the real world.

While it would be unethical to create abuse situations with the goal of later seeing what happens, research psychologist and memory expert Elizabeth F. Loftus, Ph.D., did a field experiment that more closely approximates what happens in therapy.

> The technique involved a subject and a trusted family member who played a variation of "Remember the time that . . ." To appreciate the methodology, consider the implanted memory of fourteen-year-old Chris. Chris was convinced by his older brother, Jim, that he had been lost in a shopping mall when he was five years old. Jim told Chris this story as if it were the truth: "It was 1981 or 1982. I remember that Chris was five. We had gone shopping at the University City Shopping Mall in Spokane. After some panic, we found Chris being led down the mall by a tall, oldish man (I think he was wearing a flannel shirt). Chris was crying and holding the man's hand. The man explained that he had found Chris walking around crying his eyes out just a few moments before and was trying to help him find his parents."
>
> Just two days later, Chris recalled his feelings about being lost: "That day I was so scared that I would never see my family again. I knew that I was in trouble." On the fourth day, he recalled a conversation with his mother: "I remember Mom telling me never to do that again." On the fifth day: "I also remember that old man's flannel shirt." On the sixth day, he started remembering the mall itself: "I sort of remember the stores." In his last recollection, he could even remember a conversation with the man who had found him: "I remember the man asking me if I was lost. . . ."

A couple of weeks later, Chris described his false memory and he greatly expanded on it. Thus, in two short weeks, Chris now could even remember the balding head and the glasses worn by the man who rescued him. He characterized his memory as reasonably clear and vivid.

Finally, Chris was debriefed. He was told that one of the memories presented to him earlier had been false. When asked to guess, he guessed one of the genuine memories. When told that it was the getting-lost memory, he said, "Really? I thought I remembered being lost. . . ."

Dr. Loftus has repeated this experiment with at least five different individuals. While this is not a large enough sample to be considered statistically significant, it is an important experiment that approximates "real life." It indicates the threat of misinformation presented by a credible individual with no apparent motive to deceive. Those are the "real" world conditions for therapy.

Granted, the trauma of being lost is not the same as the trauma of being abused. But, the fact that people can be convinced of something untrue by someone they trust who has no apparent motive to deceive is at the heart of the controversy. It is also interesting to note that as the belief of having been lost settled in with Loftus's subjects, more and more details of the "memory" began to surface.

TIMING IS EVERYTHING

The suggestive techniques I have described in this chapter do not occur in a vacuum. Rather, they are typically introduced once a trusting and caring relationship has been established, which adds to their power. Make no mistake about it: It is not as if the therapist threw out a suggestion of abuse and it was automatically accepted by the client. In most of the cases I have seen, it is a perspective that evolves gradually. The notion that an entire false history could be instantly implanted is, as its critics contend, unlikely. Rather, it is more typically a belief that evolves over time, as a result of continuous pressure to believe.

In almost all of the cases in which I have been involved over the past decade, repressed memories of abuse were "discovered" only after many therapy sessions and *well after the therapist first introduced it as a possibility.* A variety of suggestive methods such as those described earlier in this chapter were employed.

People don't just join the Moonies when someone knocks on their door and says, "Hey, do you want to be a Moonie?" It is a subtle, gradual process, and the name Reverend Moon is never mentioned at all in the beginning. You are given lots of affection and lots of attention, a process commonly known as "love bombing." You are made to feel important, accepted, and even loved by the recruiters over the course of many separate interactions. Much later, after you feel bonded to these wonderful people, when you genuinely care about them, as they seem to care about you, it is only mildly confusing when they introduce you to the Reverend Moon's teachings. Cognitive dissonance, discussed earlier, prevents you from reaching almost any conclusion other than, "These are great people, and they're Moonies. So, Moonies are great." But until the relationship is strong enough to endure the disclosure of the Reverend Moon's connection to these wonderful people, his name is simply not mentioned. It takes quite some time to absorb newcomers into a belief system. Interestingly, in the same *PrimeTime Live* segment I mentioned earlier, the one in which a therapist was professing his skills as a mind reader, one client candidly responded to a question about her efforts to recover repressed memories by saying, "I don't have that many memories. I'm new at this diagnosis!" It would be comical, if it weren't so tragic.

Sometimes, however, a therapist who lacks finesse altogether may suggest abuse right off the bat. Even in the absence of a well-developed relationship with the therapist, such suggestions can make a client question his or her memories. Many patients have sought out therapy from me for abuse they really don't think happened but fear might have because another therapist told them that it did. Recall the woman who asked to be hypnotized to find out whether she was abused? When she called another therapist to get help in improving her self-esteem, the therapist told her— over the phone and never having met her—that she must have been abused, and since she can't remember it she should be hypnotized! Dropping a bombshell like that—on someone who isn't even a client—is inexcusable.

The symptom checklists also play a role, both by encouraging therapists to make superficial diagnoses and, via magazine articles or talk shows, by promoting self-diagnosis. People are going to therapy and joining recovery groups with a predisposition to find abuse at the root of their problems simply because they seem to fit "the profile."

I know therapists who pride themselves on being able to spot an abuse survivor in a crowd, just from the way he or she walks or talks. The therapist may even feel smug about "knowing" something that even the "afflicted" individual does not. By and large, though, the discovery of abuse through therapists' suggestions occurs gradually, unfolding with increasingly detailed memories and images over time. The therapist typically presses to recover as much detail as possible, so that every session goes further and further into the abyss of memory and confabulation. Neither therapist nor client can ever really know which is which, and, most troublesome of all, I think, neither seems to think it matters. The only important thing, it seems, is to continue the process.

The therapeutic relationship can be a complex one that invites the expression of conscious and unconscious needs and drives in its participants. It is a context that can alter what previously appeared to be stable traits, and it can bring out in people parts of themselves they didn't even know they had. This makes for both the potential benefits and liabilities of therapy, depending on how the process is managed.

Mental health professionals are in a position of power they can too easily underestimate or even deny. Many therapists would love to believe they are merely providing a safe context for repressed memories of abuse to surface. They would love to believe that their own attitudes and beliefs have no bearing on whether a client recovers repressed memories of abuse or not. But given what we know about suggestibility, interpersonal influence, memory, and the therapy process, no such beliefs can be justified. Shall we say, then, that therapists who don't quite grasp these important points are "in denial"?

KEY POINTS TO REMEMBER

- Therapists are often hypersensitive to issues of abuse because of pressure from the legal system, backlash against past disbelief of abuse, peer pressure, and the value of abuse frameworks for explaining symptoms and dictating a specific path of healing.
- Therapists have a variety of communication devices to convince clients they were abused, including direct and indirect suggestion, "mind-reading" (presupposition), analogy, and misinformation presented with certainty and logic.
- Misinformation presented as fact to a confused client is the most potent means of building receptivity to suggestions of abuse.
- False memories of abuse are generally not likely to be quickly accepted. It takes time to build credibility and rapport, the necessary ingredients for influence.
- Therapists generally don't like to think of themselves as having the capacity to use power malevolently, yet clearly they do. It is irresponsible to fail to consider the potential misapplications of the power inherent in the therapist's role.

CHAPTER 6

Why Believe It

If It Isn't True?

*I*f *you are unlucky enough to have been falsely accused of abuse,*
or you know someone who has been, you may find it difficult
to accept that anyone would come to believe he or she was
abused if it wasn't true. Your pain may be compounded by people's assumption that no one would believe something so horrible
if it weren't at least *partially* true. "Even if only 10 percent of it is
true," the reasoning may continue, "that is enough to crucify the
bastard who did it." The erroneous assumption is that there must
be *some* measure of truth in the allegations, even if they have
been exaggerated or otherwise distorted.

Most people seem to agree wholeheartedly with the statement
"Sometimes innocent people are falsely accused." They are also

aware that millions of people believe in astrology, past lives, and spirit possession, and that Jim Jones and David Koresh had scores of followers willing to die for their obviously irrational belief that these two men were messiahs. Yet they are still apt to regard a mere accusation as a guilty verdict or at least to believe that it inevitably contains an element of truth.

On March 9, 1993, the television program *Inside Edition* aired a story on a religious group in Florida that had undertaken a "holy mission" to rid Satan from an "evil tree" in their hometown. Apparently, the preacher believed and was able to convince his congregation that a particular nearby tree was evil and harbored demons. The "evidence"? (1) A murder had occurred near it, (2) a suicide had taken place under it, and (3) strange markings alleged to be those of devil worshipers were found nearby. Congregation members eventually clearly "saw" the tree as "a place of darkness" that required an exorcism. Many of the congregation's members reported having powerful visions (images and dreams) of the evil spirits residing there. The preacher and his congregation conducted an elaborate exorcism ritual involving anointing the tree with holy water, vigorously praying to it, and singing hymns at it. There was no follow-up report as to whether the tree has returned to a state of goodness.

It is difficult to discuss irrational beliefs logically. Strong reflexes come into play—the need to defend what you deeply believe and the desire to attack whoever challenges your belief. I recognize that I am challenging some very basic beliefs you may hold about memory, abuse, and therapy, as well as the overall value of your arbitrary and subjective beliefs. I can only hope you and some other individuals and families will be spared pointless devastation as a result.

Once the client comes to believe that he or she must have been abused and repressed the memories, he or she is typically encouraged to confront the perpetrator with this new awareness. If the memories are genuine, this can be an empowering, though painful, experience. If, however, the memories are a product of suggestion or confabulation, the situation can rapidly deteriorate into chaos. The effects can be devastating to both the accuser and the falsely accused.

Those who are falsely accused will naturally try to make sense out of the shocking accusations. Typically, they review the history of their relationship with the accuser, seeking a rational explanation. "How could this happen?" they ask themselves. "How could a child for whom I did everything I could even imagine that I could do the things I am being accused of? How could we have had such a normal relationship all our lives and then come to this?" It is natural for these questions to surface and for confusion to follow in the wake of false allegations of abuse.

HISTORY MAY NOT HELP YOU BETTER UNDERSTAND THE PROBLEM

One of the biggest mistakes that the falsely accused and their families typically make is to look for the answers to their questions in the history of their relationship with the accuser. They wonder whether they gave another of their children preferential treatment, whether they should have taken more family vacations, or whether they should have been more loving, and so forth. They erroneously believe that the past will somehow provide an explanation for the present. While this is sometimes true, more often than not the relationships of the past have little bearing on the insanity of the present. Raking up the past in the search for clues is to rewrite the past, just as the accuser has done, since in the process memories are inevitably filtered selectively to fit the current picture.

The accuser is responding *not* to the past, but rather to the needs of *right now*. Family members ask, "How could this have happened? We were always so close." I often believe them. They frequently present letters, cards, and pictures, even recent ones, in which the accuser expresses love and affection, even appreciation, for them. And then, inexplicably, things change.

We might just as well ask, how does it happen that a young man who grew up on a farm in the Midwest goes off to college and ends up becoming a Hare Krishna? There is nothing in this man's background that would have predisposed him to choose to be a Hare Krishna specifically. But he's at an impressionable age when he is searching for answers to life's toughest questions: "What is the meaning of my life?" "Why am I here?" "What will make me happy?" "What do I believe about life and death?" So, one night he goes to a Krishna meeting at the suggestion of an interested friend. Lo and behold, he meets people who say things that somehow fit his needs to understand himself and to find purpose in life. He doesn't immediately become a member, but he starts to attend more and more of their lectures and meetings. He learns how to think, dress, conduct relationships, pray, contribute, and how to do everything else the "right" way, meaning the Krishna way. Over time—but faster than anyone else can understand—he has become deeply immersed in his life with Krishna.

It is easy for us to dismiss such groups as the Hare Krishnas and the Moonies as fanatics or cultists. But, many "mainstream" religious and spiritual leaders are equally skilled in manipulating people's need to believe, and the process by which they win "converts" is similar, even when their values are more accepted socially. Therapy that provides a rigid belief system is no different.

The answer to the question why someone would make a false allegation of abuse lies not much deeper than the therapist's explanation to the client: "From your symptoms, it is clear that you were abused." It provides a clear and specific scapegoat—someone else to blame for one's own failures. It provides a specific identity—that of an "abuse survivor." It provides an instant support network of empathetic and sympathetic people in this cold, impersonal world, namely all the others who show up at recovery meetings. It provides an apparently safe outlet for exploring and communicating one's feelings.

CHOICES AND
SITUATIONAL INFLUENCES

I have suggested that the past does not matter so much in trying to understand the rise of false beliefs in response to suggestions of abuse. Why not? To truly understand this, we must first
consider the roles of character (trait) and situational influences
(state) in scenarios of suggested abuse.

The branch of psychology called social psychology has addressed the issue of "trait versus state" through some excellent research for many decades. The "trait" perspective suggests that
people's personalities are largely fixed and predictable. For example, if you believed in the trait model, you would predict that
someone with the trait of honesty would likely be honest in all
life situations. But there is much evidence to support a "state"
perspective of personality, which suggests that personality varies
with the context. For example, a normally honest person might,
in a particular situation, behave dishonestly. If you rigidly subscribed to the trait theory, you might find it impossible to believe
that your "honest" child (brother, sister, whoever) would ever lie
about something as serious as abuse ("Why would she say it if it
wasn't true?"). But consider that situational influences may very
well have led the accuser to believe something that is not at all
true. In other words, there is a state, a context, in which this person can be led to believe things that, under other circumstances,
he or she never would.

Suppose you considered yourself a basically honest person. If
you were absolutely assured you could get away with it, would you
steal $10 million? What if you stumbled upon untraceable money
from a drug deal gone bad? What if you got a tax refund in error?
Can you imagine *any* circumstances under which you could justify stealing $10 million? What if it were the only way to help
someone you loved who was going to die without extensive treatment you otherwise could not afford?

I am describing a phenomenon known as "situational specificity," which is the recognition that the demands of a current sit-

uation generally outweigh your previous history in determining your response. A normally peaceful person becomes violent when his or her children are threatened. A normally honest person declares a false deduction on his or her income tax. A normally sensitive person snubs an acquaintance at a cocktail party. A person who is normally quite sensible and deliberate follows a wild impulse and buys a sports car he or she really can't afford.

It should be clear by now that the history of the relationship between the accuser and the accused is far less significant to understanding why false accusations arise than what current needs of the accuser are being met by believing he or she was abused. The fact that the accuser doesn't "know" of the abuse until he or she sees a therapist makes the accuser much like the fellow from the Midwest who doesn't "know" we are all reincarnated until he goes to a Hare Krishna lecture. If he has sufficient need or desire to believe that there is more than just this life, he will find the concept and "reality" of reincarnation reassuring, enlightening, and *true*. The Midwest values he grew up with, his close family relationships, his old friends and way of life, are quickly abandoned for the "truth" he now believes, a truth that everyone else is simply too blind to see. His rigid and noncritical new belief leads him to think, "When they are enlightened as I am they will know what I know and believe what I believe."

One of the most dramatic examples of situational specificity relating to repressed memories of sexual abuse is a case described by Richard Ofshe, a sociologist at the University of California, Berkeley.

Paul Ingram, the father of six children, served as chief civil deputy of the Thurston County, Washington, Sheriff's Department. In September 1988, his twenty-two-year-old daughter, Ericka Ingram, attended a church-sponsored retreat intended to raise and address issues of sexual abuse. During the retreat, Ericka accused her father of having raped her when she was a child. In the following weeks and in response to further questioning, Ericka expanded her accusations and reported that recently her father had been raping her on a near nightly basis. Contacted by police in November, Ericka's allegations again grew when she claimed that her father had been raping her continuously since she was the age of five.

Julie, Ericka's younger sister, attended the same church retreat and was aware of Ericka's accusations. In a letter to a high school teacher in which she apologized for her misconduct, Julie claimed that the cause of her problems was the fact that she was raped at the age of four. She claimed that *all* of the men who participated in weekly poker games with her father, most of whom were law enforcement officers, would enter her bedroom, one or two at a time, and rape her while her father observed. She further wrote that even though Ericka slept in the upper bunk of their bed, she had slept throughout *all* of Julie's weekly multiple rapes.

Starting in January 1989, Ingram's two daughters further expanded the allegations to include satanic ritual abuse involving their father and many of his law enforcement associates. They reported witnessing the murders of twenty-five infants and one adult. They reported being tortured, observing mutilations of fetuses and dead babies, and being scarred with knives and fire. Questioning about inconsistencies in their stories led to revisions of their narratives.

Despite the highly questionable nature of their allegations, Paul Ingram told detectives he was willing to believe what his daughters said—why would they say it if it weren't true?—even though he had no memory of any such events. He was told repression is common among perpetrators.

Ingram underwent intensive questioning for memory enhancement, and up came memories of events even worse than what his daughters described. He became convinced he was an agent of Satan and presented numerous stories of his involvement in a violent satanic cult. Ingram also implicated a dozen other law enforcement officers as members of the satanic cult.

Ofshe, however, strongly doubted Ingram's guilt. He recognized how Ingram's highly suggestible nature, religiosity, and inability to separate fantasy from reality could lead him to accept the accusations against him. To prove how easily false memories can be created in some individuals, he suggested to Ingram that he had committed an additional crime: He had made one of his sons and one of his daughters have sex together while he watched. Ingram again claimed he remembered no such event, but accepted that it must be true if he was told it was so. He was encouraged to keep trying to remember, to try to "see" it happening. The next day Ingram came in and confessed to the fictional crime Ofshe had suggested. He stated he remembered vividly what had happened, and also that he was confident his memory of the act was accurate.

What a twist! I've been describing people succumbing to false suggestions of having been abused, and here's a man who succumbs to false suggestions of having *perpetrated* abuse. A man who under any other circumstances would never see himself as a sexual abuser of children translates his preexisting beliefs in Satan, repression, and his children's honesty into profound self-doubt that leaves him vulnerable to the suggestions—in the form of interrogation questions—of professionals he trusts. Ingram is now serving a twenty-year prison term for crimes he claims he now knows he never committed. He is appealing his conviction.

MOST ACCUSERS—LET ALONE THOSE THEY ACCUSE—ARE AT least somewhat reluctant to accept suggestions of abuse at first. Family members (most often siblings) frequently point out that the accuser did not want to believe it and, in fact, denied it for a long time. Therefore, they go on to reason, if he or she ultimately believes it, it *must* be true. Therapists have frequently asked me, "Don't you understand? This client doesn't want this. Why would *anyone* want this?" What, then, makes the client change his or her mind?

Allow me to digress a moment to make a point. I was a student at the University of Michigan many years ago, in the so-called "hippie era." Men routinely wore their hair quite long, to identify themselves as members of a youthful and rebellious generation whose mottos were "Let it all hang out" and "Question authority." One day I was sitting in a class on advanced psychoanalytic techniques in which the professor was discussing latent homosexuality. One thing you need to know about psychoanalysis—in case you don't already—is that it's a way of thinking in which almost everything means something else, psychologically speaking. A cigarette can be viewed as symbolic of a mother's nipple. A sarcastic joke can be viewed as thinly veiled aggression. And so on. According to the professor, "A male who grows his hair long has an unconscious wish to be a woman and is probably a latent homosexual." I wrote that in my notes, like a good student, and that was that. It wasn't until hours later that I realized, "This guy's interpretation is absolutely *nuts!*" What about our culture? What about the conformity that comes from social pressure and the need to belong? I realized then that one of the problems with the psychoanalytic training I had received was that it focused almost entirely on individual issues. It ignored almost completely the role of social context, which was clearly (to me, anyway) the greater factor in determining hair length at that time. My point is this: Before we speculate about what must be going on in one person's head, we must first consider the environment—the cultural context—in which this person exists.

AMERICA: THE LAND OF VICTIMS

The August 12, 1991, *Time* magazine carried a cover story entitled, "Busybodies and Crybabies: What's Happening to the American Character?" It featured a story entitled "Crybabies: Eternal Victims" which began with this vignette:

> There, in a grocery store in suburban Portland, OR, was cashier Tom Morgan, more or less minding his own business. And there also was cashier Randy

Maresh, who seemed to delight in tormenting Morgan. At length Morgan got fed up, hired a lawyer and sued Maresh for $100,000 in damages. The complaint: Maresh "willfully and maliciously inflicted severe mental stress and humiliation . . . by continually, intentionally and repeatedly passing gas directed at the plaintiff." Not only that: Maresh would "hold it and walk funny to get to me" before expressing himself.

The defense countered with the argument that breaking wind is a form of free speech and that the right to flatulence was protected, in theory if not in so many words, by the First Amendment. After listening patiently to both sides, the judge concluded that the unusual form of aggressive expression was "juvenile and boorish," but he could find no Oregon law prohibiting it. Case dismissed. . . .

This is the age of the self-tort crybaby, to whom some disappointment—a slur, the loss of a job, an errant spouse, a foul-tasting can of beer, a slip on a supermarket floor, an unbecoming facelift—is sufficient occasion to claim huge monetary awards.

It is also the age of the all-purpose victim: The individual or group whose plight, condition or even momentary setback is not a matter that needs to be solved by individual effort but constitutes a social problem in itself. "We're not to blame, we're victims" is the increasingly assertive rallying cry of groups who see the American dream not as striving fulfilled but as unachieved entitlement. Crybabyhood is all blame, no pain, for gain. And all too often it works.

I HAD ALREADY BEEN TALKING PUBLICLY IN MY WORKSHOPS ABOUT my observations of shifts in societal values and personal conduct for several years, and was happy to see that the author of the article, Jesse Bernbaum, skillfully captured the essence of the trend. Bernbaum's epithet in the article for people who habitually blame others for their problems is "crybaby," a name nearly every angry, pouting kid who didn't get his way has been called. His use of the same term to describe angry, pouting adults is at first startling, but it seems to fit. Although that fellow over there may look like an adult on the outside, as John Bradshaw keeps reminding us, there's inevitably and invariably a little child in there somewhere. But when does the "inner child" grow up, leave home, and assume adult responsibilities?

Our culture has been sending us a terribly mixed-up set of signals. We are encouraged to take charge of our lives, but we should find fault elsewhere when we get hurt or disappointed. The mental health profession has played a central role in propagating this confusion. Since psychotherapy started to become more widely accepted and available a couple of decades ago, therapists have intensely emphasized personal fulfillment, personal happiness, and being "brave enough" to "follow your feelings" and "do your own thing." Overwhelmingly, the message has been, "Yes, you have a right to be happy and, no, you don't have to live up to anyone else's expectations." So, you don't have to honor commitments that later become inconvenient, you don't have to do things you find unpleasant, you don't have to put up with others' foibles—and don't let anyone tell you any different.

The widespread result of such beliefs should be self-evident: The country is *not* better off, although the number of therapists has more than doubled in the last decade. The divorce rate exceeds 50 percent, drug abuse is rampant, families are an expendable commodity (particularly those troublesome kids from the last marriage), and relationships are short-term bargains begun in classified ads. In this terribly overcrowded world, people are dying of loneliness and apathy.

Unrealistic and unfulfilled expectations of easy, carefree lives have given rise to a culture of blame. With no sense of personal responsibility, only a sense of entitlement, it is all too easy to pass the blame for personal failures to someone else. Consider these true and highly publicized examples:

- A driver gets stopped for weaving recklessly in and out of traffic. Obviously drunk, he is arrested. He is quickly released, and the bartender is fined for serving the man too much alcohol and letting him drive off.
- An intoxicated man falls in the New York subway and is run over but survives. He sues the city for not preventing his falling on the tracks.
- Jim Bakker, famed televangelist, blames his affair with Jessica Hahn on his enemies who "conspired to betray me into a sexual encounter."
- When $13 million cannot be found during an IRS audit of his financial misdeeds, Bakker suggests that the devil has gotten into his computer.
- A man sues McDonald's because he spilled his milkshake on himself and got into a traffic accident. He contends that McDonald's should have printed warnings on the cups about the dangers of drinking their milkshakes while driving.
- Mike Tyson, convicted of rape, contends he did nothing wrong. After all, he maintains, it is clear from the victim's lack of broken bones or bruises that "I didn't hurt her."
- George Bush contends he was not "out of touch" with the disastrous economy. Rather, he claims, the recession was "hyped by the media."
- A very drunk football fan falls from an escalator and sues the stadium for failing to fence off the escalator area.
- Senator Bob Packwood, accused by twenty-three women of lewdness and sexual harassment, blames the disease of alcoholism for his poor judgment.

- Leona Helmsley contends she is not guilty of tax evasion, but rather is the victim of everyone's jealousy of her wealth.
- Parents of a child in Ohio sue the makers of Cracker Jack, because when their child opened a box of the snack, there was no toy surprise inside. The child is alleged to have suffered "emotional distress."

WALTER OLSON, IN HIS BOOK *THE LITIGATION EXPLOSION*, describes well the skyrocketing number of lawsuits filed, often over outrageously trivial matters. Of course there *are* true victimizers who ought to be brought down. In such cases, taking an active role in one's own care and defense by fighting back not only is desirable, but may be emotionally necessary to recover from hurt, anger, and shame. Stepping out of the victim role and taking control can be the biggest step toward a healthy life and should be encouraged by therapists, families, friends, and anyone else who cares. But too many cases illustrate that too many people will go to almost unbelievable lengths to avoid taking personal responsibility.

Turning people into victims has become nothing short of an industry in this country. We encourage people to view others as oppressors and themselves as diseased. The trend in mental health to define problems in "disease" terminology was well addressed by Stanton Peele in his important book, *The Diseasing of America*. To view your problems as a product of disease implies both a biological adversary and an inevitability that is anything but empowering. So, now we have "sex addicts," "shopping disease," and all the other newly termed addictions and diseases for seemingly everything people do too much of. Recovery groups abound to absorb the afflicted, demanding conformity to a common philosophy, adoption of a common language, and adherence to a rigid protocol. I have seen too many clients who became worse trying to conform to a program that just didn't fit them, and then blamed themselves for being "too sick, even for a recovery group."

The false premises and arbitrary beliefs that can unintentionally create false memories and allegations of abuse unintentionally creates victims as well. Once they "believe," they have acquired an unalterable identity—that of "abuse survivor." The euphemistic shift in terminology from "victim" to "survivor," although more accurate and politically correct, may offer little actual benefit. It's still an identity rooted in negative circumstances. We are much more than our histories, but from that label you'd never know it.

Why are stories of repressed memories of abuse so common now? The cultural climate invites them by encouraging individuals to believe they are entitled to whatever they want, however unrealistic and irresponsible. We are encouraged to lay the blame elsewhere when we are disappointed. But to focus only on the individual and not the larger social context in which we live is to see only a portion of the overall problem. And as long as the legal system, the educational system, the health system (including mental health professionals), and the workplace allow—and even encourage—people to make excuses for, or even profit by, their own irresponsibility, the problem will get worse. Therapists could play a very important and powerful role in shaping healthier cultural perspectives, but they miss the opportunity to do so when they are caught in the grip of their own biases.

THE ROAD TO HELL MAY BE PAVED WITH A FAMILY'S GOOD INTENTIONS

I doubt there has been any greater casualty of three decades of self-absorption than the traditional nuclear family. Fewer than one in five American families fit the model of an intact family—

that is, biological parents and their children. While some cultural observers believe that this represents the progress of a society much less restricted by traditional male and female roles, it clearly is made at the expense of the individuals whose lives have been painfully disrupted by the family's breakdown.

It isn't just the high divorce rate that is the problem. Even in intact families it's the long-term effect on children and adults when relationships that should be close and loving become relationships merely of convenience or obligation. It's the statement, culturally and familially, that *every* relationship is conditional and expendable ("You may be my child, but I'll only spend some time with you this weekend if I get caught up on my work first"). How does someone who seems expendable ever come to feel love, trust, and security?

Is it coincidence that so many accusers are in the same age range—about twenty-five to forty-five? This generation of people was raised in an environment of affluence and indulgences unlike any that preceded it. As conservative political commentator George Will observed on the eve of a California election a few years back, these children of propriety have become the first generation of parents who *knowingly* make decisions that they know will *decrease* the quality of their children's lives. The very next day, the voters proved him correct by voting against environmental initiatives that would have protected the last 5 percent of old-growth trees in the state and tightened air quality measures and the regulation of toxic waste dumping. Voters didn't want to pay anything extra for these things.

Kids are angry, people are angry. Our larger culture plays a considerable role in helping to make it acceptable to desert your spouse and kids—or just to ignore them, or to abuse them physically or verbally. But it is our families that are primarily *responsible* for our well-being on all levels—physically, emotionally, intellectually, and spiritually. When the family fails to provide love, safety, nurturance, acknowledgment, stimulation, and values, people get hurt.

. . .

I HAVE A CARTOON I SOMETIMES SHOW IN MY WORKSHOPS. IT shows a huge auditorium with a banner hanging on the wall that says, "Annual Convention of Adult Children of Normal Parents." In this huge auditorium are scattered only a half-dozen attendees.

I have a client I'll call John who has a brother one year older than he. John is a very responsible man by nature. He works hard, takes his commitments seriously, and generally does exactly what he says he is going to do. John's brother is still trying to "find himself." John describes his relationship with his parents as "nothing great—just comfortable as long as I did what I was supposed to, which I always did." John does not feel his parents were openly affectionate or demonstrative of loving or tender feelings for him. He accepts that about them, though he occasionally wishes they were otherwise. He has never doubted their love for him, though, or their earnest desire to see both of their sons become happy and successful. When John and his brother talk about their parents, John is shocked to hear him portray them as "cold, heartless people who can't give love." His brother considers their childhood "abusive" and he blames them for his lack of success in establishing either a career or a relationship. John wonders if they had the same parents! When John says, "Aw, they weren't so bad. They gave us everything—even our college educations," his brother looks at him angrily and says, "You're so wrapped up in denial, I can't believe it! Well, if you have the need to remember them as anything but abusive, I wish you luck in eventually coming to terms with the harsh reality of your childhood." John actually starts to wonder whether he is repressing some terrible memories of his parents! But when the brothers compare memories, John sees that while he consistently finds in them evidence of his parents' will for them to achieve success without sacrificing humility, his brother remembers the exact same experiences as evidence of emotional neglect and abuse.

Again we see how the "inkblots" of our lives can give rise to multiple interpretations, each of them plausible. But notice how John's interpretations enhance his life, while those of his brother

144

limit him. Both views "make sense," but they clearly do not generate the same quality of consequence.

John offered a perspective about his brother's views that I found to be not only interesting but quite possibly true. John believes his brother feels better about himself by putting down his parents and thinking of his childhood as one involving emotional abuse. He makes comments about having "overcome adversity" and wanting John to see how far he's come since he left "that miserable family."

It's one of our strong cultural beliefs that personal character comes from overcoming adversity and that self-worth comes from surviving, then mastering, harsh conditions. It's like a scar competition—"You call that a scar? I've got scars on me that make that look like a freckle!" Few people are willing to say, "Yeah, I've always had it easy and I still do." There's no pride to be gained from having everything handed to you on a silver platter.

The greater the need to build self-esteem on having overcome adversity ("We were so poor, I never had a new pair of pants until I was seventeen"), and the less successfully one does so, the more bitter and resentful one is likely to be, and the more apt to place blame elsewhere. Few people want to say, "I guess I'm just a loser." It is much easier to say, "It's Mom and Dad's fault."

In this culture of blame, it is easy to appreciate how obvious a target parents present. In a survey of adults across the United States, the National Mental Health Association (NMHA) found that 65 percent, nearly two thirds of respondents, believe that "bad parenting" is the single greatest cause of all mental disorders. Again, we tend to review our personal history selectively, through our need to find the sources of our current problems or to bolster our beliefs. John reviews his history through the lens of believing that his parents encouraged his success, and with an easy acceptance that his parents were imperfect, even "toxic" in some ways. His brother reviews his own history through the lens of "emotional abuse" and selectively finds and interprets experiences to fit that framework.

The "recovery movement" consistently falls back on the claim that it does not encourage people to blame their parents for their problems. Rather, John Bradshaw says, he wants them to be held "accountable." While Bradshaw may be able to differentiate between "blame" and "accountability," a great many Americans are not quite so discriminating. They blame their parents relentlessly, and who can blame them, when leaders like Bradshaw suggest that they recover, in vivid detail, episode after episode of childhood experiences that reflect family dysfunction and parental neglect or abuse? He offers the disclaimer that parents are really not the target of the anger or rage that accompanies all these memories he cultivates while he encourages followers to view them through the lens of victimhood. It is much like telling a child about the dangers of smoking and admonishing him not to smoke while you are puffing away. "Do as I say, not as I do" has *never* been an effective strategy for shaping desirable behavior. Bradshaw's steady fanning of the flames of anger and resentment as a necessary path to eventual acceptance of things that happened and a greater sense of personal responsibility (which he claims are his goals) sends a very mixed message.

Parents can get caught in a similar trap. Claiming they have "nothing but the best of intentions," they may go on to do things that are hurtful, then defend themselves by saying, "I would *never* deliberately do anything to harm my child." Meanwhile, their children get hurt, sometimes badly, through neglect, ignorance, or their inability to live up to their parental responsibilities. I know of no job more challenging and meaningful than that of good parenting. It requires an extraordinary sense of responsibility to be aware of the potential of *each and every* interaction to enhance or diminish the child. It requires an extraordinary sense of balance between current actions and reactions and later consequences, both short-term and long-term. Unfortunately, not enough parents have the necessary wisdom, and too many children end up with an ample supply of accumulated hurts, disappointments, rejections, and humiliations. It doesn't take a therapist long to find these and amplify them in the person's awareness. Kleenex is a tool of the therapy trade, and there is simply no way to dismiss lightly or otherwise discount the pain of someone's past. In that sense, it is easy to redefine someone's past hurts as "abuse." And, once the "abuse" is identified in one area or context, the label can spread thickly over other areas as well until eventually, for some people, the entire past is covered by it.

Parents' good intentions mean little in this context. As the saying goes, "The road to hell is paved with good intentions." What was perhaps Mom's feeble attempt to "hold the family together" may well be remembered as her unwillingness to face and deal with the "abuse." What was perhaps her sheer ignorance of abuse occurring can be remembered as "passive participation" or even as a "silent endorsement." That is why when accusations surface, they are often directed at both parents, with the father most often portrayed as the perpetrator and the mother viewed as having allowed or even encouraged abuse.

The family and each of its members are necessarily part of the "conspiracy" when abuse is genuinely present. But the family and each of its members can also be falsely implicated in a conspiracy when the accuser's history has been rewritten for all the reasons we have explored. Under these circumstances, the family is likely to explode, and some of the most important relationships in it are likely to be irreparably harmed.

INDIVIDUAL RESPONSES TO SUGGESTIONS OF ABUSE

In the absence of any specific memories of abuse, it is up to the individual to decide whether to accept the interpretation of abuse and whether to get absorbed in the hunt for whatever "evidence" is assumed to lie under a blanket of repression, waiting to be uncovered. As we have seen, this is a time when a client is quite vulnerable to the suggestions of the therapist.

There is an infinite number of combinations of symptoms complicating the process of diagnosis and, subsequently, treatment. Clients come to therapy because they have very uncomfortable and troublesome symptoms that seem to be out of control. While some symptoms surface suddenly, typically they have been present for a long time. No one comes in for therapy saying, "I've only had these symptoms for four hours, but I want to nip them in the bud." On the contrary, most clients have been suffering for months or years, and usually they have already tried to effect change by reading self-help books, going to lectures, watching *Oprah Winfrey* and *Donahue*, or talking to others. They come into therapy *hurting*, and feeling both hopeless that anything will truly help and hopeful that somehow therapy will exceed their expectations.

The frustration, the emotional intensity, and the earnest desire to get better that clients bring to therapy create their vulnerability to a therapist's suggestions, *whatever* they are. Earlier, I described the power of a client's need to know, to make sense out of a seemingly nonsensical bunch of symptoms. Typically a client believes that these symptoms "happen *to* me" and does not feel any sense of connection to them. Technically, this detachment is termed "dissociation," and it is an understandable phenomenon. No one consciously or deliberately chooses to be obese, or to have rotten self-esteem. Similarly, no one consciously or deliberately chooses to be a survivor of sexual abuse. No one, on the surface, wants that for themselves. But in the same way that some people can build their lives around a pathological pattern (like binge eating or purging, or chronic depression) that hurts them and affects all of the things they do—career, relationships—an individual can build a life around being a survivor. Therapists can speculate endlessly about *why* someone would do that, but we can only say with assurance that it happens. The reasons are speculative, perhaps unconscious, and, in some ways, of secondary importance.

The speculations are, however, a focus of this book. It is therapists' speculations about "why" a client has symptoms that leads them to say, "You have these symptoms because you were abused, even if you don't know it." The client now has (finally!) an explanation for symptoms that have been so painful and confusing. And with the explanation comes the promise of recovery, a path to follow. Is it any wonder that masses of people believe, and follow?

Consider the comments of several women interviewed by correspondent Jay Schadler on ABC's *PrimeTime Live* on January 7, 1993, along with Emory University psychiatrist George Ganaway. These women had all accused their parents of abuse but later retracted their accusations. They followed an earlier woman patient in the segment (the "first patient") shown recovering traumatic memories in therapy.

> *Schadler:* I hate to be so blunt about it, but some of these therapists may be as sick as their patients.
>
> *Dr. Ganaway:* Well, the question is, "Who is hoaxing who?"
>
> *Schadler:* That question is now at the heart of a bitter feud brewing amongst patients, their families, and the therapeutic community, because, increasingly, people who while undergoing therapy recounted bizarre stories of ritual abuse, now say it was never true.
>
> *Fourth patient:* I thought I saw my father doing things to me. I really believed it. I thought—and I wrote the things down—but it wasn't true. It didn't happen.
>
> *Schadler (voice-over):* These four women are all former patients of Dallas psychotherapist Michael Moore. Moore, who is being sued for negligence and fraud, would not talk to *PrimeTime Live*, but continues to practice as a specialist in the treatment of eating disorders.

Fifth patient: He made you believe that all these pictures going on in your head was reality, was real stuff. Here I am, I'm sick, he's the specialist, he's the one that is supposed to be saving lives, you know, and I'm going to argue with him?

Schadler: So the therapist was giving you a reason, an explanation for your problem?

Fifth patient: Yes.

Schadler: And it seemed reasonable to you?

Fifth patient: I was desperate. I was desperate.

These people retracted their allegations apparently because they could not muster the conviction to fully believe the abuse occurred. Besides, believing it didn't make their symptoms go away. But, what if they *had* believed *and* their symptoms had gone away? Would that prove the truthfulness of their beliefs? No! Clearly, people get better all the time by accepting ideas that are not true or believing in things that are not accurate. The well-known "placebo effect"—improvements in the health of clients who take sugar pills, thinking them to be real medicine—highlights how sheer belief, even erroneous belief, can make you better. Just believing that you have started on a well-defined road to recovery has healing effects. This principle is true of all psychotherapies, but is particularly noticeable in those that have many rituals associated with them. Believing that you have to lie on a couch and describe your dreams, for example, makes some people feel better, merely because "it's supposed to."

At the individual level, we can speculate about other motives and mechanisms for accepting suggestions of abuse beyond those we have discussed. Psychiatrist George Ganaway offers the possibility that in some individuals, the lines between reality and fantasy are not very well established. The fantasy of having been abused makes little sense to anyone, but psychological fantasies clearly have a peculiar life of their own. They reflect needs, drives, and wishes that may seem mysterious, *especially* to the person who has them. They may reflect unconscious feelings, or they may be simply another psychological unknown. What is known, though, is that fantasies of abuse happen and they may seem entirely real to an individual whose ability to distinguish fantasy from reality is poorly developed.

Ganaway also proposes another interesting idea. He suggests that such beliefs may be a defense mechanism of sorts: Clients who believe they were abused effectively avoid dealing with some other issues or problems that may be even *more* threatening or ambiguous. It's easier to have an identified "bad guy" in your life, whether or not he or she is actually guilty.

The need, or at least the willingness, to be a "victim" has been described in clinical literature for decades. For some, it is a way of avoiding feelings of guilt for some act of victimization or abuse that they themselves have committed. For others, being a victim alleviates the anxiety associated with being responsible for oneself. For still others, it is a way to elicit sympathy and support in a world seemingly full of people who are otherwise too busy to care.

Newly identified abuse survivors (or *possible* survivors) can find in a support group (perhaps for the first time) a network of other people who are wrestling with similar issues. These other people will likely echo the therapist's belief that you have to "face it, admit it, and work through it." Those who do as others in the group push them to do get lots of hugs and praise. Those who continue to harbor doubts and are foolish enough to express them openly are chastised as still being in denial and will be pressured to "work through" their denial. The presupposition is that those who show up at such meetings must have been abused. As we have seen, the power of groups, especially to elicit conformity, is enormous. Those who are most vulnerable and in need of help are likely to be those most easily absorbed. The cultlike atmosphere of some groups has been noted by many critics of the recovery movement, perhaps most notably by Wendy Kaminer in her powerful book, *I'm Dysfunctional, You're Dysfunctional.*

Whether the need is to belong to a group and to assume its identity or to win the approval or affection of the therapist, an important authority figure, the individual's need for acceptance can be a critical source of vulnerability. The more scared, alone and confused the client, the more reassuring and fulfilling the relationship to the therapist is likely to feel. A paid confidant, someone who is there at the appointed time (and at nonappointed times, if necessary) with a seemingly endless supply of empathy, can have a very strong hold. You can get praise when you do things right, like admit you were abused; or you can get rejection when you do things wrong, like consider other reasons for your symptoms instead of accepting what the therapist "really" knows happened.

Revenge is another possible motive for alleging abuse. The number of allegations of abuse that surface during bitter custody disputes or hostile divorce settlements is increasing regularly. It is the "nuclear bomb" of the settlement process. As soon as abuse is alleged, the wheels of justice can roll right over an innocent party in the name of protecting the child. Often, a mere allegation is as good as a condemnation.

The way a therapist questions clients can, in fact, amplify negative feelings about other people, paving the way for labeling offenders' behavior as abuse. A parent who was sometimes emotionally detached, drunk, or violent is a ready-made target for allegations of sexual abuse because the accumulated lifelong anger is an eruption waiting for the right opportunity. The therapist can unintentionally create that opportunity.

Once the basic premise "You were abused" is accepted, for any or all of the reasons described in this chapter, generating the specific details and the emotional drama is not particularly difficult. But remember that the volume of detail and the degree of drama in the telling do *not* indicate the truthfulness of the account, only that it is believed by the teller.

A systemic viewpoint—one that sees everything as related, however indirectly, to everything else—is essential to good therapy. An individual is part of a larger social network (family, friends, society). We have to consider carefully the cultural climate in which abuse allegations have been made, as well as the impact of family dynamics and individual needs. It is rarely as simple as "truth" or "fiction" when such accusations arise, and so it is vital for all concerned—survivors, perpetrators, families, friends, spouses, lawyers, therapists—to consider more carefully *all* the factors underlying suggestions of abuse and their influence on the lives they so deeply touch.

KEY POINTS TO REMEMBER

- Many people assume an allegation, even if it is not entirely true, must be at least partially true. This is a false assumption.
- Examining your relationship history with the accuser is likely to be less of a source of understanding him or her than is identifying the current needs being met by the accuser's believing he or she was abused.
- Situational influences are typically more powerful in shaping responses than character is.
- Suggestions of abuse can lead to false memories, false allegations, and false confessions, as Paul Ingram's case clearly shows.
- To appreciate why someone would come to believe he or she repressed memories of sexual abuse, we must consider all levels of experience: cultural, familial, and personal.
- Our culture often encourages us to define ourselves as victims of others' abuses.

- Anger over disillusionment can lead to vindictive feelings.
- Therapy can unwittingly encourage defining oneself as a victim.
- Bad parenting is identified by the majority of surveyed Americans as the leading cause of all mental disorders.
- A family's good intentions do not compensate for its lack of skills.
- Symptoms are not a product of conscious choice; saying, "I don't want to believe I was abused," does not address whatever motivations to believe might exist outside of consciousness.
- People can have a variety of motives for adopting the belief of having been abused, including the value of abuse as an explanation for confusing symptoms; the belief that believing it will provide a cure; the lack of ability to separate fact from fantasy; revenge; the avoidance of even more threatening problems; and the relief in absolving oneself of personal responsibility for one's life decisions.

CHAPTER 7

How Can You Be Sure?

*J*ohn and Rose, *a couple in their early seventies, were obviously* distraught. As they took turns telling their shocking story, I watched closely for some sign, some clue, that would help me determine the truthfulness of their account. They desperately wanted me to believe them, and that is what made my objectivity seem all the more necessary.

They impressed upon me the frustration and anguish of their circumstances. Shortly after the birth of her own daughter, their daughter Sally, the youngest of their four children, began to have dreams of babies being hurt.

Her brother-in-law, a well-known expert on childhood sexual abuse who strongly believes that abuse can be deduced even from very indirect methods, told her that having a baby is a common catalyst for recovering memories of abuse. He was the first to suggest to her that she must have been abused, in response to some of the dreams she shared with him. He referred her to other therapists, to whom she reported her dreams and her brother-in-law's interpretations. These therapists agreed that her dreams were valid expressions of repressed memories. With their encouragement, she uncovered memories of being abused by her two uncles (Rose's brothers). Over time, through more dreams and guided imagery, she uncovered even more and increasingly bizarre stories of personal abuse. The list of abusers in her past expanded to include John and Rose, who appeared to be genuinely dumbfounded by the allegations. Sally soon refused to have any contact with them at all, and she likewise prohibited them from having any contact with their grandchild. She now believes that many of the episodes of abuse also involved satanic ritualistic abuse and torture.

Sally's two brothers and sister think she has "gone crazy." They are at least as perplexed as John and Rose by Sally's perspective of her childhood. Sally views them as pawns in the conspiracy of silence and has cut off contact with them as well.

Listening to John and Rose, observing their obvious despair, hearing their confusion, empathizing with their desire to make sense out of apparent madness, what can I conclude? Are they phenomenal liars who actually were participants in horrendous acts of abuse? Are they two nice, innocent old people utterly bewildered by a crazy situation spun out of control?

I don't know.

THE MOST TROUBLING QUESTION FOR ALL INVOLVED IS, "HOW DO I know whether these awful memories are true?" This pivotal question most needs to be asked in cases where repressed memories surface in response to *any* external influence, like a magazine article or therapy (although in a legal system that presumes innocence until guilt can be proved, it ought to be kept in mind at all times). Where the survivor has known all along that he or she was abused, but has not disclosed it out of denial, fear, or avoidance, the memory is as continuous and reliable as any other. While *any* memory may be prone to error, we have seen from the research that the likelihood of error is greatest when vulnerable people are exposed to credible misinformation.

How many cases of authentic repressed memories are there? This is one of the toughest questions posed to researchers. After all, you can't walk into a room full of people and ask, "How many of you are repressing memories of childhood sexual abuse?" You can't study directly what someone doesn't know about, which is, by definition, what a repressed memory is. While no one can know for certain just how common repression really is, it seems safe to say from a variety of studies, some of which were cited earlier, that repression is evident in only a minority of cases of genuine trauma. In the great majority, the survivor knows *and has always known* that the abuse occurred, but has never acknowledged it or discussed it openly. A background of abuse is typically a source of intense shame, self-hatred, and poor self-esteem. Survivors may develop ways to avoid dealing with the harsh reality of their abuse, but even so may still sense its perpetual presence and maintain continuous awareness for its having happened.

Determining the "truth" of allegations of abuse is easier in a general statistical sense than it is in any specific case. In 1985, the U.S. National Center on Child Abuse and Neglect published statistics that indicated that approximately two thirds of sexual abuse complaints filed were dismissed after investigation. A 1987 study done by the University of Michigan Family and Law Department indicated that more than half of the allegations of sexual abuse arising in custody cases were untrue.

An unspecified percentage of people who were defined as abuse survivors on the basis of recovering repressed memories are now retracting their accusations. (In fact, two such recanters have formed an association for others like them and publish a newsletter called *The Retractor*.) They are beginning to come to terms with the fact that they devastated their own lives and the lives of the people they most care about by getting absorbed into an overzealous therapist's belief system. So, in a general sense, we know that not every accusation can be believed, just as we know that sometimes people are imprisoned for crimes that later evidence proves they could not have committed.

But when we go from the abstract to the specific, our inability to differentiate a truth from a falsehood reliably is evident.

IT WOULDN'T BE SO CONFUSING IF IT WASN'T SO PLAUSIBLE

Remember the fiasco over Clarence Thomas's nomination to the Supreme Court? The hearings involved two highly credible witnesses, Anita Hill and Thomas, battling in the public eye over allegations that Thomas had sexually harassed Hill. Public reactions paralleled closely what happens when allegations of sexual abuse are made against a parent or other alleged offender. Friends of Hill rallied to testify in her behalf, swearing that she would never make up such charges. Friends of Thomas rallied to testify in his behalf, adamant that he would never say or do such things. People hypothesized that Hill was lying because of anger she felt over unrequited love or some other such hidden motivation. Others deduced that Thomas was lying to protect his new position of prestige. People deduced that Hill was telling the truth because her account was so calm and detailed. Others deduced that Thomas was telling the truth because his outrage over such "bizarre" allegations seemed genuine.

Who was lying and who was telling the truth? Was whoever lied doing so deliberately? Or, did Hill and Thomas genuinely believe their own stories? Is it possible that *both* were lying—or misremembering? What amazes me is that so much of the public "deduced" *anything* about either one of them. In the absence of a trail of objective evidence behind them, the only people who can know what truly went on are Hill and Thomas (and even they might not know, since they can't necessarily trust their memories!). Yet, public reaction was swift, strong, and extreme, despite plausible but contradictory narratives. Fortunately, both Professor Hill and Judge Thomas appear to have gotten on with their lives in highly visible and productive ways without either one of them having to be proved "right." Those who get "stuck" waiting to be believed by others suffer dramatically and needlessly.

On March 24, 1993, the *Sally Jessy Raphael* show featured a family with a unique problem—they claimed their house was haunted by sexually abusive demons. Margaret, the mother (a former therapist, incidentally) claimed there were demons who sexually abused her and her children on an unpredictable but regular basis. Each "victim" claimed to have been sexually assaulted while lying in bed, taking a shower, or just going about ordinary business. The family reported that the demons even followed them to other locations, so the possibility of escaping them seemed remote.

It's a strange story, isn't it? But if you listened to their accounts, as I did, you might have been impressed by their calm demeanor, the abundance of detail, their intelligent and articulate presentation. They openly acknowledged their stories as implausible, and in so doing, they became even more convincing. Much of the audience seemed persuaded, as evidenced by their comments and questions. How many more would have been convinced if the accused were not demons, but some relative or stranger?

No one knows for certain how often false allegations of abuse arise, but a number of research studies suggest the range is somewhere in the vicinity of 8 percent to 20 percent, and much higher—as much as 65 percent—if the allegations arise in the context of an acrimonious divorce or family fight. The complicating factor that makes *any* data suspect, however, is the unknown role of repression. When memories of abuse surface in response to outside influences, like therapy, after years or decades of unawareness that any such experiences ever took place, they must be regarded with some skepticism, *although they are not necessarily untrue.* Suggestion can, after all, precede the recovery of reasonably accurate memories as well as pseudomemories. How, then, can we distinguish suggested memories from authentic memories?

Let's do a quick review of what we have established to this point: (1) Memories that do not involve conscious and direct recall (such as body memories, dreams, and images) clearly rely on interpretation rather than direct, factual, or experiential evidence. Interpretation of such ambiguous experiences leaves lots of room for projection by both therapist and client. (2) Suggestibility is inherent in the therapeutic relationship, allowing (sometimes even demanding) clients to get absorbed into the therapist's belief system. (3) Greater levels of certainty, emotionalism, or detail about a memory do not necessarily indicate a greater likelihood of its accuracy. (4) Situational factors can lead someone to say or do something he or she would not normally do (i.e., something that seems partially or wholly out of character). This applies to both accusers and the accused. (5) There is no reliable means available to determine whether an account is real or imagined.

Is it necessary to prove or disprove the allegations of abuse arising from repressed memories? The question may seem outrageous to some, especially the followers of those abuse experts who see abuse nearly everywhere and assume those identified as survivors must recover and "work through" endless iterations of their trauma. But while it is immensely popular, there is nothing objectively necessary about this painful and hyperemotional "no pain, no gain" approach to recovery. In fact, in some cases I strongly suspect it to be more harmful than helpful in the long run.

Later in this chapter, I will discuss the decision *not* to pursue proving or disproving allegations of abuse. But first let's examine the issues associated with wanting to establish truthfulness.

WHEN CAN WE SAY IT'S TRUE?

Studies report conflicting conclusions regarding the effects of trauma on memory. Some seem to show that high levels of emotional arousal impair the formation of memory and subsequent recall in some people. For example, in a 1987 study of women in the Boston area in therapy groups for incest survivors, the researchers found that 28 percent of their sample reported significant memory impairment. In a 1993 study of women in outpatient treatment for substance abuse at a hospital in New York City, the researchers found that 18 percent reported forgetting and later remembering their history of childhood sexual abuse. Anecdotal accounts, such as that of E. Sue Blume in *Secret Survivors*, suggest that "half of all incest survivors do not remember that the abuse occurred."

Thus, it is still arguable how common repressed memories of abuse are and whether they are likely to be more or less accurate than memories of trauma that were never repressed.

The ideal way to confirm the truth of abuse allegations is with some kind of objective evidence. This might include (1) medical records that indicate specific injuries or complaints that verify abusive experience; (2) confirmation from siblings or others that abuse occurred. In general, it is unusual for abuse to happen only once, but, naturally, that varies in individual cases. Sometimes a sibling can quickly confirm, "Yes, it happened to me, too." It is possible, but less likely, that both siblings will have repressed the memory. It is important to be aware, however, that even raising the question is likely to generate strong reactions in either direction—confirmation or denial—that may change the relationship unalterably, not necessarily for the better. More will be said about this in the next chapter; (3) testimony from a friend or authority figure who was confided in at the time; (4) a confession directly from the lips of the offender, which is, of course, the greatest confirmation of all (although, as we saw in the case of Paul Ingram, even this may be open to doubt). It doesn't happen often, but it happens, and when it does, it is typically accompanied by some justification that attempts to excuse it ("Your mother was never a good wife to me, if you know what I mean"). By far, the most common response from perpetrators is denial, in the form of either a flat assertion ("It never happened") or a counterattack ("How could you even think such a thing about me?"). Denial permits the abuser to live with what he or she has done, however uneasily, and it isolates the survivor who is left to wonder, "Did this really happen to me?" Doubt and ambiguity are nearly inevitable when repressed memories are involved.

Unfortunately, objective confirmation is usually not possible, and in its absence, all the rest is inference. Inference can be accurate, too, of course, and how it is arrived at is critical. Gathering information skillfully is a therapist's responsibility. The specific methods used, and the *context* in which they are used, are critical variables in determining whether memories are more likely to have been recalled accurately or confabulated.

As we have noted, the therapist's use of leading or suggestive questions—"He touched your genitals, didn't he?" or "How did he go about threatening you into silence all these years?"—is the most common contaminant. A variety of studies suggest that *when recall is allowed to flow freely, it is generally more accurate than when direct questioning is involved.* Answers to direct questions tend to lean in the direction of whatever the question implies. And research shows that the more often a leading or suggestive question is repeated, the more likely the respondent is to accept as true whatever the question implies. One such study, conducted by researcher Stephen Ceci of Cornell University, involved investigating the effects of suggestive interview techniques on children aged four to six. In weekly sessions, the children were told an event happened to them, then simultaneously asked if the event had ever happened to them. For example, in one typical case involving a four-year-old boy, Dr. Ceci said each week for eleven weeks, "You went to the hospital because your finger got caught in a mousetrap. Did this ever happen to you?" In the first interview, the boy denied ever having been to the hospital. In the second interview, the boy said, "Yes, I cried." In the third interview, the boy said, "Yes. My mom went to the hospital with me." By the eleventh interview, the boy gave an elaborate description of how he came to get his finger caught in a mousetrap and then had to go to the hospital as a result. Is this elaboration on a suggested false memory unique to children? What about adults in regressive forms of therapy that encourage childlike perceptions? Dr. Ceci's research gives a strong indication that suggested memories can be incorporated as real ones by employing repeated suggestive questioning. A whopping 56 percent of the children in his study demonstrated this fact.

An atmosphere of accusation is the next greatest contaminant of memory. A therapist may say, "You'll feel much better if you just tell me how the abuse occurred" or "You trust me enough to tell me what really happened to you, don't you?" or "If you don't tell what happened, he'll just go out and abuse someone else."

Indeed, the therapist's certainty that abuse occurred is a compelling factor in generating belief in the client. It is definitely a contaminant when accuracy is desired. I believe it is best for therapists to admit that they do *not* know what happened, thereby reducing or eliminating the pressure on their clients to "pass a test" or to conform to the therapist's beliefs. It is equally important the clients be allowed to say "I don't know" without their answer being interpreted as "resistance," "denial," or some such undesirable label.

Two researchers, Davis Raskin (University of Utah) and Phillip Esplin (St. Luke's Medical Office Building, Phoenix, Arizona), have developed an instrument for analyzing reports of child abuse victims called the "Criteria-Based Content Analysis," or CBCA. The instrument, whose accuracy and usefulness is still being tested, was designed to help separate fact from fiction in children's testimony. It examines a number of dimensions of children's narratives that may help to determine more accurately whether an account is true. These dimensions include:

1. Logical structure of the report (coherence)
2. Quantity of specific details (place, time, objects)
3. Contextual embedding (i.e., recalling the specific context of the events)
4. Descriptions of interactions (conversations, actions, reactions)
5. Unusual (but realistic) details
6. Superfluous (specific but irrelevant) details
7. Mental state (one's own and the perpetrator's)
8. Pardoning (making excuses for) the perpetrator
9. Details characteristic of the offense (either patterns that support such allegations or specific details that are contrary to common knowledge)

Raskin and Esplin described many other variables as well that may help distinguish what they call "self-experienced" from invented stories. Some preliminary findings indicate that the CBCA has an ability to verify already confirmed accounts of abuse but has difficulty in verifying cases where doubt is present. More studies may sharpen its usefulness in such cases, but for now our surest protection against noncritical thinking is doubt.

In her book, *Repressed Memories*, psychotherapist Renee Fredrickson suggests eight criteria for evaluating her clients' recovered memories, but I consider many of her criteria to be too biased in the direction of automatically believing the client despite a lack of specific evidence. Her first criterion is the existence of symptoms she has listed on, yes, a checklist; they are as vague and common as most others I have described. The other seven criteria Fredrickson describes are (1) a correspondence between the person's level of emotional distress and the depth of pain the repressed memories suggest; (2) the "clinical cohesiveness of perpetrator acts"—in other words, how well the abuse memory matches what is known about perpetrator behavior; (3) the presence of inconsequential details; (4) "corroborating data in family of origin or present life"—although she goes on to say that "other siblings in the family may have similar fears, imagery or symptoms," rather than specific memories, and this in itself is support; (5) little evidence of sympathy-seeking behavior ("If you have a tendency to avoid sympathy and support, it is an indication that your memories are real"); (6) the presence of crippling disbelief ("The existence of profound disbelief is an indication that memories are real"); and (7) no internal awareness of lying.

Fredrickson goes on to say that "the most important step in deciding if your memories are real is doing memory work. . . . If you talk about your repressed memories long enough, you will intuitively know they are real." The memory-uncovering techniques she suggests (imagery, dream interpretation, journal writing, body work, hypnosis, feelings work, and drawing) are all projective processes largely prone to error. As if all this were not enough, she urges, "Try saying to yourself three or four times a day for one week, I believe this problem is about my repressed memories of abuse."

Recovery therapists Ellen Bass and Laura Davis, authors of *The Courage to Heal*, are even less rigorous than Fredrickson. They simply say, "If you think you were abused and your life shows the symptoms, then you were." That's it? Nondescript feelings of having been wronged and some symptoms are enough to label someone an abuser?

Let's review what we know about recovered memories of abuse that are least likely to be contaminated: (1) They arise on the basis of a free narrative, (2) unprompted by leading or suggestive questions, (3) in an atmosphere free of coercion, (4) with a therapist who manifests a neutral position, and (5) allows both him- or herself and the client the freedom to plead ignorance about what really happened. Memories that surface in conditions other than these are suspect (though not necessarily untrue). Memories from very early childhood (less than two or three years of age) are also suspect, since almost every piece of research available suggests that they are likely to be confabulations created in the face of ambiguity. Most of the time, the only honest conclusion to the question "Is it true?" must be "We don't know."

THE NEED TO KNOW

Some clients enter therapy saying, "I don't remember much from my childhood. I must be repressing some traumatic memories. Will you help me to recover the memories?" Many therapists would accept such a client and begin the search for repressed memories of trauma. You might recall that 43 percent of my research sample agreed with the statement that if a person can't remember much about his or her childhood, it must have been traumatic. Renee Fredrickson, in *Repressed Memories*, states this erroneous view directly to the reader:

> If you remember almost nothing or very little of
> your childhood, or if you cannot remember a period of
> time . . . you have repressed memories. . . . Time is
> lost only for very painful reasons.

As you now know, most people don't remember much from their early childhoods, but not because of repression. Rather, it may be due to the biological development of mental capacities for memory storage and retrieval. Or it may be because past experience is valued less than present or future experience and so is simply not represented consciously in detail.

I believe it best to view therapists disinclined to help a person construct a background of abuse as ethical and sensible in their response to requests to do memory work. However, those who are believers that signs of abuse are everywhere claim that if only other therapists weren't so steeped in denial, they would see them, too. Fredrickson's condescending and biased view is stated succinctly:

> If a therapist states that it is harmful to retrieve or
> clarify repressed memories, you may want to explore
> why he or she believes this. Be aware that some thera-
> pists take this approach because they do not have the

necessary skills or experience in working with repressed memories. . . .

Her view is a caricature of therapy and devalues the responsible position taken by many therapists that leads them to avoid
cocreating even worse problems for the client. Granted, there are
some therapists who don't deal with abuse issues because of their
emotional avoidance or lack of technical skill. But let's avoid accusing therapists of being in denial if they balk at the idea of doing trauma, memory, and recovery work on the basis of the
complaint "I can't remember much about my childhood."

IS KNOWING NECESSARY?

Why is it so important for a client to know "for sure" that he or
she was abused when there are no specific memories of any such
experiences? Why is it so important for therapists to believe abuse
occurred?

I described earlier the basic need people have to make sense
out of nonsense, order out of chaos, clarity out of confusion. This
fundamental drive has motivated our search for understanding in
all realms of knowledge and thought. All the world's religions are
based on a need to explain how the universe and life came to be.
The social science of psychology came to be as an attempt to explain the motivations and peculiarities of human behavior. You
are reading this book in an effort to better understand the confusing phenomenon of remembered abuse.

The need to understand is closely linked to the need to control. Maybe by understanding more about how our minds work,
we can increase our control over mental illness. Maybe by better understanding people's needs and motives, we can improve
our relationships with them. The goal of understanding *anything* is to better control what happens to us so we may avoid

harm or anguish and increase satisfaction.

This is, at bottom, the same motivation that leads people to believe abuse occurred even when it didn't. Believing gives substance to vague symptoms, and, painful as it is, promises to eliminate all the other pains in your life.

Explanations remove doubts, and doubt is everyone's enemy, it seems. People simply don't tolerate uncertainty well, and the lack of resolution or completion leaves people frustrated. Whenever *anything* happens, people immediately seek to explain why. If all of a sudden your home started to shake, after your first flash of fear, you would immediately search for a plausible reason: Maybe it was an earthquake (I'm from California) or maybe a big truck just rumbled by. But, almost no one would notice the shaking and simply leave it at that. A guess as to "why" is nearly inevitable.

As we have seen, that's how it is with clients and their symptoms. Never mind that the explanations they get are not always accurate, just so long as they appear to fit. The benefits of adopting the abuse theory to explain ambiguous symptoms serve both therapist and client. Having established a clear reason for the client's symptoms, the therapist can now offer a "road map" to treatment. The "grief process," the "recovery process," the "steps for working through denial," and all the other intricate aspects for conducting therapy have all been described in exhaustive detail in the professional literature. Lately, they have surfaced as well in the countless self-help books that provide methods for solving every conceivable problem (and some inconceivable ones, too). "Experts" who have written books (or even single articles) about some issue or area of treatment may attract a horde of followers, who in turn get trained in and begin to practice those ideas and methods.

I have asked many of this country's true experts on memory, suggestibility, and treatment of abuse survivors, "How do you distinguish a confabulation from an authentic memory?" and their well-informed unanimous answer was, "Without external corroboration, you can't." Some offered general guidelines, *but none questioned that memories can be suggested or that symptoms can be misinterpreted.* It is encouraging that so many true experts take such a cautious and respectful position on such volatile issues. Perhaps they have enough self-esteem and awareness of the complexity of the issues that they can be comfortable admitting, "I don't know." They openly acknowledge that some people are falsely accused, but offer no estimate as to how often. They admit that too many of their colleagues are misinformed and underinformed, and through good intentions but poor methodology create victims, but they don't know what to do about it. They know memory can be unreliable, but they stress that we know little about the effects of trauma or repression on the accuracy of memory. There is little or no relevant research, and in the absence of objective evidence, they say, the issues are simply too sensitive to be treated on the basis of some therapist's—or charismatic speaker's or writer's—arbitrary beliefs. Given where the unbridled need for certainty can lead us, perhaps the most appropriate goal is to *learn to live with the uncertainty and get better anyway.*

Doubt is perceived as the enemy in the eyes of those therapists who suggest abuse to their patients. Their zealousness in providing compelling rationales to believe and eliminate doubt often sound like those religious leaders who tell you that you won't get into Heaven if you doubt. No, to get into Heaven, you must *believe* and banish all doubts; similarly, to "get well," you must banish all doubts and *believe.*

The rationale necessitating that you believe without doubt is plausible, even compelling. Those who have genuinely been abused were typically abused in an atmosphere that demanded secrecy. One way or another, it was made clear that the abusive interactions were not to be talked about to anyone. Failure to maintain secrecy might mean you might face violence, abandonment, or worse. As a result, the abused individual was isolated. There was no open talk of the abuse, no acknowledgment of it. There was only denial. To avoid confrontation and all the potential hazards associated with it, victims may have minimized the abuse in their own minds. They may have accepted it as the price of being in the family, or detached (dissociated) from it psychologically (enabling repression to occur). Or they may have convinced themselves that "this isn't happening," perhaps setting the stage for a lifetime of self-doubt. Or they may have so emotionally blended with and lost themselves to the will of the abuser that the abuse became redefined as affection, breaking down the boundaries necessary to a healthy self-definition. They may have been seduced by their seemingly powerful position or have come to believe they invited the abuse. These and other negative consequences of abuse are real and are truly some of the most gut-wrenching aspects of treating survivors in therapy.

What is compelling to many therapists about the need to eliminate doubt as a "vital" component of treatment is that there is already so much doubt in the minds of survivors. They doubt themselves; they doubt their memories and feelings; they doubt their motives for raising allegations; and, they doubt whether they can recover. And yet, convincing themselves (or letting themselves be convinced) clearly raises some potential problems; primarily, attaining certainty despite being wrong.

DENIAL AND DOUBT

It is not common for criminals of any sort to admit what they have done. If you walk into a jail or prison and talk to the inmates, very few will admit to having committed a crime. Rather, most seem to have had incompetent attorneys, biased judges, bought-off juries, or someone lurking in the shadows who "framed" them. (They often proudly brag to their fellow inmates, however.) Obviously guilty people routinely plead "not guilty."

Denial of any wrongdoing from the offender is typical. Denial from family members is also typical. And there is rarely external proof, like admissions of guilt, medical records, or confirmation from siblings of abusive events. When previously repressed memories surface in therapy, survivors are usually told to directly confront the offender and any family members who actively or passively support the offender and thereby allow the denial to go on. The accused and the rest of the family are given a choice either to confess or to face an immediate break-off of all relations. The advice from some experts is, "Break all contact with those in denial," encouraging a severance from those who may truly be guilty and in denial. As we have seen, there are cases where parents confessed to some improprieties just to keep the relationship going. (Remember Paul Ingram's case described in the last chapter?) It is a brutal game of emotional extortion.

Consider a letter received by an accused parent, which set forth the following guidelines for the child to even consider the possibility of a reconciliation:

A) Admit you molested me (maybe get hypnosis to help you remember).
B) Seek professional help.
C) Apologize to me.
D) After all the above I would consider doing therapy with you with my therapist.
E) Perhaps we could work things out although I'm not sure.

You can probably understand why someone who received such a letter might even falsely admit some guilt rather than lose his or her child forever.

ABUSE "SPECIALISTS" WANT THEIR PATIENTS TO BE CERTAIN AND solid in their convictions, and to accomplish this they help cut them off from parents or family and thereby prevent any dissenting or doubt-raising opinions. Parents thought of as perpetrators are no longer allowed to see their children or grandchildren, and with no avenue of communication between the accuser and the accused, there is no chance for reconciliation or closure. In one recent case in which I was involved, a seventy-three-year-old man was accused by his daughter on the basis of some dreams she had. He died, a tortured soul, before the issue was resolved. And for all her pain, she will never have the confession she felt entitled to.

IS CONFRONTING THE PERPETRATOR ALWAYS NECESSARY?

How often are people's lives ruined by the need to eliminate doubt and belief? No one knows. Clearly, however, the need to eliminate doubt and confront the alleged offender has led to too many confrontations based on arbitrary inferences rather than facts. Therapists often view it as "empowering" to confront the offender, and it usually is, especially when other children are in the perpetrator's sphere of influence who may be at risk—but only when the person now knows and has known all along that abuse occurred. But, when abuse memories arise in response to suggestions from the therapist, or from other suggestive sources (like dreamwork or imagery), or the memories originate in the earliest months of infancy, being a confident believer is questionable, and eliminating doubt may not be the most appropriate goal. Learning to live with doubt and instead working with the implications of suspected abuse may be more appropriate goals. Many of the therapists I interviewed stated, in essence, "I can't know if the client's memory is genuine or not. It isn't nearly as important to me to try and verify its accuracy as it is to deal with its significance for the person." Instead, they ask, "Suppose it's true? What would it mean to you? What would knowing it allow you to do that you can't do now? What do you *want*?" These experts want the client to know that what is most important is his or her ability to choose how to deal with the memory, to reach an independent resolution that may or may not involve stirring up a family crisis.

Perhaps surprisingly, John Bradshaw himself provides some perspective on this very issue in an interview he gave to Jann Mitchell, published in *Changes* magazine (April 1993).

> [People who blame their parents] are missing the point, which is that the intention of your parents isn't even relevant. . . . If you call your dad after a [recovery] workshop and read him off, you're missing the whole point. . . . The inner child is a beginning, not an end. Your adult is the new source of potency in your life. You must become the head of your own household. That's the whole point of doing the work. . . . The goal of this work is for you to become the parent of your own life—your own self-nurturer. . . . [Regarding] the uncovery. . . . I thought this was more the answer than I do now. The goal is to move on with your life and not stay stuck in it. Now I see it as much larger than I did then. I see there's lots of different ways of getting there: Gestalt therapy, your divorce, religious conversion.

DOGMATISM, WHETHER IN POLITICS OR THERAPY, IS DOOMED, FOR too many of our experiences fall outside the narrow lines of extremism. I think Bradshaw (in this instance) makes the point well that there are multiple paths to recovery, and that confrontation is *not* an absolute necessity for recovery to take place.

I found this particular viewpoint common among many of those who regularly deal with trauma. I find it enlightening that they don't necessarily advocate confrontation as essential to the recovery process. My own clinical experience leads me to a similar conclusion.

When I work with cases involving repressed memories that

have surfaced under conditions I am not sure about, I try to communicate to my clients that they are more than their histories. I want them to know that regardless of what they have experienced, good or bad, they have more dimensions than the definition "abuse survivor" connotes. In the process of therapy, I want them to discover that the personal significance they attach to their experience is an even greater determinant of the quality of their lives than the events themselves.

I present confrontation as a choice, not a necessity. Some individuals choose not to confront an offender directly for a variety of reasons. These include uncertainty the abuse actually occurred, fear of being labeled a "traitor" of sorts and being ostracized from the rest of the family, a personal belief that dealing with what happened is their own personal challenge and that no one else should be involved in the recovery process, the lack of availability (through death or separation) of the offender, or the fundamental belief that confrontation would yield nothing of value that couldn't be obtained in other, less explosive ways.

Either choice, to confront or not to confront, is one I will respect and work with in therapy. And, of course, if my client's perspective changes later, I will allow for that as well.

NO PAIN, NO GAIN?

The divergence of opinion among experts suggests that the "no pain, no gain" philosophy is suspect. The necessity of having to recover every detail of every abusive memory may actually lead to greater confabulation and greater traumatization, as in the questioning of the children of the now infamous McMartin preschool case, and in the questioning of adults who allege virtually impossible acts of abuse in satanic cults.

Many of the most well-respected clinicians wisely avoid the trap of trying to validate what appear to be suggested memories of abuse. They focus instead on clarifying and working toward the client's goals, building up the client's resources, and empowering the client to go beyond *whatever* the past might (or might not) have involved. Rather than being guilty of "denial," these cautious therapists are avoiding getting absorbed into an unprovable hypothesis that holds far too much potential for destruction. They resist the temptation to believe even though the explanation of repressed memories of abuse would be plausible and convenient. And, perhaps most important, they are keenly aware of the ability of the client to make progress even in the absence of having to believe.

Doubt is *not* the enemy. There is so very much the experts don't yet know about these complex issues. What is known is that people are suggestible and can be convinced to believe things that seem reasonable but are, nonetheless, untrue. What is also known is that sometimes reasonably accurate memories surface after years of repression. I believe it is a more sophisticated—and ethical—mind that can accept uncertainty and suspend belief or disbelief. When suggestions of abuse are made in suspicious circumstances, the question "How do you know if it's true?" is often best answered with "I really don't know."

KEY POINTS TO REMEMBER

- While we know that some percentage of allegations of abuse are false, it is extremely difficult to determine truth reliably in a given case.
- As evident in the Anita Hill/Clarence Thomas hearings, convincing witnesses giving plausible accounts may not necessarily be providing objective "truth."
- It remains unclear whether repressed memories of abuse are likely to be more or less accurate than

memories of trauma that were never repressed.

- Seeking objective corroboration is one way of confirming abuse, but it may be impossible—or have negative consequences for personal relationships.
- The need to know for certain can be so great in either the therapist or the client that it may lead to a noncritical acceptance of what could be misinformation. Doubt is *not* the enemy.
- While confronting the alleged offender has been routinely prescribed as a necessary step of the recovery process, confrontation may not always be desirable or necessary, and benefits should be weighed against liabilities.

CHAPTER 8

Shattered Lives

Dear Dr. Yapko:

. . . The excerpt from your book [*Trancework*] is the best written material I've read, and describes exactly what has happened to our daughter. She now views herself as an AMAC (Adult Molested as a Child), and appears consumed with her new "role" and hatred for us. Our daughter refuses to communicate with us. We saw her in court recently (we were trying to get visitation with our grandchild). We were shocked at her appearance—much too thin, no makeup, cowering down behind her attorney, crying and biting her nails. A year ago, she was a beautiful, smiling, loving daughter full of self-confidence. The judge ordered a psychological evaluation of us, our daughter and her child. He also ordered that we be allowed to visit our grandchild on two specific dates. She left town with her child rather than allow the visit. She has told others she will go to jail rather than permit us a visit. So we are dropping the legal request because it seems futile. (We completed the psychiatric evaluation, but she only went in once. We've received no results as of yet.) We have many notes from our daughter thanking us for being such wonderful parents, etc., etc. We cared for her child almost daily until she cut off contact last year. (They lived with us for several months when she and her husband separated.) Thanks to a local counseling group who call themselves Christians, she has cut herself off from her supportive extended family, and we have lost our beloved daughter and only grandchild. Our family has been destroyed. We are overwhelmed with grief.

Where are the healers??

ONCE THE ACCUSATION OF SEXUAL ABUSE ON THE BASIS OF RE-pressed memories is leveled against someone, there is a chain reaction that is as inevitable and as lethal to the entire family as that of a nuclear explosion. If you have been accused, or you are coming to believe that you are an abuse survivor and are preparing to confront the offender, or you are a family member who is being drawn into the turbulence—or you are involved with the issue of abuse professionally in some way (perhaps as a therapist or an attorney)—there are many deep and sensitive issues for you to consider in managing your dealings with all those who are (or will be) affected.

There are few things more intensely painful and damaging to the emotional well-being of a person than the experience of being sexually abused, particularly by someone who is trusted. The majority of those who have suffered a history of sexual abuse will spend at least some of their lives working painfully hard to re-build themselves on many levels. As a psychologist who works with such people, I can tell you it is a privilege to be a part of the reconstruction process. But for the reasons we have discussed, a (probably) small percentage of accusations are made against in-nocent people in response to undue influences. Unfortunately, even a "small percentage" translates into tens of thousands of in-nocent people being accused of one of the most despicable of all crimes. And these innocent people are part of families, inevitably linked to many others who are immediately and powerfully af-fected by the accusation as well. Beyond their families, these in-dividuals are connected to friends and colleagues in an ever-larger network of people who eventually come to hear of the allegations of abuse. They may jump to the same damning con-clusion that so many people do: that mere accusation is sufficient evidence of guilt.

If you are a survivor of sexual abuse, you must not think even for a moment that I am lacking empathy for you or that I am not offering my support to your difficult life struggle. I am deeply in-volved in helping men and women deal with the aftermath of abuse, and I am very aware of and responsive to their pain. In that respect, I encourage getting support from others, reading reason-able self-help books, and being in therapy with a qualified and aware professional. However, what I am addressing in this book in general, and in this chapter in particular, is what happens when an individual comes to believe abuse occurred when it never actually did. In this chapter, I will consider the aftermath of false allegations of abuse. I will discuss the allegations' effects on those who are most affected—husbands, wives, brothers, and sis-ters. In each instance, I will attempt to provide some insight about relevant issues and some practical assistance.

IF YOU ARE A SURVIVOR

Before you accuse someone publicly or confront an individual privately and set into motion a complex and devastating process, it is very important that you have a well-considered plan. How will you confront and when? Publicly or privately? Who else do you want there and why? Perhaps most important—*what do you want?* To "dump" and run? An admission of guilt? Do you want simple acknowledgment of what really happened? Do you want an apology? How will you feel and how will you respond if and when you don't get one, since it is so unlikely? How will you respond if you get an admission of guilt but it is followed by some stupid excuse? How will you respond to others' reactions, particularly if they are skeptical or even flatly disbelieving? Can the relationships continue, or will they have to end? Is reconciliation later going to be possible? There are no "right" answers to all these questions, only well-considered responses that reflect some forethought on your part.

Is confrontation really necessary to recover? Is it necessary to say to those close to you, in essence, "You are either with me or against me"? If you are certain that this is what you need to do, then do so. But if it is more important to your therapist than it is to you that you do so, you can legitimately question why. If it is described as "necessary" in order to recover, you can rightfully consider whether there really is "only one path to recovery."

In all my years of clinical practice, I have never demanded confrontation or even suggested it was essential. If my client chooses it as an option, I will respect and support that choice, but I will also prepare him or her for all the inevitable consequences of that choice by raising and discussing all the questions that I have posed in these pages. Often, my client will choose not to confront. The point is, I don't say, "You must," because I know that this person can heal and grow in lots of other ways that don't involve confrontation. It isn't my therapy, it's my client's. I respect the client's choice regarding whether to confront or not, because either way I know this person I care so much about is going to recover. Each of us is unique and in unique circumstances. There is no map to follow other than the unique one we create for ourselves.

The arguments that "you are in denial" and that "you are enabling others' denial, especially the offender's," are offered by some therapists in order to underline their mandate to confront. The rationale sounds plausible. In truth, there *is* a massive denial that typically exists in families where abuse occurs. Confronting the denial and bringing out into the open what has happened can be intensely therapeutic and personally empowering. But, it can also be devastating if it causes your family to splinter. Now you have not only memories of abuse to deal with, but a family that has disintegrated. It is a tough choice to make, and it is an intensely personal one. There is no formula that requires you to follow a therapist's agenda.

If you do decide to confront, be sure you take the time to anticipate and plan for the possible consequences. Typically, accusers hope for an admission of guilt, an apology, or some such response that can help ease recovery. Remember that you are unlikely to get that, and you may lose your family in the process. If you are ready to risk that and you feel it's necessary, then do what you feel you must, but *be prepared*.

If you are plagued by doubts about whether abuse really happened, or you are unprepared to splinter your family—or your therapist is considerably more certain about your abuse than you are—you are not ready to confront your suspected abuser. If you require validation and support for your allegations from others in your family, you are not ready.

I think it is terribly destructive that so many abuse specialists encourage accusers to cut themselves off from any who have doubts about the allegations. Why *shouldn't* they have doubts? What else can they do but consider their own experiences with the accused in making their judgments? Understand that and *don't personalize it*. They simply have no frame of reference for relating to the accusation—it isn't how they experienced that person. That is why it is *so* important that you work with what you believe to be true and do what you can to empower yourself and work through the consequences of the abuse in your own way. But do not assume that you must cut yourself off from your family as a necessary part of your recovery. If you feel you need or want to cut them off from having contact with you for your own reasons (not because it is deemed necessary to recovery in general but rather because it seems essential to your own recovery in particular), then, again, do what you feel you need to. Always bear in mind, though, there are lots of ways of making your life better that don't necessarily involve confrontation at all. And if your memories are of the questionable variety discussed in earlier chapters, it is generally wise not to take them as sufficient evidence that abuse occurred, before you start a process that quickly develops a destructive momentum all its own.

IF YOU ARE ACCUSED

There is probably no moment in your life that more powerfully defines your personal integrity than the moment in which you first respond to the accusation. The mechanisms that lead people to believe they were abused when they never actually were are those that can lead *anyone* to misrepresent—to themselves and to others—what they have done. In other words, abusers can confabulate a history of nothing but good deeds and a loving demeanor just as readily as accusers can confabulate a history of abuse. It *definitely* works both ways.

In this section, I focus on the accusation scenario of a child accusing a parent. Likewise, I discuss the issues from the standpoint of a female accuser and male perpetrator. While these relational and gender typings do not represent all abuse scenarios, they are the most common.

If you are accused and you now know and have known all along that you instigated or participated in acts directly or indirectly involving abuse, the painful but moral response is to admit it. To let your child go on wondering and go on suffering in order to protect yourself would be the cruelest injustice heaped onto other cruel injustices. Admitting that abuse occurred is often an opportunity for an offender to make important life changes. For the survivor, to be offered the chance to get confirmation of what may seem like unreal memories and an opportunity to discuss openly what really happened, is to be given a turning point toward recovery. If you can find it in yourself to admit abuse happened, do not make excuses for it—there simply aren't any acceptable ones. Instead, participate in your child's therapy (if she wants you to), face up to her anger, and look to the future possibility of a healthier and more honest relationship with your child. You can demand of yourself that you endure the pain and shame of acknowledging what you did in what, by now, may seem like another lifetime. You can apologize and do so sincerely and abundantly, and you can participate in your child's recovery in whatever way your child defines as helpful. The best you can do is to be honest and participate, even when the going gets tough, which it undoubtedly will. And, you'll need your own therapy, too.

If, however, you believe you are being falsely accused, you must be careful to respond intelligently and not out of emotional defensiveness. Appreciate first and foremost that your accuser is not intentionally lying, but actually believes in the truth of the allegations. Likewise, you must appreciate that any denial you offer will likely be interpreted as further evidence of your presumed guilt, and will trigger a predictable subsequent accusation that you are "in denial" and maintaining the "conspiracy of silence." If your accuser is following the recovery "formula" outlined by many groups and self-help books, she is now likely to cut off any further communication. I strongly encourage you to make it your goal to keep the lines of communication *open*. Stunned, shocked, hurt as you might be by the allegations, a cooler head must prevail. You can share your surprise ("This catches me totally off guard"). You can share your confusion ("I don't even know how to respond to this"). You can express your concern ("This must be horrible for you to have to talk to me about, and I want to respond in the best way possible"). And finally, you can express your desire to talk about it more openly in the presence of someone more neutral, like a therapist ("There is so much to say about all of this. When can we meet with someone skilled at dealing with these sensitive issues?"). Get an appointment as quickly as possible with a therapist, and make sure that both of you commit to attend. (How to choose a therapist is discussed in the next chapter.) If the only therapist your child will agree to see is the one that she has already been working with, then go. In the next chapter, I will discuss things to consider in meeting with your child's therapist, who may also seem to have predetermined your guilt.

The important thing is to keep the lines of communication open between *all* family members, and especially with the accuser. Reaffirm your love for your child, your desire to help, and your desire and willingness to continue the relationship, even under these terrible circumstances. Your door has to remain open to the possibility of a later reconciliation, even if for now it seems hopeless.

For the falsely accused, it is all too easy to get trapped in a "no-win" scenario. Admit to the abuse just to hold on to your child and you're forever branded a monster. Deny it and you're forever branded a monster *and* a coward. The safest immediate solution is neither to confirm nor to deny the abuse, but to get someplace fast where these issues can be dealt with as openly and fairly as possible.

DRAWN INTO THE LINE OF FIRE

The moment of accusation is exceptionally powerful for other family members as well. Their typical immediate reaction is massive confusion: "Is it true? How can this be? Why would she lie? Is it possible? He would never do that! Or, would he? Whom do I believe? What should I do?"

The questions about what to believe and what to do are intensely emotionally charged. Some of your most powerful and important relationships are now teetering on the edge of destruction. The anxiety about what to say and do can be extreme. It is no surprise, then, that the first overt reaction for most family members is denial. Understandably, people are highly motivated to avoid as best as they possibly can such an upheaval to their personal lives as having to acknowledge and deal with something so profoundly painful as the sexual abuse of a family member. At some level, they know their lives will never be quite the same; no one wants that kind of change forced on them, and no one seeks it out voluntarily. But, it *is* forced upon them, and sooner or later it will have to be dealt with. My advice is to deal with it sooner rather than later, and as sensitively as possible.

For the family members who get drawn into the crisis, the gut-wrenching division of self is almost audible. They have to ask themselves questions like: "Do I believe the accuser or the accused? Do I actively and openly support one or the other? Or, do I keep quiet and let them work it out themselves somehow?" Complicating the problem is the fact that a carefully plotted position of neutrality is not often viewed as such. Rather, an attempt to be neutral is apt to be seen as an indirect vote for maintaining the status quo: Neither the accused nor the accuser will feel supported. As suggested earlier, the psychology of these explosive situations is typically "If you're not with me, you're against me." This is how families begin to tear apart at the seams. If you take a position, you lose, and if you don't take a position, you lose. It is truly the exceptional accuser or accused who can insulate family members from the need to align themselves with anyone.

Is there a distinction between being "in denial" and being skeptical? Is it disloyal to have doubts about the validity of the memories of abuse of the accuser? Each family member must form some conclusion about what is going on and why, and what the best way is to respond. Each member of the family can play a role, albeit a limited one, in facilitating family cohesiveness or destruction.

IF YOU ARE THE SPOUSE OF THE ACCUSED

How often we hear of spouses who discover, after decades of marriage, that the person they have lived with for years has led a secret life: She finds out he is gay, or he finds out she has been engaging in prostitution, or they find out some similarly shocking revelations about someone they thought they knew well. An allegation of *any* sort almost forces us to consider, "Maybe something *has* been going on." Doubt and uncertainty are the precursors to belief, and some measure of doubt is *inevitable* when your spouse has been accused. After all, you weren't there, you really don't know what happened, and you really don't know that he or she *didn't* do it. And, as the (faulty) reasoning goes, "It's always the person you least suspect."

While the impulse to doubt your spouse is understandable, perhaps even necessary, how you work through your feelings of uncertainty will have a profound impact on what happens in the long run with the accuser and what happens in the short run with everyone else. Yours is a key role. To support your spouse blindly is wonderful but potentially misplaced loyalty. To support your child noncritically is to destroy your marriage—the most important of all family relationships. The pressure on you is enormous. It is *vital* to get some objective help in sorting through whatever evidence is being used against your spouse as well as whatever evidence there is in support of your spouse. Be prepared, for the evidence in either direction is likely to be flimsy or nonexistent, perhaps leaving you more uncertain than ever. In some cases, you can bide your time and stay out of it, but, most often, an apparent lack of belief in the integrity of your spouse will erode any sense of trust or closeness between you and lead to the eventual demise of the relationship.

In some of the marriages I have worked with, the accused were quick to grasp that a spouse's doubt is both natural and inevitable. In the case of a couple I'll call Jane and Mark, married nearly thirty years, both were flabbergasted at their daughter Cindy's allegations. Jane could not believe Mark would ever do the awful things he was accused of doing (nearly daily rapes, torture, threats of extreme violence), but she also couldn't believe her daughter would make up such horribly graphic things. Jane pulled away from Mark as an instinctive response to her confusion. Rather than taking it personally as a statement of Jane's lack of belief in him, Mark took quick action and arranged for both therapy and a lie detector test. Mark passed two different lie detector tests easily, and as Cindy's accusations became increasingly wild and impossible to take seriously, Jane became convinced of Mark's innocence. They are the lucky ones—their marriage survived the accusations. Many do not. Lie detector test results are not considered reliable enough for admission in court proceedings, yet they are often a valuable convincer when doubt is present.

In another case example, a couple I'll call Elliot and Shelly were both accused by their youngest daughter, Cary, of sexual abuse throughout her early life, starting at the age of eighteen months and continuing until she was fifteen. Cary claimed she was made pregnant at thirteen by her father, and that she had subsequently suffered a miscarriage. She also claimed that her mother would photograph her having sex with her father, and show the photos to neighbors.

Elliot and Shelly were shocked, and to the detriment of their marriage, each suspected the other of some grievous error in parenting that would account for the venomous nature of Cary's accusations.

Shelly quickly called a family meeting, asking her other two grown children to fly in from their respective homes in other cities to discuss Cary's allegations. Cary chose not to attend the family meeting, but the discussion brought both Elliot and Shelly great relief. It was apparent the other children did not believe any of Cary's story, and they gave their own views about her beliefs.

One important piece of information that Shelly had forgotten about until the meeting was that soon after Cary was born, Elliot had had a vasectomy. Elliot couldn't have gotten Cary—or anybody else—pregnant. Remembering this, remembering Cary's wildly impossible inclusion of the neighbors in the "conspiracy of silence," and getting reassurance from her other children helped convince Shelly that the problem was primarily Cary's. Elliot and Shelly got their marriage back on solid ground. They were unified in their concern for their daughter, but they were certain that they were not the source of her deluded perspectives.

The doubt that both Elliot and Shelly felt about each other at first is absolutely normal. It may be comforting for you to know, incidentally, that Cary eventually retracted her accusations and is now reconciled with her family. They are still working at resolving the aftereffects of the accusations, but communication is becoming increasingly open and things are progressing.

As the spouse of the accused, you can help the accused to understand that doubt is inherent in the situation (meaning it would be there *no matter who* was accused) and is not a statement about his or her own integrity. Ally yourself with any attempt by the accused to gather objective corroboration as described in Chapter 7. Having him or her take a lie detector test, obtaining your child's relevant medical records and school records, arranging for interviews conducted by a neutral party (a skilled and unbiased therapist) of siblings, relatives, and friends, and assisting with any other efforts to gain some objective basis for *legitimately* denying the allegations is an important role for a spouse to take. The necessary mental discipline in such situations is for you to remain nonjudgmental until there is enough evidence to be reasonably convinced of guilt or innocence.

It takes discipline to avoid jumping to conclusions or getting overwhelmed by painful and unanswerable questions. One of the quickest paths to constant fear and agitation is to keep asking, "Did he do it?" Therapy can help a lot in assisting you in sorting out your fears and doubts and in developing a realistic game plan for coping with uncertainty. The important short-term goal is to maintain your marriage in the face of intense adversity. That means working together *against* the problem instead of working *against* each other *because* of the problem.

What your accusing child typically wants from you and others is to be believed right from the start. He or she wants to form an alliance and establish a support system that isolates the accused. Do not immediately say you believe. Nor should you just dismiss the allegations, or you open yourself up to the accusation that you are in collusion with your guilty spouse. Again, the most important thing is keeping the lines of communication open. If your child wants you to go with him or her to see the therapist, I would suggest going in an effort to keep communication open. Beware, though, that the therapist may not be a neutral party, a condition I'll discuss in the next chapter. Beware also, that if your spouse is excluded, your participation can create a perceptible split in your demonstrated loyalties. Delicately remind your spouse that the goal is to prevent the collapse of communication if possible (sometimes it isn't). Without some credible third party present to mediate the accusations and counteraccusations, the situation can easily escalate to the point of no return. You can be the one to suggest that communication needs to take place in a more neutral environment where you can have some guidance and gain some better understanding of what is going on. There is too much at stake not to treat this situation carefully and with the respect it deserves. You can communicate caring and empathy for your child without either validating or rejecting his or her beliefs. Neutrality is important, but it should be an *active neutrality* that says, in essence, "We are going to work to find out what is going on here." Your spouse will then know you have not presumed guilt, and your child will know that you are taking the allegations seriously. Presuming guilt or trivializing the allegations are the biggest potential mistakes the spouse of the accused and parent of the accuser can make. It is a difficult but necessary tightrope to walk.

IF THE ACCUSER IS YOUR SIBLING

A woman named Nancy sought me out at one of my workshops recently to tell me about some allegations of abuse made against her father and mother by her younger sister, Ellen. Ellen had gone through the breakup of a relationship not long ago, and around the same time she was laid off from her job. She became very depressed and sought therapy. In therapy, Ellen was told that her difficulty in maintaining relationships with men and her employers indicated a history of abuse she must have repressed. She did not believe it at first but thought it must be possible, since she clearly was without a man or a job. Ellen told Nancy what the therapist had said, and Nancy's reaction was "That's ridiculous!" Ellen did not raise the issue again until a few months later. Ellen was now sure abuse occurred and told Nancy so. She intended to confront her parents when more details became available. She described having been made to perform oral sex on her father from the age of two months to two years. These memories surfaced in some therapy sessions in which guided imagery was used to find out the "cause" of Ellen's problems. Nancy was flabbergasted, and told Ellen that her accusations were crazy and impossible. When Ellen expanded the allegations to include their mother, whom she claimed had allowed the sexual contact to occur, Nancy exploded. Ellen expressed openly her disappointment and regret that Nancy was so mired in denial that she couldn't face the truth about Mom and Dad. She interpreted Nancy's denial as part of "the family conspiracy to keep dirty secrets." That Ellen's "memories" from infancy might not be accurate and might have been suggested by the therapist was never a consideration. Confronting all the presumed coconspirators was apparently the only option generated in her therapy.

Nancy wavered for a little while, but just a little while. Her dilemma as a sibling of the accuser was not unlike that of an accused person's spouse. She first spent an inevitable period of time actively considering the possibility that the allegations might be true. But, as she questioned Ellen, Ellen became wilder and wilder in her accusations. In the next round of stories, Dad was not the only one she was forced to perform oral sex on: Ellen claimed he also had his friends over to the house to use her sexually. She further claimed that sometimes their wives were there, too, just watching and getting sexually aroused. She went even further, claiming that some of the couples would then have sex near her crib and call to her to watch them. She claimed Dad was the main culprit, but Mom allowed it to go on, so she was just as guilty. Nancy soon realized that even though Ellen seemed to believe all she said, it was clearly too fantastic a yarn to give any credibility to. Ellen applied a great deal of pressure to convince Nancy of the truth of her infantile memories, but she could not. Now, they were no longer speaking to each other at Ellen's request. Ellen didn't want to condone Nancy's staying "in denial" about their mom and dad. Nancy cried when she described how the sister she used to be close to had now been ripped from her life.

It is typical for the accuser to want to rally support against the accused. As a brother or sister to the accuser, you may get caught in a bind as to whose story to believe.

Nancy was a little luckier than most. The increasingly bizarre details Ellen supplied with each new therapy session made it relatively easy to dismiss her stories as fabrications. Often, though, stories seem plausible enough to warrant serious consideration, and so they are anything but easy to dismiss. *Doubt is inevitable and is inherent in the situation.* But, uncertainty increases suggestibility, and so it may lead you to be more responsive to either the accuser or the accused than the evidence warrants.

As the brother or sister of the accuser, you may be able to play a more powerful role in keeping communication going than your nonaccused parent (if there is one). Yet when feelings are so intense and extreme this may not be possible. Your relationships with both the accuser and the accused are on the line, making for a very precarious situation. Your accusing sibling will typically believe that you are less biased than the parent who is the spouse of the accused. Likewise, your accused parent will typically believe that you can be counted on to believe him or her, since you have no such tainted memories (assuming you don't—for if you do, then you can corroborate the allegations and lend support to their essential truth). Both sides will likely look to you for support, and no matter what you say or do, you stand to lose a relationship with members of your family.

Again, I urge *active neutrality* based on a lack of knowledge. Admit that you are confounded by the allegations. Acknowledge the "no-win" scenario in which you have been placed and openly state your need to address all the relevant issues in a more controlled environment. The emotional power of the situation typically exceeds any one family member's ability to direct it, and so it is important that you take the position of encouraging a dialogue between all parties concerned. The "hit and run" tactic of dropping the accusation bombshell and then precluding any further communication about it is terribly destructive. Feelings get churned up, loyalties are divided, family relationships are breaking up, and an arbitrary "gag rule" is imposed by the accuser. If you can, use your position as a caring sibling to encourage communication in whatever form the accuser will permit. Because you are less likely to be viewed as biased, you may be able to encourage your accusing sibling to open the door to further discussion. Your sibling may not permit your parents access to the therapist with whom he or she is working, but he or she may permit access to you. Any foot you can get in the door can keep circumstances fluid and prevent them from getting "set in concrete," a most valuable contribution to your family in crisis.

KEEPING THE FAMILY TOGETHER

My focus on the nuclear family is not coincidental. The family has taken most of the blame as the identified perpetrators in cases where abuse has been suggested by therapists and other external forces. All of the family can be judged as guilty by assuming that members all knew—or *should* have known—abuse was occurring. The fact that they did nothing to stop it is popularly known as "the conspiracy of silence." That's why when one member is accused, typically *all* family relationships suffer.

Should the family seek and evaluate evidence? Of course. Whatever can be learned about the nature of the accuser's therapy, the details of the allegations, the evidence the accuser is using to maintain a belief in his or her abuse, and anything else that will point the way to a more objective approach to handling the crisis is desirable.

As of this writing, over three hundred civil cases involving repressed memories have been filed. Most involve children suing their parents for alleged damages arising from newly recovered memories of childhood abuse. I don't condone the practice by any means, but I recognize its potential value for providing some survivors a sense of vindication and reparation in legitimate cases of abuse. Should the accused sue therapists for causing or contributing to the accusers' false beliefs? While I am aware that such suits are threatened by parents who feel terribly wronged, there is currently no legal basis for such suits. The therapist's obligation is to the patient, not to the patient's family. (This may change, however, based on a few test cases being filed now that will be litigated in the years to come.) Can someone who believed suggestions of abuse made by the therapist and later retracted his or her accusations claim the therapist is guilty of malpractice and sue? Yes.

Lawsuits are not good vehicles for keeping families together in cases of false allegations, however. It is much more productive in the long run to keep the lines of communication open.

Families in crisis can, and probably should, use outside help to stabilize them. Getting into family therapy and forming support groups with other families who have been similarly struck with fragmenting abuse allegations are two very good options for coping with some very painful circumstances.

Realistically, there are times when the lines of communication cannot be kept open. Sometimes the accuser is so filled with rage that he or she refuses contact under *any* circumstances. In such cases, there is little that can be done. You can't communicate with someone who refuses your phone calls, visits, and mail.

However, I want to reiterate the potential value of reassuring the accuser that "the door will always be open." Even though right now he or she may seem light-years away, it is important to appreciate with some realistic hopefulness that the potential exists for a later reconciliation. Allow for that possibility as best you can and for now don't try to force the issue. It usually only creates more backlash. But you can still send birthday cards and notes. You can still pass along a "hello" through siblings or other relatives.

Likewise, *you* may be the one to cut off contact, at least temporarily, if you find yourself so lost and confused or so angry that you cannot deal sensibly with the accuser. All the things I have said thus far about understanding the accuser's frame of reference are meant to empower you to take purposeful action. If the interactions go nowhere and deteriorate into threats and manipulations, then a "cooling off" period may be necessary. Beware, though, that cooling off periods can sometimes let positions harden, making eventual resolution even more difficult. It is a matter of individual judgment, so discover and weigh your options carefully.

Crisis holds equal potential to strengthen or destroy families. Recognizing the complex interplay of issues and feelings is a necessary step in dealing realistically with circumstances that can seem too crazy to take seriously. Be assured that how you respond will determine to a significant extent—*but not entirely*—what the future will bring. I wish you luck.

KEY POINTS TO REMEMBER

- There are many sensitive issues to consider in responding to the situation of allegations of abuse. It is generally best to have a plan of response rather than simply reacting impulsively.
- Survivors of abuse need to take a variety of factors into account in deciding to confront the perpetrator, including where to confront, the purpose of the confrontation, the desired response and how to respond if it is not forthcoming, and how to respond to other family members who do and do not take positions of support.
- Cutting off communication with family members is generally counterproductive. It prevents resolution of issues and makes later reconciliation more difficult.
- There is no established formula for recovery. Each person must discover what works in his or her own particular case. A skilled therapist can provide both guidance and support in the recovery process.
- If you are rightly accused, admitting and taking responsibility for your past actions is essential for the eventual recovery of the accuser and all the other family members involved.
- For the falsely accused, simple denial is likely to be seen as self-protection and will not be accepted.

You must move quickly to create a context for exploring and addressing the allegations without closing down communication—not an easy task. The value of a neutral third party cannot be overstated.

- Pressures of this intensity can splinter or strengthen families, depending on their collective and individual responses. Address issues sooner rather than later so that positions do not get so deeply entrenched that there is no basis for resolution.

- The spouse of the accused will naturally have doubts about his or her guilt or innocence, as will everyone else involved. Doubt is natural, and to be expected. It should be used as motivation to communicate, seek answers, seek evidence. A spouse's push for clarity can show both the accused and the accuser that he or she takes the allegations seriously and wants to play an active role in helping.

- The siblings of the accused are placed in a no-win scenario right from the start. Believing one party means discounting the other, which will not go unnoticed. The siblings' key role is to keep communication as open as possible; it may not be possible when feelings are so intense and extreme.

- In all instances, regardless of the seeming disintegration of the family right now, keep the door open to the possibility of later reconciliation. It *does* happen.

CHAPTER 9

Therapy That Hurts and

Therapy That Helps

*T*he headline read *"Alleged murder-plot target says he's victim of 'memory' therapy."* It appeared in the San Diego *Union-Tribune* on December 15, 1992, above a case involving a prominent psychiatrist and professor at Stanford University who is also, ironically, a child-abuse specialist.

Two men acting suspiciously were stopped by police near the psychiatrist's home and were arrested when they were found to have items in their possession obviously relating to an intended violent crime—knives, gloves, ski masks, handcuffs. Unbelievably, one of the two men arrested was the psychologist treating the psychiatrist's daughter!

In her therapy, the daughter began, at the psychologist's urging, to recover "memories" of having been sexually abused by her father and other family members as well. She became openly hostile and eventually made two separate, and apparently sincere, death threats against her father and mother.

The psychologist and his accomplice were tried for conspiracy to commit murder, the daughter is more convinced than ever of her history of abuse, and the father is dumbfounded that he has become a victim in his own area of expertise. The whole story reads like a bad movie script, but it is really happening as you read this.

IT WOULD BE EASY ON THE BASIS OF THE THINGS I HAVE SAID about some therapists and their questionable approaches to treatment to conclude that therapy is dangerous and best avoided. That would be an incorrect and unfortunate conclusion to draw, however. When approached intelligently and with some insight into the potential hazards, therapy is often not only desirable, but necessary. This is especially true *after* allegations of abuse, when the feelings and views of all involved are so far apart and so intense that there is no obvious way to bridge the gap. As a general principle, *time is crucial.* The longer you wait to respond to allegations of abuse, or the longer you wait after the initial confrontation to further communicate about your allegations, the more time there is for others' positions to become entrenched and unyielding. In such instances, there are no winners, only losers. The goal, first and foremost, is to keep communication going. The next most important priority, elaborated in Chapter 7, is to find ways to move forward without having to be proved right or wrong.

BE REALISTIC ABOUT THERAPY

As I've stressed throughout this book, therapists are people first, therapists second. We are just as prone to errors in thinking and judgment (in some ways, perhaps even more so) as the rest of humankind. Therapists typically become therapists because we want to help people. All our years of formal education and clinical training are meant to develop that desire into a powerful and benevolent force for producing positive results. During professional training, we get exposed to a formidable array of theories and methods that represent the collective wisdom of the field. It is quite difficult to assert your own beliefs and methods during training when there seems to already be an established "correct" way of interpreting and treating a client's symptoms. Clinical training thus involves deferring to the judgment and methods of perceived authorities. It demands conformity to established views and procedures, it requires establishing a hierarchy of priorities that puts the therapist-client relationship above nearly all else, and it encourages maintaining a consistency of approach that makes it very difficult to switch methods midstream even if you observe that what you are doing isn't working very well. Think of how long some people stay in therapy for relatively simple problems with ineffective therapists who simply keep doing more of what already isn't working, just because that's what they spent years learning to do!

To complicate matters, there are many people practicing therapy who do not have the credentials (the formal education and clinical training) to do so effectively. While a license to practice is not the utmost guarantee of competence, it at least suggests a familiarity with a variety of clinical approaches and legal and ethical issues. It's hard enough to be a good therapist when you've been properly trained. The lack of such a background is even more likely to subject the consumer to mistakes born of ignorance.

The situation suspected abuse poses for therapists is a most delicate one. Mistakenly encouraging an accuser to return to an abusive relationship, or mistakenly encouraging him or her to damage or even end a relationship with an innocent parent is an error that concerns most therapists. The potential for damage, as we have seen, is immense: Families can be bitterly divided and individual lives can be shattered. For the abuse survivor, therapy can become an exclusive focus, decreasing one's quality of life while draining one's resources of time and money. People's lives hang in the balance.

So the process of confronting allegations of abuse is an emotionally harrowing and stressful one for therapists as well. Is someone lying? Is someone misremembering? It takes skill to find ways to move such volatile situations in constructive directions, and not a lot of people seem to envy our job in such cases.

THE ROLE OF THE THERAPIST

A Florida teacher filed a lawsuit in San Diego against Kentucky Fried Chicken. She said she came to San Diego with her husband in order to be with her mother-in-law, who had suffered a major stroke. After going to church and stopping at the restaurant for lunch, she slipped and fell on some barbecue sauce on the floor. Her advanced age, her apparent physical afflictions resulting from the fall, her inability to continue to practice her teaching profession, her medical records detailing her many untreatable injuries, and her psychiatric report detailing the deep depression arising from her now very limited capabilities combined to make what seemed a clear case of negligence on the part of the fast-food chain. It would no doubt cost them millions.

A strange thing happened, though, just as settlement time was nearing. As it turned out, the same eminently believable woman had recently filed a lawsuit in Florida against a bowling alley where she allegedly suffered disabling injuries after tripping over some torn carpeting there. The defendant's attorneys in that case hired private investigators who secretly videotaped this woman and her family vacationing at Disney World in Orlando. With obvious agility and enjoyment, she was doing things that, according to her lawsuit, she should not have been able to do. When she was shown the videotape of herself, she promptly dropped the lawsuits both in Florida and in San Diego. It became instantly clear that she was actually a well-practiced scam artist staging accidents for settlement money. (She and her family are being charged with perjury and conspiracy to bring a false lawsuit; if they are convicted, they will face up to eight years in prison.)

Here is an example of brazen deceit, conscious and deliberate. The woman *knew* she was lying, unlike those who make false allegations of abuse. But what about the conduct of the professionals in the case? No fewer than thirty-eight medical doctors and one psychiatrist evaluated this woman. All were fully prepared to testify in her behalf. The psychiatrist said she was severely depressed at the prospect of being crippled for life as a result of her fall.

Remember the case of the Vietnam vet who was never actually in Vietnam, as I described it way back at the beginning of this book? Why *shouldn't* psychiatrists and psychologists involved in such cases believe their clients? Why *should* a therapist be skeptical about the client's narrative? Is that the therapist's responsibility?

Under normal circumstances and where only the individual well-being of the client is concerned, therapists have been very clear in their collective conviction that their job is to do therapy and *not* investigative work. You may recall that only 37 percent of the therapists I surveyed said they do anything at all to figure out whether their clients are giving them truthful information. Is it the therapist's duty to support the client by believing his or her narrative uncritically and in its entirety? Or, is it the therapist's role to challenge the client's narrative, look for discrepancies and contradictions, and serve as a challenger who helps define what is true? Simply put, how therapists define the role they play in the process dictates to a huge extent their responses to the client's narrative and the direction their therapies take. Therapists who "believe" are far more likely to side with the accuser in a prescribed confrontation with the accused parent(s). Therapists who want to investigate further and who value keeping an open mind are far more likely to initiate a dialogue between all involved.

All parties involved need to understand the precarious position the therapist is in. The therapist naturally wants to provide support to the client, but may easily be viewed as anything but supportive if he or she delays jumping to the survivor's side or suggests that the allegations be investigated further, perhaps in the presence of the accused. Therapists place great value on the relationship they have with their clients. They tend to fight the notion of being an investigator of sorts. They will likely claim, "I do therapy with, not fact-finding about, my clients." And, as a therapist, I understand their negative reaction to the idea. In the case of the phony veteran, should the psychologist have spent time and money checking the records? Why would it ever have occurred to him, especially with the intensity of that client's symptoms and his detailed memories? And if he had a couple of dozen clients like that per month, what then? The practical limitations of expecting therapists to be investigators are self-evident.

But, the phenomenon of suggested memories of abuse isn't quite the same. My colleague did not suggest a false history to his client. And although he was abusive to his wife, this man did not accuse others of horrible crimes, destroying their reputations and their lives. Therapists must come to terms with the fact that while the abuse survivor's well-being is of utmost importance, it is also important to prevent innocent people from being falsely accused. Once the accusations are made, there are too many lives forever altered in traumatic ways. With so much at stake, it is now time for therapists to expand the definition of their role to include greater objectivity as investigators of some of the most serious accusations that one person can level against another. Even though the odds may seem to be against most such accusations being false or confabulated, before playing the odds noncritically, therapists need to be more deliberate and skillful in suspending judgment and gathering information.

CHOOSING A THERAPIST

For an unbelievably long time, therapists fooled themselves into believing they could assume the role of therapist yet keep themselves from influencing their clients. Many therapists believed they should merely serve as "mirrors" to their clients—reflecting but not directing. If a client asked for advice ("Doctor, what should I do about this?"), the therapist "skillfully" dodged the question by answering with another question ("What do *you* think you should do?"). Their desire to avoid influencing their clients was entirely unrealistic given that clients come in for help and answers—in other words, *expecting* to be influenced *in positive ways*. Influence in therapy is inevitable, but many therapists *still* don't recognize their ability to influence their clients, and so avoid feeling responsible for the direction the therapy moves in. They actively deceive themselves and believe their own self-deception.

How do you find a therapist? The best way, of course, is by referral from a client or colleague who has worked with the therapist and can attest to his or her competence. Be realistic, though. Your experience of the therapist may not be the same as another person's. Each therapy relationship is as different as the two people who comprise it. Another source of referral is your local (city or county) psychological and psychiatric societies, which usually maintain a list of practitioners according to specialty. Given the family-oriented nature of abuse issues, the American Association for Marriage and Family Therapy (AAMFT) can be especially helpful in providing a local family therapist who is sensitive to these issues. Their address and phone number is: 1100 17th Street, N.W., 10th Floor, Washington, D.C. 20036; (202) 452-0109. AAMFT has local chapters in most major cities that you can contact as well.

It is important as a starting point to know that your therapist can and will offer support and direction as needed. The therapist has to be comfortable in acknowledging that he or she has important information and valuable perspectives. He or she has to be able and willing to share them responsibly and have a good sense of timing about doing so. Information introduced too early or too late may lose its therapeutic impact.

I think it is clear from the data presented in Chapter 2 that what a therapist knows and believes is more important than what professional degree he or she has (despite the established hierarchy, M.D.'s are not automatically better therapists than Ph.D.'s, and Ph.D.'s are not automatically better therapists than M.A.'s). If a therapist believes, for example, that the path to recovery includes processing memories from infancy or even "past lives," or that memory isn't influenced by suggestion, he or she is misinformed and should be avoided. Abuse issues are far too important and volatile to be diverted onto paths involving esoteric and arbitrary beliefs. There is far too much real work to do to help individuals and their families deal with these devastating issues to go off chasing past incarnations or give air time to misinformation.

Thus, it is not only desirable but *necessary* that you interview therapists before you commit to working with one. Some you will get a "feel" for as you talk to them on the telephone, others you might need to spend a session or two with before you have a sense of their unique style. Whether you are sure you are an abuse survivor, suspect abuse but aren't really sure, or have been accused, you should ask the following questions of potential therapists:

1. Do you have substantial experience working with issues of sexual abuse? What kind of experience?
2. How do you typically approach these problems? What are your typical therapeutic goals in such situations? Do you favor individual or family therapy?
3. Are you aware of the intense controversy surrounding repressed memories of abuse that surface after many years of being buried? What is your position on these matters?
4. Are you generally more or less likely to encourage

the recovery of repressed memories? If more likely, under what conditions?

5. Do you believe you can recognize the signs of abuse even in someone who has no such memories? If so, how?

6. Do you have a particular method for working with abuse survivors? Can you describe the process?

7. Do you encourage survivors to confront their families or to resolve the issues independently? Do you encourage family members to participate in treatment? Why or why not?

8. How long does your approach to treatment typically take in terms of time or number of sessions?

9. Can I tape our sessions for later review?

10. Do you tend to seek any additional evidence of an objective nature in order to facilitate cases such as ours?

Although asking these questions may provide some insight into therapists' beliefs and practices, be aware that there can be a substantial difference between what therapists *say* they do and what they *really* do. It may take a few sessions before you conclude that a particular therapist's approaches are not for you or that you can work with him or her comfortably. The most important point to remember is that you are not obliged to blindly obey. Do not get swept up in therapeutic double-talk or let yourself get convinced of anything that violates your own beliefs. The therapist can and should be responsive to your feedback and wishes, not necessarily agreeing, but certainly giving them respectful consideration. If you experience subtle—or not so subtle—pressure to comply with an individual treatment plan that you did not cocreate, the therapy relationship holds greater potential for harm than good. And if the therapist does not respond to your reasonable questions with clear, straightforward answers, then you have your answer: Find another therapist. There is no legitimate basis for a therapist's withholding information about his or her methods and intentions.

Choosing a therapist requires some patience, a willingness to ask questions and think critically about the answers, and a greater desire for things to get better than to be "right." A *good therapist can be an invaluable ally* in the toughest of times, so it is most worthwhile to be a "smart shopper."

Some Therapy Guidelines for the Abuse Survivor

If you are currently in therapy, or are considering going into therapy, and you are starting to face the harsh reality that you were abused, it is essential that you get skilled help. If you have always known you were abused, this book has less relevance for you. It is primarily for the person who has discovered what seem like repressed episodes of abuse in his or her past as a result of either therapy or some other such external source, like a talk show or magazine article. Even so, the specific path you choose to follow when you are coming to terms with what happened to you is critical in determining what your therapy is like, meaning *where* it focuses, *how* it progresses, and *what* it helps you to accomplish. By now you know that not all therapies are alike. There are serious consequences associated with choosing a therapist and the kind of therapeutic process you will undergo while in his or her care. Be assured that a skilled therapist can do a world of good for someone needing to come to terms with a history of abuse. It is a complex, multifaceted problem that generally precludes quick and simple interventions. Having survived abuse affects one's self-image, mood, relationships, sexuality, motivation, and almost every other aspect of human experience. People are typically unaware of their own "blind spots," and a good therapist who is experienced in working effectively with abuse survivors can do a great deal to expand your range of vision while supporting you emotionally as you reach new conclusions about old experiences. Therapy obviously can't change what happened to you, but it can do a lot to change the way you look at it and how you feel about it.

The conventional wisdom in the recovery field has been that you must recall and work through nearly every detail of every abusive experience you suffered. Sometimes the process involves vivid imagery and recall, and sometimes it involves screaming and kicking and crying. Other times it's simply gut-level insight that shifts people's ideas about themselves and their experiences. Is it necessary to spend hour after hour, day after day, dredging up more and more details of the terrible past to work on in therapy? Sometimes it *is* desirable, but *necessary?* No, *not always.* To ignore or discount your feelings, your body sensations, or your perceptions is obviously undesirable. But, amplifying feelings of hurt or shame about the past in order to promote a sense of well-being in the present is not a particularly sensible strategy of recovery, either. Some therapists who work with abuse survivors have expressed their concerns to me that bad therapy can be one more trauma for the client. They suggest this is most likely to happen when the therapist requires the client to follow a formula of some sort that the therapist thinks is important despite the client's openly expressed disinclination to do so.

How do you find a good recovery group? Follow the same recommendations I provided earlier about finding a therapist. Call individual therapists whose names you have obtained and ask them to recommend some therapists who run groups for survivors. Then contact them and ask to attend a meeting or two.

You don't have to sign your life over to a recovery group just because you attend some of its meetings. Go to a meeting or two, and get the flavor of what goes on there. Talk to other members and find out things like:

- How long has each person been in the group? (If the answer is years, it may indicate the group fosters more dependence than independence. Be alert to see if that is the case.)
- How would each member describe what goes on in the group? (Is there direction? Methods taught for

building resources? Emotional support? Valuable
feedback offered safely and respectfully?)
- Is the process rigid or flexible? (Do you have to follow a preconceived plan or does the program adapt
to individual needs and preferences?)
- How is progress measured? (Are group members
expected to stay indefinitely, or are there clear
bench marks of success?)

Dealing with your past is an inescapable part of treatment: The
crucial variables are *how much* focus on the past and *when* in the
therapy process. When an abuse survivor is already overwhelmed
with flashbacks and nightmares, crippled with fear, and on the
verge of falling apart, does it make any sense to go digging up
more painful memories? The client is clearly already overwhelmed
and lacking the necessary abilities to cope effectively. On this basis alone, it has been and continues to be my practice to *build coping resources first before dredging up more of what is already too much
to handle.* Getting into all the painful details of what happened to
you may be necessary *at times*, but certainly not all or even most
of the time. When you do get into hurtful memories, it is best to
do so armed with the necessary resources to use them to your best
therapeutic advantage.

One commonly expressed piece of information stated as fact by
some in the recovery movement is that memories of abuse surface
only when the person is ready to deal with them. This position is
stated succinctly in the following quotation published by the Association for Humanistic Psychology:

When children are traumatized, they repress their
memories longer than adults and on average do not
recover their memories until their thirties or forties. It
appears that their subconscious minds somehow know
when they are mature enough to process the memories consciously.

While this is an interesting viewpoint, it is hardly true. People do not have a subconscious that wisely recognizes opportunities. Symptoms exist, the abuse survivor seeks help, and the alert therapist determines whether he or she has the resources necessary to resolve them yet.

When I say build coping resources first, what kinds of resources am I referring to? Such skills as

1. the ability to maintain a comfortable emotional distance, whereby memories can be considered, detached from the hurtful feelings associated with them;

2. the ability to create emotional attachments, whereby some positive feelings (e.g., self-worth, ability to cope with adversity) may be amplified within the person or attached to the memory;

3. the ability to personalize or depersonalize, in this case meaning the ability to discriminate with insight and clarity between what is appropriate to take personally and what is not. Often, survivors make the mistake of thinking the abuse was somehow their fault or a statement about them or their worth, rather than recognizing it as a statement about the character of the offender. This personalization leads to the self-blame and guilt that can be some of the most destructive aspects of being a survivor;

4. the ability to "reattribute" the experience, meaning reinterpreting both *why* it happened and *what* it means. The ability to view both the abuse and the abuser from perspectives other than the hurtful one you got "stuck" in is a very important therapeutic goal;

5. the ability to orient to the future, so that the hurtful past no longer continues to prompt unhealthy or self-destructive decisions for the future. The future

needs to become detached from the past to some extent, which becomes more possible with the realization that the future is *not* simply going to be "more of the same." New perspectives and skills can lead you to make new choices and seek out new experiences that open your future up to unlimited possibilities; and,

6. the ability to compartmentalize, meaning the ability to separate different aspects of yourself from each other and focus on and amplify whatever aspect(s) will serve you best in a given situation.

When is it important to be in touch with your feelings, and when is it best to set them aside (compartmentalize) in order to responsibly do what must be done? Or when is it desirable or necessary to set aside your personal interest and make a sacrifice of sorts, and when is that unhealthy self-denial? Knowing which "part" of yourself to access at a given moment for a given purpose is a most powerful way of going through life. If you think about it, symptoms often arise when someone taps into the "wrong" part—for example, so-and-so gets into her feelings when they are irrelevant, or she gets into her rational self when she would be better off following her heart. Each part of you is valuable at some time, in some place—even the parts of you that right now you don't like very much. A good therapist can help you come to recognize that and teach you how to access the "best" part(s) at the "right" time.

There is no precise formula for abuse therapy. Despite the popular term "recovery process," the process is as individual as each person who undertakes it. When you find a therapist who can work with you *as an individual* and is more interested in your well-being than in following "the process," you have found someone worth working with. And when you have found a support group (which I would recommend doing) that speaks English and not "program," then you have found a group worth participating in.

Some Therapy Guidelines for the Doubtful

In light of everything I have described about suggestibility and the potential harmful influence of the therapist's perspectives on the client, you can easily appreciate that you are more vulnerable to untoward influence when you are in doubt. If you are starting to uncover what seem to be—and very well could be—previously repressed memories of abuse, try as best you can to be objective. Consider these questions: (1) What are the memories? Are they vague impressions or vivid recollections? (2) How did the memories surface? Are they directly available to you as memories, or are they something you deduced from confusing symptoms? (3) Did the memories arise through external influences (like a therapist suggesting them through some memory recovery process, or through a magazine article you read or a television program you saw), or did they surface independently? (4) Is your mind already made up that your memories are (or are not) true? (5) Are the abuse scenarios feasible, or have they gotten increasingly bizarre and improbable as time goes on? (6) Do they involve memories exclusively from early infancy?

I have discussed the implications associated with your answers to each of these questions. I have suggested that when the line between reality and fantasy is blurred, it is best not to work at having to "believe." If you are doubtful and you are in therapy, note the position your therapist takes. Consider these questions: (1) Does your therapist seem certain abuse occurred even if you aren't? (2) Is your therapist condescending in some way, suggesting that "when you are ready, you'll come to accept it"? (3) Is your therapist so intent on your believing it that he or she is willing to terminate the therapy relationship if you don't? (4) Is your therapist gently pressuring (or even bullying) you into removing all doubts and believing it "or else you'll never get well"? (5) Is your therapist forcing you to confront your family and risk losing them forever, even though you're not really sure it happened? (6) Is your therapist leading you to believe that the explanation of child abuse is the *only* way to explain your symptoms? (7) Does your therapist seem so stuck in the belief you must have been abused that he or she is unable to view your problems in any other way?

If you answered "yes" to any of the above questions, your therapist may be making the very mistakes that can lead you to get absorbed in a potentially destructive situation. It is very important, *especially* when you are uncertain, that the therapist be as objective as possible and *not* impose his or her beliefs on you at such a vulnerable time. The common denominator underlying all the questions above is *coercion*. It is important that you feel the freedom to choose what to accept or reject in the therapy relationship, rather than feel pressured to conform to a belief that you feel uncertain about.

Some Therapy Guidelines for the Falsely Accused

It is the worst sort of nightmare to be accused of something you know you did not do. To prove you *didn't* do something is nearly impossible, and once the false accusation is made, it alters your life forever. At this time when your emotions are explosive and rationality is hard to come by, you most need to keep your wits about you. I strongly encourage you to seek professional help. You can't realistically expect your family and friends to experience no doubts about you at all once the allegations are made, and you will need an outside source of both support and objectivity. You would be wise not to demand or expect an immediate and unwavering statement of support from your family or friends, or you will likely push them in the opposite direction. That is *not* because they are being disloyal to you or because they immediately believe you did what you are accused of doing. Rather, it is because *doubt is inevitable in the situation*. It is not personal, even though since it affects you, it *feels* personal. Do not make the mistake of isolating yourself from others because you are feeling abandoned while they work through their own reactions to the allegations. Reread Chapters 7 and 8 and try to understand why each person will likely have doubts. If you happen to garner immediate support from others and no one hesitates to affirm their belief in your innocence, consider yourself unusually lucky. Doubt is the most typical reaction, with disbelief and denial following right behind. Expect it, allow it, and don't personalize it, even though it may hurt.

Getting support is crucial to staying sane while dealing with this sort of trauma. Your therapist can be a very valuable source of emotional support and a good costrategist for dealing with the circumstances. A support group of others who have also been falsely accused can provide further support as well as an exchange of information and strategies for coping. Your therapist will likely know of such local support groups, but in the event he or she does not, you can contact the False Memory Syndrome Foundation (FMSF) in Philadelphia. Their address and phone number is: 3401 Market Street, Suite 130, Philadelphia, PA 19104; (215) 387-1865. They provide current information and valuable support, publish a newsletter, and can most likely refer you to a support group in your area.

Meeting Your Accusing Child's Therapist

If your child has been in some sort of therapy through which he or she has recovered memories of abuse that you know never actually occurred, it is entirely possible that you may be invited to meet with your child's therapist. Therapists often prescribe such meetings to enable your child to confront you and to extract a confession of your guilt as well as an apology. There are many potential hazards in meeting the therapist involved in your child's memory work, and you need to know what they are if you are to have any hope of handling the interaction well. You should work out ahead of time what you will say and do (and *not* say and do) in response to the wide range of things that can happen in such meetings. If you go into such a meeting without a realistic plan, you run the risk of getting blindsided.

Take the time to sort out and think about the facts available to you. Your child has been in therapy and has developed the idea that you sexually abused him or her. Preposterous as this might seem if you know you are truly innocent, your child believes it. Do you expect the therapist to be neutral in this matter? Or can you safely predict that the therapist is largely responsible for your child's coming to believe what he now believes? If the therapist is neutral, there is room for discussion. If the therapist has already predetermined your guilt, there is not going to be much room to change his or her mind.

It helps to know who wants the meeting and why. Was it suggested by the therapist? Did your child ask to arrange it? For what purpose? These are questions you can and should ask ahead of time.

Go to the meeting, but be prepared for the worst. The therapist may already believe you are guilty. You can easily feel ganged up on and backed into a corner. If you react by getting angry or defensive, then you merely confirm for them that you cannot deal with your feelings rationally. You thereby confirm your guilt in their minds. Heads, they win; tails, you lose.

I suggest you try to tape the session, so bring a tape recorder. At the outset of the meeting, you can ask for permission to record the session for your later review. Of course, the meeting is confidential and taping it without permission is a violation of that confidentiality. If the reaction you get is negative or defensive, then don't press it. Some therapists will welcome the chance to have a record of the conversation, but others will fear it and refuse to allow taping. Let it go if you're told no taping will be permitted.

If it soon becomes clear to you that the meeting was called so that you can confess, you must take charge and bring focus back to the session. You must say clearly and nondefensively, "I did not do the things I am being accused of. I don't know why this is happening, but I have no intention of letting my future relationship with my child be held hostage in order to coerce a false confession out of me. Now, are you open to any other possible explanations for these allegations or my child's symptoms, or are you fully intent on maintaining the abuse explanation despite its being untrue?" Make your denial firm and clear, for to not do so can be taken as a passive confession.

Do your best to encourage further objective exploration by the therapist. Ask that other family members be interviewed, that medical and school records be obtained, that childhood friends be interviewed, and that other sources be used to investigate the false allegations. Remind the therapist that while his or her intentions are obviously to help your child, he or she cannot take the role of rigidly confirming the allegations without allowing room for open discussion. Hopefully you will appeal to some objectivity on the part of the therapist.

In the event that the predetermined verdict is that you are guilty and there is simply no avenue open for further discussion or consideration, then you can verbalize your disappointment that the session was unproductive because the agenda was so rigidly predetermined, precluding an honest exchange and a deeper look into the matter. Calmly, but matter-of-factly, state your willingness to talk again anytime it might be helpful, but only on the condition that the meeting have a purpose beyond seeking a confession for something you never did. Provide an address and telephone number to the therapist should he or she want to reconsider his or her approach, and provide your child with the assurance that despite the pain and confusion involved in the situation, you would welcome the chance to reconcile in the future. Do not blame your child as wrong or crazy and do not attempt to employ guilt by asking variations of "How could you do this to me?" Say your piece and then go.

The analogy of losing your child to a religious cult is an apt one. Why people become cult members is a topic I touched on earlier. You can't just kidnap and deprogram cult members, despite whatever hype you sometimes hear. You can't control the choices another person makes, and though it is heartbreaking when an impasse is reached, all you can really do is continue to make yourself available. Continue to send birthday cards, send greetings, do the little things generously that let your child know you are still there. No one can predict the future, and you never can tell whether an eventual reconciliation may be possible. Keep your options—and your door—open. And, in the meanwhile, get on with your own life. Making a painful situation that is out of your control the centerpiece of your life is a guaranteed path to depression. Take charge of your life and make sure you have more to it than heartache from a mixed-up kid.

A NOTE TO THERAPISTS

Therapy can hurt people, as I suspect you already know. Who hasn't had to clean up someone else's botched case? As you read the case histories in this book and evaluate the advice I give here to people caught in the trap of suggested abuse, I hope you are touched by the realization that things are not always as they seem. I implore you to appreciate these basic points regarding therapy: (1) Clients typically come to therapy believing they are personally powerless to effect meaningful change in their lives; (2) clients believe that a trained "expert" can, through an "objective" perspective and refined techniques, help resolve their problems; and (3) clients assume they must conform to the therapist's perceptions and comply with the therapist's treatment plan if they are to improve.

In the unique context of therapy, conformity and obedience are often defined as necessary in order to recover from one's symptoms. Thus, your perspective as the therapist is critical in determining the focus of treatment.

There are no reliable means for determining whether a previously repressed memory is authentic or confabulated. In light of everything I have stated here about the role of suggestion in making the diagnosis of abuse when that was not a presenting problem, it seems prudent and respectful that you avoid becoming a basis for the kinds of problems described throughout this chapter.

I would encourage you *not* to (1) preclude open communication at all times among family members; (2) act as your client's "hired gun"; (3) act as if corroboration of allegations of abuse were unnecessary; (4) jump quickly to the conclusion abuse occurred simply because it is plausible; (5) suggest a history of abuse to someone who is not your client; (6) refer a client out for hypnotic confirmation or disconfirmation on the false premise that hypnosis is some kind of lie detector; (7) ask leading or suggestive questions; (8) assume repression is in force when someone does not have much memory from childhood; (9) rely on your memory of the interaction. Tape your investigative sessions and review them later for any evidence of possible unintentional contamination of your client's recollections.

As a therapist, too, I want our work to be taken seriously and be favorably regarded by the rest of the society in which we live. We are now embroiled in intense controversy over the issues of memory, trauma, and recovery. How we deal with these sensitive issues will determine in large part how we will all eventually be viewed. Let's admit openly that there is much we don't yet know and use our advanced knowledge to create avenues of objective exploration. In the meanwhile, let's try not to destroy people's lives by presuming guilt on the basis of inadequate evidence and arbitrary subjective beliefs.

KEY POINTS TO REMEMBER

- Despite some of the hazards associated with therapy, skilled and sensitive therapists can be invaluable sources of information, support, perspective, and treatment.
- Time is a critical variable. Move to resolve things sooner rather than later. Letting too much time

pass allows perceptions to solidify and become more difficult to change.

- Therapists may well have to take on the additional task of being investigators of sorts, seeking objective information about people and situations when necessary or desirable.
- Not all therapists are equally skilled or equally "tuned-in" to the relevant issues. Choose a therapist using the guidelines provided.
- Therapy is indicated when the problems you face exceed your ability to manage or solve them. Therapy that builds resources for coping with and solving problems (goal- and solution-oriented) is most relevant for the circumstances of suggested memories of abuse.
- If you have been falsely accused, the analogy of losing a child to a religious cult is an apt one. It highlights the need to keep communication open rather than cutting it off. It is generally wise to leave your door open to the possibility of eventual reconciliation.
- It is important to have a well-thought-out plan for conducting your meeting with your child's therapist.
- Specific guidelines are provided to therapists to help them avoid becoming another problem rather than a means to a solution.

CHAPTER 10

The Memories

of Your Future

*L*ee's family had always enjoyed a close relationship. His daughter Nancy, thirty, was a professional woman. His daughter Amy, however, had yet to find herself at twenty-eight. He'd seen her get into school and drop out of school, take jobs and quit jobs. She basically followed the wind, or the snow, to be more precise—the only constant in her life seemed to be skiing.

Amy had been involved with various men throughout her adult life. Each relationship would last a year or two, then she'd move on to the next one. Finally, though, she thought she'd found a guy with whom she could marry and have a family. When he broke up with her, she was devastated. In her grief, she sought the support of a therapist, who matter-of-factly suggested that her

219

checkered history with men had its origins in sexual abuse by her father.

I'll spare you the by now familiar details, but Amy eventually came to believe sexual abuse had occurred when she was two years old. She believed Lee had digitally penetrated her several times when diapering her, despite the lack of specific memories. Eventually she accused him directly in a face-to-face confrontation.

Lee was dumbfounded, to say the least. His wife, unsure what to believe, no longer felt close to him, though she did not outright abandon him. The same was true of Nancy.

In emotional agony, Lee began to look for answers as to how such a thing could happen to him. In a local medical school library, while reading up on hypnosis and its effect on memory, he came across my book, *Trancework*. He read the section on creating false memories and felt he had to talk to me.

He flew out from the East Coast, where he lives, to see me in California. He sought information and support, in that order.

We met for nearly two hours, while he learned about memory, suggestibility, the suggestibility of memory, and suggestions of abuse. He was given strategies for gaining support from his wife and older daughter, for contacting Amy's therapist, for trying to reestablish communication with Amy, and most important, for not personalizing circumstances over which he had so little control. He would have to find ways to go on with his life while Amy made all the decisions affecting their mutual relationship.

Lee's situation has not yet healed, but he has already been helped greatly by acquiring facts, perspective, and support. He still hopes for a positive resolution to the agonizing events that almost consumed him. Who knows? Maybe he'll be one of the lucky ones who has a happy ending.

I am acutely aware of how mixed my feelings are as I write this final chapter. I think I have presented a fair consideration of the issues at hand, yet I am concerned whether my views will be perceived accurately. My greatest fear is that some readers won't understand my deep concern for the plight of abuse survivors. I don't think it's an entirely unrealistic fear, either. Over the course of the last two years, I have given quite a few lectures to professional audiences on the subject of suggested memories of abuse. I have pointed out the dangers of assuming we know more than we really do in these matters, and I have discussed the need for us to be cautious in our methods of clinical practice. By and large, my audiences have responded favorably to my pleas, yet there is invariably a small but noteworthy percentage of listeners who apparently find themselves threatened by my remarks. They get angry and they accuse me of being in denial as to how widespread the phenomenon of abuse really is. They claim I am serving as a willing pawn of abusers by giving them more compelling rationales for denying their terrible deeds. They fear I will make it more difficult for genuine abuse survivors to come forward and tell their stories out of the fear that they will not be believed. They suggest I am part of a backlash against feminism.

All of the criticisms sound plausible, yet none are true. The Hippocratic oath of health professionals demands that above all else, we should do no harm. My first concern is the welfare of our clients, and I am acutely aware that the ability to do harm is ever present when one is in a position of influence. We are irresponsible *unless* we examine our methods and assumptions, precisely because these issues are so emotional and have such great potential for harm. Unless we do so *now*, I am concerned that we will see more and more of what have come to be called "retractors"—those who, as a result of irresponsible therapy, came to believe they were abused, and who eventually came to realize they had not. The reputation of therapists in general—and all the good that they can do—will suffer. All it will take is more broadcasts like the CNN *Special Assignment* segment that aired on May 3, 1993.

CAUGHT IN THE ACT

The report was called "Guilt by Memory," and it captured a prime example of the excesses of the mental health profession that I have been describing. Correspondent Kathy Slobogin sent one of her news producers, posing as a client, to see a therapist who was well known for interpreting almost any problem presented to her as rooted in repressed memories of sexual abuse.

The following is taken directly from the transcript of the segment:

> *Slobogin:* The therapeutic community itself has difficulty overseeing what goes on inside the privacy of a therapist's office. The question whether some therapists are leading clients towards memories is a sensitive one and difficult to prove.
>
> Because such a large number of families have been wrenched apart through this process, we decided to go into therapy undercover. Before taking that step, CNN consulted a psychologist with extensive expertise in this area. We asked him to help us define symptoms for our undercover producer which would not necessarily point to child abuse.
>
> *CNN producer:* Basically, I've just been kind of depressed. I guess it started about eight months ago.
>
> *Slobogin:* Our CNN producer took a hidden camera to tape this therapist, whose identity we decided not to reveal. But she's typical of the type of therapist causing concern. She has counseled at least six people we know of who went to her for other reasons and came out accusing their parents of sexual abuse. The words here are her own, but we've substituted another voice.
>
> *Second therapist* ["first therapist" was interviewed earlier in the segment]: You mean your sexual intimacy?

CNN producer: Yeah.

Slobogin: Our producer said her depression had affected her marriage and lessened her interest in sex. She discussed her family history, and the therapist asked about childhood memories. At the end of the very first session, the therapist suggested a diagnosis.

Second therapist: It seems to me that you have the symptoms of someone who could have experienced some sexual trauma.

Slobogin: Our producer never suggested she had been sexually abused and said she had no memory of it.

CNN producer: Do you get many women like this?

Second therapist: Many, many.

CNN producer: And they forget?

Second therapist: Yes, yes, they forget. They have no idea. In fact, I mean, what you've presented to me, Leanne, is so classic that I'm just sitting here blown away actually.

Slobogin: The therapist then told our producer to read a book about repressed memories.

CNN producer: It didn't seem like me.

Slobogin: In a second session, our producer expressed strong doubts about the possibility of abuse. The therapist didn't force it, but she went on to describe how repressed memory works.

CNN producer: I mean, if something bad happened to you, I would think that you'd remember it.

Second therapist: You're right. You're right. If something bad happens, you really remember it. But if something too bad happens to you, so bad that you can't cope with it, you forget it.

Voilà—another survivor. Later in the same segment, Slobogin interviewed two retractors:

> *Slobogin* [interviewing]: But why would people be so willing to believe their own parents had abused them?
>
> *Melody Gavigan:* I thought it was the only way I could get better. That's what the books said, to, you know, uncover more memories and more memories.
>
> *Slobogin:* Melody Gavigan and Lynn Gondolf call themselves retractors. They're part of a small but growing network of former clients who say their abuse memories were false, created by therapists who pressured them to imagine abuse.
>
> *Slobogin* [interviewing]: Did you have doubts?
>
> *Lynn Gondolf:* Yeah, and when you ask them, they've got a good answer for that, too. It's normal. It's natural. It's denial.
>
> *Slobogin* [interviewing]: Why would anybody make up these memories if they weren't true?
>
> *Ms. Gavigan:* Because it gives you a simple explanation for the pain that you're in.
>
> *Ms. Gondolf:* You go to the right therapist at a right time in your life seeking answers and believing the answers you're given. You're susceptible to this. This can happen to anybody, not—it's not people who have "problems." This can happen to anybody.

This fine segment succeeded in bringing to life in front of the camera what I know has been going on for much too long a time.

As we saw in Chapter 5, there are many ways clients can be led to consider and then to adopt the belief that abuse occurred, and one of the most common mechanisms—misinformation—is clearly evident in the session Slobogin captured on tape ("What you've presented to me, Leanne, is so classic . . ."). Is there any mistaking what the "client" was to conclude about the reasons for her symptoms? And, in the case of a bona fide client, how long would it have been before "memories" started to surface?

Compelling reasons to believe precede the recovery of apparently repressed memories. The most compelling reason of all is "believe and you will be healed." As the popular book title says, you must have "the courage to heal." Not the facts, not the objectivity to examine what might or might not have happened, not the willingness to consider perspectives carefully, only the courage to believe. Conviction, not truth. The reality is, healing from a history of abuse *does* require courage. It takes strength and drive to transcend a horrible past. But leading people to believe they were abused when they were not is *not* courageous or noble. It's malpractice.

A POWERFUL LESSON

What started out as a local San Diego news story sounded an alarm that served as a wake-up call to the entire nation. An independent grand jury in San Diego had investigated San Diego County's child protection network and issued a series of highly critical reports about it, describing it as a system "out of control, with few checks and little balance." They noted far too many cases of alleged sexual abuse by parents who later were proved innocent of the charges. In many cases, children had been removed from their custody.

The story broke nationally on CBS News, which aired the case of Alicia. Alicia had been severely raped and sodomized at the age of eight. She claimed that the perpetrator was a strange man who climbed through her bedroom window, and footprints of an adult male were found near her window. But her father, Jim Wade, was home with her at the time. Jim was a petty officer in the Navy who was known to have a drinking problem, and he was immediately suspected by the authorities of being Alicia's attacker. Her story was viewed as a thinly veiled attempt to protect him. Therapists "know" that survivors too often will "enable" or defend the incestuous parent, and Alicia's story fit that profile.

Jim Wade vehemently denied his guilt. "Denial, of course," said the therapists. Alicia vehemently denied that her dad was the perpetrator. "Denial and fear," said the therapists.

Alicia was taken from her parents and placed in foster care. She was assigned to a county therapist, who repeatedly told Alicia she'd feel better if she'd just admit that "Daddy did it." After thirteen months of such "treatment," Alicia lay on the floor, assumed a fetal position, and mouthed the words she was told to say: "Daddy did it." Jim Wade's guilt was now "confirmed."

Jim was understandably devastated. But two years later, someone found in an evidence bag the panties Alicia had been wearing the night she was attacked, which had somehow been overlooked. DNA tests conducted on the semen found on them proved beyond any shadow of a doubt that Jim Wade could not have been the rapist. Alicia was a week away from adoption by another family.

Suggested realities. The power of authority. Conformity. Guilt until proven innocent. Alicia's case is just one of many, but it is unique in that in the end the accused was vindicated. What about all those for whom no such objective evidence exists?

ALL THAT WE DON'T KNOW

The specter of confabulation looming behind memories of abuse that arose in response to a therapist's (or some other external) influence can cause self-doubt, splits within families, suspicion of one's therapist, and fears of facing painful facts. All that I said in Chapter 7 about the uncertainty inherent in the situation is critical in considering all the issues from all the angles.

How can you distinguish a real memory from a confabulation? As we have seen, no objectively reliable method for doing so currently exists. This conclusion represents the unanimous response of the many experts I have interviewed on both sides of the repression issue.

The mental health profession does not yet know very much about the repression of traumatic memories. In fact, some question the very existence of repression. Therapists do not yet know how common repression of childhood sexual abuse really is. We do not currently know the authenticity of memories that have been buried twenty or thirty years that suddenly and dramatically surface in response to a lecture, a self-help book, or a therapy session. We do not know whether repressed memories always exist where symptoms are present, or whether the same symptoms can exist independently of negative experiences that might have been repressed. We do not definitively know how to characterize the differences between repression and merely forgetting. We do not know from what age repression is even possible. We do not know if trauma makes a repressed memory less or more accurate in a given individual. We do not know which techniques for recovering repressed memories will alter them in significant ways merely by using the techniques. We don't know why some people repress a particular type of trauma and others do not. We do not know why some people never recollect traumatic memories that are objectively known to exist in their backgrounds, while others have memories that do eventually return. These many unknowns all represent areas badly in need of further research.

When there is so much still to be learned, how can so many therapists be so comfortable, even adamant, in their belief that what they are doing is objective, sound, and therapeutic?

THE MEMORIES OF YOUR FUTURE

The things you do today will be the memories you recall years from now. Every person touched by the question of abuse—survivor, therapist, family members, the accused—needs a plan for coping with the terrible strain of what has happened. Throughout this book I have strongly urged restraint from jumping to what may be erroneous conclusions, and I have emphasized the value of getting help from someone skilled and objective who can guide the search for answers. The point is, only you can decide what your goals should be. You're the only one who can decide just how pervasive an influence on your life all these issues will ultimately have. You're the only one who can assess whether you are being unduly influenced to follow someone else's agenda.

Take a few minutes to imagine your life a year—five years—ten years—from now. Can you identify what has happened as a result of the decisions you made? Be as specific as you can be. Over time, have your ideas or feelings changed? If so, how? Are you better or worse off as a result?

I believe there is great value in thinking ahead, if you do so as realistically as possible. I want you to be able to look back over how you handled things and to feel good about yourself. I would want you to handle the delicate situations you now face with finesse and clarity, and to be able to respect yourself for doing so. May a strong sense of appreciation for your own integrity be your dominant memory in the future, and may this book help you to accomplish that.

APPENDIX A

DEMOGRAPHIC DATA
DESCRIBING THERAPIST RESPONDENTS

Table I. Ages of Respondents

Ages	MAQ		HAQ	
	Number	Percent	Number	Percent
20–29	40	4.6	43	4.9
30–39	211	24.4	206	23.7
40–49	374	43.3	375	43.2
50–59	174	20.1	181	20.8
60+	50	5.8	52	6.0
No answer	15	1.8	12	1.4
Total	864	100	869	100

Table II. Levels of Formal Education of Respondents

Degree	MAQ		HAQ	
	Number	Percent	Number	Percent
Master's	553	64.0	560	64.4
Ph.D.	210	24.3	208	23.9
M.D.	37	4.3	34	3.9
B.A./B.S.	41	4.7	41	4.7
Other	10	1.2	17	2.0
No answer	13	1.5	9	1.1
Total	864	100	869	100

Table III. Number of Years in Clinical Practice

Years	MAQ		HAQ	
	Number	Percent	Number	Percent
1–9	336	38.9	337	38.8
10–19	311	36.0	314	36.1
20–29	124	14.4	122	14.0
30–39	13	1.5	12	1.4
40+	1	.1	0	0
No answer	79	9.1	84	9.7
Total	864	100	869	100

Table IV. Respondent Work Settings

Setting	MAQ		HAQ	
	Number	Percent	Number	Percent
Hospital	117	13.5	110	12.7
Clinic	52	6.0	49	5.6
Agency	215	24.9	223	25.7
School	37	4.3	40	4.6
Private practice	397	45.9	406	46.7
Other	23	2.7	19	2.2
No answer	23	2.7	22	2.5
Total	864	100	869	100

APPENDIX B

DATA FREQUENCIES AND AVERAGES FOR THE MEMORY ATTITUDE QUESTIONNAIRE*

Demographics

Is your knowledge of the workings of memory:
Below Average 149 (17.2) Average 574
(66.5) Above Average 102 (11.8) NA 39 (4.5)
Do you use hypnosis in your work?
Yes 454 (52.5) No 395 (45.7) NA 15 (1.7)
Do you work hypnotically to recover memories?
Often 60 (6.9) Sometimes 238 (27.5)
Rarely 189 (21.9) Never 344 (39.8) NA 33 (3.8)

Below are 10 statements which you are asked to state your relative agreement or disagreement with. Please place a check mark in the appropriate place by each item.

Items	Agree Strongly	Agree Slightly	Disagree Slightly	Disagree Strongly	No Response
1. The mind is like a computer, accurately recording events as they actually occurred.	107 (12.4)	179 (20.7)	220 (25.5)	349 (40.4)	9 (1.0)
2. Events that we know occurred but can't remember are repressed memories— i.e., memories that are psychologically defended against.	187 (21.6)	326 (37.7)	244 (28.2)	89 (10.3)	18 (2.1)

*Numbers in parentheses represent the percentage of total responses for that item.

231

Items	Agree Strongly	Agree Slightly	Disagree Slightly	Disagree Strongly	No Response
3. Memory is a reliable mechanism when the self-defensive need for repression is lifted.	103 (11.9)	316 (36.6)	281 (32.5)	144 (16.7)	5 (2.3)
4. If someone doesn't remember much about his or her childhood, it is most likely because it was somehow traumatic.	81 (9.4)	291 (33.7)	276 (31.9)	193 (22.3)	23 (2.7)
5. It is necessary to recover detailed memories of traumatic events if someone is to improve in therapy.	27 (3.1)	138 (16.0)	300 (34.7)	388 (44.9)	11 (1.3)
6. Memory is not significantly influenced by suggestion.	17 (2.0)	66 (7.6)	294 (34.0)	461 (53.4)	26 (3.0)
7. One's level of certainty about a memory is strongly positively correlated with that memory's accuracy.	35 (4.1)	173 (20.0)	310 (35.9)	310 (35.9)	36 (14.2)
8. I trust my client such that if he or she says something happened, it must have happened, regardless of the age or context in which the event occurred.	44 (5.1)	176 (20.4)	351 (40.6)	278 (32.2)	15 (1.7)
9. I believe that early memories, even from the first years of life, are accurately stored and retrievable.	106 (12.3)	244 (28.2)	272 (31.5)	228 (26.4)	14 (1.6)

Items	Agree Strongly	Agree Slightly	Disagree Slightly	Disagree Strongly	No Response
10. If a client believes a memory is true, I must also believe it to be true if I am to help him or her.	110 (12.7)	204 (23.6)	260 (30.1)	274 (31.7)	16.(1.9)

Do you attempt to distinguish between what appear to you to be true memories and false memories?

Yes 323 (37.4) No 489 (56.6) NA 52 (6)

If yes, how do you do so? Please write your response on the back of this form. Thank you. Include your name, address, and telephone number if you are willing to discuss your response.

Wrote: 250 (29)

Did not write: 614 (71)

DATA FREQUENCIES AND AVERAGES FOR THE HYPNOSIS ATTITUDE QUESTIONNAIRE*

Demographics

Are you formally trained in hypnosis?
  Yes 372 (42.8) No 485 (55.8) NA 12 (1.4)
Do you use hypnosis in your work?
  Yes 463 (53.3) No 382 (44.0) NA 24 (2.7)
Do you work hypnotically to recover memories?
  Often 66 (7.6) Sometimes 246 (28.3) Rarely 173 (19.9)
  Never 350 (40.3) NA 34 (3.9)

Below are 15 statements which you are asked to state your relative agreement or disagreement with. Please place a check mark in the appropriate place by each item.

Items	Agree Strongly	Agree Slightly	Disagree Slightly	Disagree Strongly	No Response
1. Hypnosis is a worthwhile therapy tool.	665 (76.5)	179 (20.6)	15 (1.7)	3 (.3)	7 (.8)
2. Hypnosis enables people to accurately remember things they otherwise could not.	211 (24.3)	442 (50.9)	123 (14.2)	50 (5.8)	43 (4.9)
3. Hypnosis seems to counteract the defense mechanism of repression, lifting repressed					

*Numbers in parentheses represent the percentage of total responses for that item.

Items	Agree Strongly	Agree Slightly	Disagree Slightly	Disagree Strongly	No Response
material into conscious awareness.	248 (28.5)	470 (54.1)	87 (10.0)	23 (2.6)	41 (4.7)
4. People cannot lie when in hypnosis.	30 (3.5)	126 (14.5)	355 (40.9)	308 (35.4)	50 (5.8)
5. Therapists can have greater faith in details of a traumatic event when obtained hypnotically than otherwise.	74(8.5)	333(38.3)	273(31.4)	148(17.0)	41(4.7)
6. When someone has a memory of a trauma while in hypnosis, it objectively must actually have occurred.	42 (4.8)	225 (25.9)	334 (38.4)	228 (26.2)	40 (4.6)
7. Hypnosis can be used to recover memories of actual events as far back as birth.	157 (18.1)	310 (35.7)	208 (23.9)	139 (16.0)	55 (6.3)
8. Hypnosis can be used to recover accurate memories of past lives.	63 (7.2)	180 (20.7)	170 (19.6)	366 (42.1)	90 (10.4)
9. It is possible to suggest false memories to someone who then incorporates them as true memories.	310 (35.7)	378 (43.5)	96 (11.0)	47 (5.4)	38 (4.4)
10. Hypnotic age regression has positive value as a therapeutic tool.	410 (47.2)	322 (37.1)	63 (7.2)	34 (3.9)	40 (4.6)
11. Someone could be hypnotically age regressed and get "stuck" at a prior age.	44 (5.1)	121 (13.9)	247 (28.4)	401 (46.1)	56 (6.4)
12. Hypnotically obtained memories are					

Items	Agree Strongly	Agree Slightly	Disagree Slightly	Disagree Strongly	No Response
more accurate than simply just remembering.	68 (7.8)	309 (35.6)	287 (33.0)	145 (16.7)	60 (6.9)
13. Hypnosis increases one's level of certainty about the accuracy of one's memories.	128 (14.7)	404 (46.5)	210 (24.2)	68 (7.8)	59 (6.8)
14. There is legitimate basis for believing that hypnosis can be used in such a way as to create false memories.	200 (23.0)	356 (41.0)	178 (20.5)	59 (6.8)	76 (8.7)
15. The hypnotized individual can easily tell the difference between a true memory and a pseudomemory.	30 (3.5)	146 (16.8)	406 (46.7)	214 (24.6)	73 (8.4)

Do you know of any cases where it seemed highly likely that a trauma victim's trauma was somehow suggested by a therapist rather than a genuine experience?

Yes 164 (18.9) No 655 (75.4) NA 50 (5.8)

If yes, could you briefly describe such a case scenario on the other side of this form? Thank you. Include your name, address, and phone number if you are willing to be contacted about your scenario.

Wrote: 151 (17.4) Did not write: 718 (82.6)

NOTES

PREFACE

Page 15   *He told his wife:* See "Closer Look Strips Glory from Vietnam War 'Hero,' ": in the San Diego *Evening Tribune* (October 10, 1989).

    19   *Many therapists believe:* See *Bradshaw On: The Family*, by J. Bradshaw (1988, Health Communications, Inc.).

    20   *In ever-increasing numbers:* See *The Courage to Heal*, by E. Bass and L. Davis (1988, Harper & Row), and *Repressed Memories*, by R. Fredrickson (1992, Fireside Books).

CHAPTER 1

Page 27   *Why is the mental health profession:* See "Beware the Incest-Survivor Machine," by C. Tavris, in *The New York Times* (January 3, 1993).

    32   *Consider the following letter:* See "Wife Who Regrets Sex Still Loves Her Husband," in the San Diego *Union-Tribune* (July 20, 1993).

    33   *If the client noncritically:* See "Cry Incest," by D. Nathan, in *Playboy* (October 1992).

    37   *Consider the trends:* See *Diseasing of America*, by S. Peele (1989, Lexington Books).

    37   *Right now, our culture:* See *Bradshaw On: The Family*, by J. Bradshaw (1988, Health Communications, Inc.).

    38   *Many therapists now accept:* See *Secret Survivors*, by E. Blume (1990, John Wiley & Sons).

CHAPTER 2

Page 42   *This ad appeared:* San Diego California Association for Marriage and Family Therapists *Newsletter* (October 1992).

45   *The HAQ was created:* Dr. Ernest Hilgard, personal communication, 1988.

52   *Does repression:* See *Hidden Memories,* by R. Baker (1992, Prometheus Books); "The Reality of Repressed Memories," by E. Loftus, in *American Psychologist* (May 1993); and *Trauma and Recovery,* by J. Herman (1992, Basic Books).

56   *Considerable research:* See "Hypnotic Hypermnesia and Forensic Hypnosis: A Cross-examination," by J. Watkins, in the *American Journal of Clinical Hypnosis* (1989); "The Investigative Use of Hypnosis: A Word of Caution," by M. Zelig and W. Beiderman, in the *International Journal of Clinical and Experimental Hypnosis* (1981); and "The Use and Misuse of Hypnosis in Court," by M. Orne, in the *International Journal of Clinical and Experimental Hypnosis* (1979).

57   *The majority (54 percent) also agreed:* See *Repressed Memories,* by R. Fredrickson (1992, Fireside).

58   *A commonly held misconception:* See *Trancework: An Introduction to the Practice of Clinical Hypnosis,* by M. Yapko (1990, Brunner/Mazel).

CHAPTER 3

Page 64   *Can memories, or even just the belief:* See "The Reality of Repressed Memories," by E. Loftus, in *American Psychologist* (May 1993); and "When Belief Creates Reality?" by M. Snyder in L. Berkowitz (ed.), *Advances in Experimental Social Psychology* (1984, Academic Press).

65   *Unfortunately, the computer as a metaphor:* See *Memory,* by E. Loftus (1980, Addison-Wesley).

66   *First, what is memory?:* See *Trance on Trial,* by A. Scheflin (1989, Guilford Press); and "Children's Memory for Witnessed Events," by C. Brainerd and P. Ornstein, in J. Doris (ed.), *The Suggestibility of Children's Recollections* (1991, American Psychological Association).

67   *The primary reason:* See *Memory,* by E. Loftus (1980, Addison-Wesley); *Trance on Trial,* by A. Scheflin (1989, Guilford Press); *Cognition,* by A. Glass and K. Holyoak (1986, Random House); and *Human Cognition: Learning, Understanding and Remembering,* by J. Bransford (1979, Wadsworth).

72   *In experiments conducted:* See "Influences of Misleading Postevent Information: Misinformation Interference and Acceptance," by R. Belli, in the *Journal of Experimental Psychology: General* (1989); "Misleading Suggestions Can Impair Eyewitnesses' Ability to Remember Event Details," by D. Lindsay, in the *Journal of Experimental Psychology: Learning, Memory and Cognition* (1990); and "Misinformation and Memory: The Creation of New Memories," by E. Loftus and H. Hoffman, in the *Journal of Experimental Psychology: General* (1989).

73   *The objective accuracy:* See "A Case of Misplaced Nostalgia," by U. Neisser, in *American Psychologist* (January 1991); and "Phantom Flashbulbs: False Recollections of Hearing the News About *Challenger,*" by U. Neisser and N. Harsch in E. Winograd and U. Neisser (eds.), *Affect and Accuracy in Recall: Studies of "Flashbulb" Memories* (1992, Cambridge University Press).

75   *When does memory begin?:* See "The Earliest Recollection: A New Survey," by J. Kihlstrom and J. Harackiewicz, in the *Journal of Personality* (1982); *Play, Dreams and Imitation in Childhood,* by J. Piaget

(1962, Norton); "Voices, Glances, Flashbacks: Our First Memories," by P. Hughe, in *Psychology Today* (September 1985); and "The Development of Event Memory," by J. Morton, in *The Psychologist* (1990).

77 *Therapists are just as likely:* See *True and False Accusations of Child Sex Abuse*, by R. Gardner (1992, Creative Therapeutics); *Repressed Memories*, by R. Fredrickson (1992, Fireside); and "An Indirect Method of Discovering Primary Traumatic Experiences: Two Case Examples," by D. Cheek, in the *American Journal of Clinical Hypnosis* (1989).

79 *The San Diego Union reported:* See "Are Past Lives Weird Truth or Mass Delusion?" by S. LaFee, in the *San Diego Union* (January 19, 1992).

84 *Despite the lack of intention:* See "The Evidence for Repression: An Examination of Sixty Years of Research," by D. Holmes, in J. Singer (ed.), *Repression and Dissociation: Implications for Personality, Theory, Psychopathology, and Health* (1990, University of Chicago Press); *Repressed Memories*, by R. Fredrickson (1992, Fireside); and *Adult Children of Abusive Parents*, by S. Farmer (1989, Ballantine).

86 *There is a well-known phenomenon:* See "When Belief Creates Reality?" by M. Snyder, in L. Berkowitz (ed.), *Advances in Experimental Social Psychology* (1984, Academic Press); "Hypothesis-Testing Processes in Social Interaction," by M. Snyder and W. Swann, in the *Journal of Personality and Social Psychology* (1978); and "Confirmatory Bias in Hypothesis-Testing for Client-Identified and Counselor Self-Generated Hypotheses," by B. Haverkamp, *Journal of Counseling Psychology* (1993).

88 *Adding new perspective:* See "Is Therapy Turning Us into Children?" by J. Hillman and M. Ventura, in *New Age Journal* (June 1992).

89   *It is unknown:* See "Childhood Trauma: Memory or Invention?" by D. Goleman, in *The New York Times* (July 21, 1992).

90   *In one study:* See "The False Memory Debate: Social Science or Social Backlash?" by J. Herman and M. Harvey, in the *Harvard Mental Health Letter* (April 1993); and "Amnesia in Adults Molested as Children: Testing Theories of Repression," by J. Briere and J. Conte, a paper presented at the 97th Annual Convention of the American Psychological Association, New Orleans (August 1989).

90   *In still another study:* See "Memory and Its Distortions," by E. Loftus, in A. Kraut (ed.), G. *Stanley Hall Lectures* (1982, American Psychological Association).

CHAPTER 4

Page 93   *One fact the letter doesn't mention:* See *Communion*, by W. Strieber (1987, Avon Books), and *Out on a Limb*, by S. MacLaine (1986, Bantam).

94   *Consider the power:* See "One on One with John Bradshaw," by J. Mitchell, in *Changes* (April 1993).

96   *Researchers in the field:* See *Trance on Trial*, by A. Scheflin (1989, Guilford Press).

96   *In the British television documentary:* See *Hypnosis on Trial*, produced by M. Barnes (1982) for the British Broadcasting Corporation.

97   *Dr. Herbert Spiegel:* See *Trance on Trial*, by A. Scheflin (1989, Guilford Press); and "Hypnosis and Evidence: Help or Hindrance?" by H. Spiegel, in the *Annals of the New York Academy of Sciences* (1980).

98   *Further research is showing:* See "Pseudomemory in Hypnotized and Task-Motivated Subjects," by J. Weekes, S. Lynn, J. Green, and J. Brentar, in the *Journal of Abnormal Psychology* (1992); "Reality vs. Suggestion: Pseudomemory in Hypnotizable and

Simulating Subjects," by S. Lynn, J. Weekes, and M. Milano, in the *Journal of Abnormal Psychology* (1980); and "Hypnosis and Suggested Pseudomemory: The Relevance of Test Context," by K. McConkey, L. Labelle, B. Bibb, and R. Bryant, in the *Australian Journal of Psychology* (1990).

98   *In many studies:* See "Pseudomemory in Hypnotized and Task-Motivated Subjects," by J. Weekes, S. Lynn, J. Green, and J. Brentar, in the *Journal of Abnormal Psychology* (1992); "Hypnotically Created Memory Among Highly Hypnotizable Subjects," by J. R. Laurence and C. Perry, in *Science* (1983); and "Duality, Dissociation and Memory Creation in Highly Hypnotizable Subjects," by J. R. Laurence, R. Nadon, H. Nogrady, and C. Perry, in the *International Journal of Clinical and Experimental Hypnosis* (1986).

98   *Critics of this type:* See "The False Memory Debate: Social Science or Social Backlash?" by J. Herman and M. Harvey, in the *Harvard Mental Health Letter* (April 1993); and "Concerns About the Application of Research Findings: The Issue of Ecological Validity," by J. Yuille and G. Wells, in J. Doris (ed.), *The Suggestibility of Children's Recollections* (1991, American Psychological Association).

101   *People want to alleviate confusion:* See *The Social Animal,* by E. Aronson (1992, Freeman & Co.), and *A Theory of Cognitive Dissonance,* by L. Festinger (1957, Stanford University Press).

102   *People have a strong desire:* See *The Social Animal,* by E. Aronson (1992, Freeman & Co.).

103   *Milgram's experiment:* See *Obedience to Authority,* by S. Milgram (1974, Harper & Row).

105   *One of the most potent forms:* See *Trancework: An Introduction to the Practice of Clinical Hypnosis,* by M. Yapko (1990, Brunner/Mazel).

107   *One of the more interesting pieces:* See *Social Psychology,* by J. Goldstein (1980, Academic Press), and *Understanding Social Psychology,* by S. Worcher and J. Cooper (1979, Dorsey Press).

108   *Here's a positive example:* See *Cognitive Therapy and the Emotional Disorders,* by A. Beck (1976, International Universities Press), and *Cognitive Therapy of Depression,* by A. Beck, J. Rush, B. Shaw, and G. Emery (1979, Guilford Press).

CHAPTER 5

Page 114   *Partly we have Sigmund Freud to thank:* See *Secret Survivors,* by E. Blume (1990, John Wiley & Sons); "Incest Resolution Therapy and the Objectification of Sexual Abuse," by J. Haaken and A. Schlaps, in *Psychotherapy* (1991); *The Assault on Truth: Freud's Suppression of the Seduction Theory,* by J. Masson (1984, Farrar, Straus, and Giroux); and *Freudian Fraud,* by E. Torrey (1992, HarperCollins).

115   *Therapists are now obliged:* See *True and False Accusations of Child Sex Abuse,* by R. Gardner (1992, Creative Therapeutics); *Sex Abuse Hysteria,* by R. Gardner (1991, Creative Therapeutics); and *Wounded Innocents,* by R. Wexler (1990, Prometheus Books).

117   *To better understand:* See "Beware the Incest-Survivor Machine," by C. Tavris, in *The New York Times* (January 3, 1993); *Secret Survivors,* by E. Blume (1990, John Wiley & Sons); *Repressed Memories,* by R. Fredrickson (1992, Fireside); and *The Courage to Heal,* by E. Bass and L. Davis (1988, Harper & Row).

118   *One prominent therapist:* See ABC News *PrimeTime Live,* aired January 7, 1993 ("Devilish Deeds," Transcript #279).

122   *It has been frequently stated:* See "Is Childhood Sexual Abuse a Risk Factor for Bulimia Nervosa?" by H.

Pope and J. Hudson, in the *American Journal of Psychiatry* (1992); and *The Evolution of Consciousness*, by R. Ornstein (1991, Prentice-Hall).

124 *The technique involved:* See "The Reality of Repressed Memories," by E. Loftus, in *American Psychologist* (1993).

126 *People don't just join the Moonies:* See *Combating Cult Mind Control*, by S. Hassan (1990, Park Street Press); and "Cults and Zealous Self-Help Movements: A Psychiatric Perspective," by M. Galanter, in *The American Journal of Psychiatry* (1990).

CHAPTER 6

Page 132 *We might just as well ask:* See *Cults: Faith, Healing and Coercion*, by M. Galanter (1989, Oxford); *Combating Cult Mind Control*, by S. Hassan (1990, Park Street Press); and the *Social Animal*, by E. Aronson (1992, Freeman).

133 *The branch of psychology:* See *Understanding Social Psychology*, by S. Worchel and J. Cooper (1983, Dorsey), and *Social Psychology*, by D. Sears, L. Peplau, J. Freedman, and S. Taylor (1988, Prentice-Hall).

134 *One of the most dramatic examples:* See "Inadvertent Hypnosis During Interrogation: False Confession Due to Dissociative State, Mis-Identified Multiple Personality and the Satanic Cult Hypothesis," by R. Ofshe, in the *International Journal of Clinical and Experimental Hypnosis* (1992), and "Remembering Satan, Parts I & II," by L. Wright, in *The New Yorker* (May 17 and May 24, 1993).

137 *There, in a grocery store:* See "Crybabies: Eternal Victims," by J. Birnbaum, in *Time* (August 1991).

139 *The widespread result:* See *We've Had a Hundred Years of Psychotherapy and the World's Getting Worse*, by J.

Hillman and M. Ventura (1992, HarperCollins).

141 *Walter Olson:* See *The Litigation Explosion,* by W. Olson (1991, NAL-Dutton).

141 *Turning people into victims:* See *The Diseasing of America,* by S. Peeles (1985, Lexington Books); *I'm Dysfunctional, You're Dysfunctional,* by W. Kaminer (1993, Vintage Books); and "Recovery Movement Makes Us All Victims, Say Its Critics," by M. Muro, in the San Diego *Union-Tribune* (May 24, 1992).

142 *I doubt there has been any greater casualty:* See *Family Therapy: An Overview,* by I. Goldenberg and H. Goldenberg (1985, Brooks/Cole); and *Divorce-Busting,* by M. Weiner-Davis (1992, Summit Books).

143 *Is it coincidence:* See "Long-Delayed Memories of Abuse: True Recall or Artifacts of Therapy?" by L. Orange, in *Clinical Psychiatry News* (March 1993).

145 *In this culture of blame:* See "PT Stats: Mentally Unhealthy," in *Psychology Today* (March/April 1993).

145 *The "recovery movement:"* See *Bradshaw On: The Family,* by J. Bradshaw (1988, Health Communications, Inc.).

149 *Consider the comments:* See ABC News *PrimeTime Live,* aired January 7, 1993 ("Devilish Deeds," Transcript #279).

150 *At the individual level:* See "Historical versus Narrative Truth: Clarifying the Role of Exogenous Trauma in the Etiology of MPD and Its Variants," by G. Ganaway, in *Dissociation* (1989).

CHAPTER 7

Page 157 *How many cases:* See "Recovery and Verification of Memories of Childhood Sexual Trauma," by J. Herman and E. Schatzow, in *Psychoanalytic Psychology* (1987); and "The Reality of Repressed Memories," by E. Loftus, in *American Psychologist* (1993).

157 *Determining the "truth"*: See *Hidden Memories*, by R.
Baker (1992, Prometheus Books), *Sex Abuse Hysteria*, by R. Gardner (1991, Creative Therapeutics);
and *Wounded Innocents*, by R. Wexler (1990,
Prometheus Books).

159 *No one knows*: See "A Question of Abuse," by N.
Wartik, in *American Health* (May 1993).

161 *Studies report conflicting conclusions*: See "Recovery
and Verification of Memories of Childhood Sexual
Trauma," by J. Herman and E. Schatzow, in *Psychoanalytic Psychology* (1987); "Memories of Childhood
Sexual Abuse: Remembering and Repressing," by E.
Loftus, S. Polonsky, and M. Fullilove, unpublished
manuscript, University of Washington and Columbia
University School of Public Health (1993); "What
Happens to Early Memories of Trauma? A Study of
20 Children Under Age Five at the Time of Documented Traumatic Events," by L. Terr, in the *Journal
of the American Academy of Child and Adolescent Psychiatry* (1988); and "Why Do Traumatic Experiences
Sometimes Produce Good Memory (Flashbulbs) and
Sometimes No Memory (Repression)?" by E. Loftus
and C. Kaufman, in E. Winograd and U. Neisser
(eds.), *Affect and Accuracy in Recall: Studies of Flashbulb Memories* (1992, Cambridge University Press);
Secret Survivors by E. Sue Blume (1990, John Wiley
& Sons).

162 *As we have noted*: See "Studies Reveal Suggestibility
of Very Young as Witnesses," by D. Goleman, in *The
New York Times* (June 11, 1993).

163 *Two researchers*: See "Assessment of Children's
Statements of Sexual Abuse," by D. Raskin and P.
Esplin, in J. Doris (ed.), *The Suggestibility of Children's Recollections* (1991, American Psychological
Association).

169   *Doubt is perceived as the enemy:* See *Repressed Memories,* by R. Fredrickson (1992, Fireside).

173   *Perhaps suprisingly:* See "One on One with John Bradshaw," by J. Mitchell in *Changes* (April 1993).

174   *The divergence of opinion:* See "Studies Reveal Suggestibility of Very Young as Witnesses," by D. Goleman, in *The New York Times* (June 11, 1993); and *True and False Accusations of Child Sex Abuse,* by R. Gardner (1992, Creative Therapeutics).

CHAPTER 8

Page 193   *As of this writing:* See *Sonya Live* (television program), guest attorney H. MacLean (July 19, 1993); "Buried Memories, Broken Families," by S. Salter, in the *San Francisco Examiner* (April 4–9, 1993); and *The Courage to Heal,* by E. Bass and L. Davis (1988, Harper & Row).

CHAPTER 9

Page 197   *The headline read:* See "Alleged Murder-Plot Target Says He's Victim of 'Memory' Therapy," by J. Okerblom in the San Diego *Union-Tribune* (December 15, 1992).

199   *To complicate matters:* See "Haunting Accusations," by J. Okerblom and M. Sauer, in the San Diego *Union-Tribune* (September 13–15, 1992).

200   *A Florida teacher:* See "Plaintiffs Slip and Fall into Defendants' Role," by B. Callahan, in the San Diego *Union-Tribune* (April 10, 1993).

208   *One commonly expressed piece of information:* See "Resolving Childhood Trauma," by L. Finney, in AHP *Forum* (March/April 1993); and "Dangerous Obsession," by C. Safran, in *McCall's* (June 1993).

209   *When I say build coping resources:* See *Resolving Sexual Abuse,* by Y. Dolan (1991, Norton).

217   *I would encourage you* not *to:* See "The Seductions of Memory," by M. Yapko, in *Family Therapy Networker* (September/October 1993).

CHAPTER 10

Page 222   *The report was called:* See CNN "Special Assignment," aired May 3, 1993, ("Guilt by Memory," Transcript #302, Segment #1).

225   *What started out as a local San Diego news story:* See "When Authorities Browbeat Children into a Lie," by N. Hentoff, in *The Washington Post* (December 26, 1992).

BIBLIOGRAPHY

Aronson, E. (1992). *The Social Animal* (6th ed.,). San Francisco: W.H. Freeman and Co.

August, R. and Foreman, B. (1989). "A Comparison of Sexually Abused and Nonsexually Abused Children's Behavioral Responses to Anatomically Correct Dolls." *Child Psychiatry and Human Development, 20,* 39–47.

Baker, R. (1992). *Hidden Memories.* Buffalo, NY: Prometheus Books.

Barclay, C. and Wellman, H. (1986). "Accuracies and Inaccuracies in Autobiographical Memory." *Journal of Memory and Language, 25,* 93–103.

Bass, E. and Davis, L. (1988). *The Courage to Heal: Women Healing from Sexual Abuse.* New York: Harper & Row.

Baxter, J. (1990). "The Suggestibility of Child Witnesses: A Review." *Journal of Applied Cognitive Psychology, 3,* 1–15.

Beck, A. (1976). *Cognitive Therapy and the Emotional Disorders.* New York: International Universities Press.

Beck, A., Rush, J., Shaw, B., and Emery, G. (1979). *Cognitive Therapy of Depression.* New York: Guilford.

Belli, R. (1989). "Influences of Misleading Postevent Information: Misinformation Interference and Acceptance." *Journal of Experimental Psychology: General, 118,* 72–85.

Blume, E. (1990). *Secret Survivors: Uncovering Incest and Its Aftereffects in Women.* New York: John Wiley & Sons.

Bohannon, J. (1988). "Flashbulb Memories for the Space Shuttle Disaster: A Tale of Two Theories. *Cognition, 29,* 179–96.

Bonanno, G. (1990). "Remembering and Psychotherapy." *Psychotherapy, 27,* 175–86.

Bower, G. (1981). "Mood and Memory." *American Psychologist 36,* 129–48.

Bowers, J. and Bekerian, D. (1984). "When Will Postevent Information Distort Eyewitness Testimony?" *Journal of Applied Psychology, 69,* 466–72.

Brainerd, C. and Ornstein, P. (1991). "Children's Memory for Witnessed Events: the Developmental Backdrop." In J. Doris (ed.), *The Suggestibility of Children's Recollections* (pp. 10–20). Washington, D.C.: American Psychological Association.

Bransford, J. (1979). *Human Cognition: Learning, Understanding and Remembering.* Belmont, CA: Wadsworth.

Brewin, C., Andrews, B., and Gotlib, I. (in press). Psychopathology and Early Experience: A Reappraisal of Retrospective Reports. *Psychological Bulletin.*

Briere, J. (1989). *Therapy for Adults Molested as Children: Beyond Survival.* New York: Springer Publishing Co.

————. (1992). "Methodological Issues in the Study of Sexual Abuse Effects. *Journal of Consulting and Clinical Psychology, 60,* 196–203.

Briere, J. and Conte, J. (1993). "Self-Reported Amnesia for Abuse in Adults Molested as Children." *Journal of Traumatic Stress, 6,* 21–31.

Bruhn, A. (1990). *Earliest Childhood Memories, Vol. 1: Theory and Application to Clinical Practice.* New York: Praeger.

Calof, D. (1993, September/October). "Facing the Truth about False Memory." *Family Therapy Networker, 17,* 5, 39–45.

Campbell, T. (1992). "Therapeutic Relationships and Iatrogenic Outcomes: The Blame and Change Maneuver in Psychotherapy. *Psychotherapy, 29,* 474–80.

Ceci, S. (1991). "Some Overarching Issues in the Child Suggestibility Debate." In J. Doris (ed.), *The Suggestibility of Children's Recollections.* Washington, D.C.: American Psychological Association.

Ceci, S., Leichtman, M., and Nightingale, N. (1993). "Age Differences in Suggestibility." In D. Cicchetti and S. Toth (eds.), *Child Abuse, Child Development, and Social Policy.* (pp. 117–37). Norwood, NJ: Ablex.

Ceci, S., Ross, D., and Toglia, M. (1987). "Suggestibility of Children's Memory: Psycholegal Implications." *Journal of Experimental Psychology: General, 117,* 38–49.

Ceci, S., Toglia, M., and Ross, D. (1988). On "Remembering . . . More or Less." *Journal of Experimental Psychology: General, 118,* 250–62.

Cheek, D. (1959). "Unconscious Perception of Meaningful Sounds During Surgical Anesthesia as Revealed Under Hypnosis." *American Journal of Clinical Hypnosis, 1,* 101–13.

———. (1974). "Sequential Head and Shoulder Movements Appearing with Age Regression to Birth." *American Journal of Clinical Hypnosis, 16,* 261–66.

———. (1989). "An Indirect Method of Discovering Primary Traumatic Experiences: Two Case Examples." *American Journal of Clinical Hypnosis, 32,* 1, 38–47.

———. (1992). "Are Telepathy, Clairvoyance and 'Hearing' Possible in Utero? Suggestive Evidence as Revealed During Hypnotic Age-Regression Studies of Prenatal Memory." *Pre- and Perinatal Psychology Journal, 7,* 2, 125–37.

Claridge, K. (1992). "Reconstructing Memories of Abuse: A Theory-Based Approach." *Psychotherapy, 29,* 243–52.

Coleman, L. (1992). "Creating 'memories' of Sexual Abuse." *Issues in Child Abuse Investigations, 4,* 169–76.

Council of Scientific Affairs (1985). "Scientific Status of Refreshing Recollection by the Use of Hypnosis: A Council Report." *Journal of the American Medical Association, 253,* 1918–23.

Courtois, C. (1988). *Healing the Incest Wound: Adult Survivors in Therapy.* New York: Norton.

Courtois, C. (1992). "The Memory Retrieval Process in Incest Survivor Therapy." *Journal of Child Sexual Abuse, 1,* 15–32.

Daro, D. (1988). *Confronting Child Abuse.* New York: Free Press.

Doe, J. (1991). "How Could This Happen?: Coping with a False Accusation of Incest and Rape." *Issues in Child Abuse Accusations, 3,* 154–65.

Dolan, Y. (1991). *Resolving Sexual Abuse.* New York: Norton.

Doris, J. (ed.) (1991). *The Suggestibility of Children's Recollections.* Washington, D.C.: American Psychological Association.

Dywan, J. and Bowers, K. (1983). "The Use of Hypnosis to Enhance Recall." *Science, 222,* 184–85.

Edwards, D. (1987). "The Dream as a Vehicle for the Recovery of Childhood Trauma." *Clinical Social Work, 15,* 356–60.

———. (1990). "Cognitive Therapy and the Restructuring of Early Memories Through Guided Imagery." *Journal of Cognitive Psychotherapy, 4,* 33–50.

Farmer, S. (1989). *Adult Children of Abusive Parents.* New York: Ballantine.

Festinger, L. (1957). *A Theory of Cognitive Dissonance.* Stanford, CA: Stanford University Press.

Forward, S. and Buck, C. (1988). *Betrayal of Innocence: Incest and Its Devastation.* New York: Penguin Books.

Fredrickson, R. (1992). *Repressed Memories: A Journey of Recovery from Sexual Abuse.* New York: Fireside Books.

Ganaway, G. (1989). "Historical Versus Narrative Truth: Clarifying the Role of Exogenous Trauma in the Etiology of MPD and Its Variants." *Dissociation, 2,* 205–20.

Gardner, R. (1991). *Sex Abuse Hysteria: Salem Witch Trials Revisited.* Cresskill, N.J.: Creative Therapeutics.

———. (1992). *True and False Accusations of Child Abuse.* Cresskill, N.J.: Creative Therapeutics.

Glass, A. and Holyoak, K. (1986). *Cognition (2nd ed.).* New York: Random House.

Goldenberg, I. and Goldenberg, H. (1985). *Family Therapy: An Overview.* Belmont, CA: Brooks/Cole.

Goldstein, E. (1992). *Confabulations.* Boca Raton, FL: SIRS Books.

Goldstein, J. (1980). *Social Psychology*. New York: Academic Press.

Goleman, D. (1992, July 21). "Childhood Trauma: Memory or Invention?" *The New York Times*.

———. (1993, June 11). "Studies Reveal Suggestibility of Very Young as Witnesses." *The New York Times*.

Gordon, J. (1991). "The UFO Experience." *The Atlantic Monthly, 268*, 82–92.

Gudjonsson, G. (1992). *The Psychology of Interrogations, Confessions and Testimony*. Chichester: John Wiley & Sons.

Haaken, J. and Schlaps, A. (1991). "Incest Resolution Therapy and the Objectification of Sexual Abuse." *Psychotherapy, 28*, 39–47.

Harsch, N. and Neisser, U. (1989, November). "Substantial and Irreversible Errors in Flashbulb Memories of the Challenger Explosion." Poster presented at the Psychonomic Society Annual Meeting.

Hassan, S. (1990). *Combating Cult Mind Control*. Rochester, VT: Park Street Press.

Haverkamp, B. (1993). "Confirmatory Bias in Hypothesis Testing for Client-Identified and Counselor Self-Generated Hypotheses. *Journal of Counseling Psychology, 40*, 3, 303–15.

Herman, J. (1992). *Trauma and Recovery*. New York: Basic Books.

Herman, J. and Schatzow, E. (1987). "Recovery and Verification of Memories of Childhood Sexual Trauma." *Psychoanalytic Psychology, 4*, 1–14.

Hilgard, J. (1979). *Personality and Hypnosis: A Study of Imaginative Involvement (2nd ed.)*. Chicago: University of Chicago Press.

Hillman, J. and Ventura, M. (1992a). *We've Had a Hundred Years of Psychotherapy and the World's Getting Worse*. New York: HarperCollins.

Hillman, J. and Ventura, M. (1992b). "Is Therapy Turning Us into Children?" *New Age Journal, IX*, 2, 60–65, 136–141.

Holmes, D. (1990). "The Evidence for Repression: An Examination of Sixty Years of Research." In J. Singer (ed.), *Repression* and Dissociation: Implications for Personality, Theory, Psychopathology, and Health* (pp. 85–102). Chicago: University of Chicago Press.

Hornstein, G. (1992). "The Return of the Repressed." *American Psychologist, 47,* 254–263.

Howe, M. and Courage, M. (1993). "On Resolving the Enigma of Infantile Amnesia." *Psychological Bulletin, 113,* 305–26.

Huyghe, P. (1985, September). "Voices, Glances, Flashbacks: Our First Memories." *Psychology Today, 19,* 9, 48–52.

Kaminer, W. (1993). *I'm Dysfunctional, You're Dysfunctional.* New York: Vintage Books.

Kihlstrom, J. and Evans, F. (1979). "Memory Retrieval Processes During Posthypnotic Amnesia." In J. Kihlstrom and F. Evans (eds.), *Functional Disorders of Memory* (pp. 179–218). Hillsdale, N.J.: Erlbaum.

Kihlstrom, J. and Harackiewicz, J. (1982). "The Earliest Recollection: A New Survey." *Journal of Personality, 50,* 135–48.

Klatzky, R. and Ederlyi, M. (1985). "The Response Criterion Problem in Tests of Hypnosis and Memory." *International Journal of Clinical and Experimental Hypnosis, 33,* 3, 246–57.

Kline, M. and Gaze, H. (1951). "The Use of Projective Drawing Technique in the Investigation of Hypnotic Age Regression and Progression." *British Journal of Medical Hypnosis, 3,* 10–21.

Kluft, R. (ed.) (1990). *Incest-Related Syndromes of Adult Psychopathology.* Washington, D.C.: American Psychiatric Press.

Labelle, L., Laurence, J.-R., Nadon, R., and Perry, C. (1990). "Hypnotizability, Preference for an Imagic Cognitive Style and Memory Creation in Hypnosis." *Journal of Abnormal Psychology, 99,* 222–28.

Laurence, J.-R., Nadon, R., Nogrady, H., and Perry, C. (1986). "Duality, Dissociation, and Memory Creation in Highly Hypnotizable Subjects." *International Journal of Clinical and Experimental Hypnosis, 34* (4), 295–310.

Laurence, J.-R. and Perry, C. (1983). "Hypnotically Created Memory Among Highly Hypnotizable Subjects." *Science, 222,* 523–24.

————. (1988). *Hypnosis, Will and Memory*. New York: Guilford.

Lindberg, M. (1991). "An Interactive Approach to Assessing the Suggestibility and Testimony of Eyewitnesses." In J. Doris (ed.), *The Suggestibility of Children's Recollections* (pp. 47–55). Washington, D.C.: American Psychological Association.

Lindsay, D. (1990). "Misleading Suggestions Can Impair Eyewitnesses' Ability to Remember Event Details." *Journal of Experimental Psychology: Learning, Memory and Cognition*, 16, 1077–83.

Lindsay, D. and Read, J. (in press). Psychotherapy and Memories of Childhood Sexual Abuse: A Cognitive Perspective. *Applied Cognitive Psychology*.

Linton, M. (1982). "Transformation of Memory in Everyday Life." In U. Neisser (ed.), *Memory Observed: Remembering in Natural Contexts* (pp. 77–91). New York: W.H. Freeman.

Loftus, E. (1975). "Leading Questions and the Eyewitness Report." *Cognitive Psychology*, 7, 560–72.

————. (1979). *Eyewitness Testimony*. Cambridge: Harvard University Press.

————. (1980). *Memory*. Reading, MA: Addison-Wesley.

————. (1982). "Memory and Its Distortions." In A. Kraut (ed.), *The G. Stanley Hall Lecture Series*. Washington, D.C.: APA.

————. (1986). "Ten Years in the Life of an Expert Witness." *Law and Human Behavior*, 10, 241–63.

————. (1991). "Commentary: When Words Speak Louder than Actions." In J. Doris (ed.), *The Suggestibility of Children's Recollections* (pp. 56–59). Washington, D.C.: American Psychological Association.

————. (1991). "Made in Memory: Distortions of Recollection After Misleading Information." In G. Bower (ed.), *Psychology of Learning and Motivation*, Vol. 27 (pp. 187–215). New York: Academic Press.

————. (1993). "The Reality of Repressed Memories." *American Psychologist*, 48, 5, 518–37.

Loftus, E. and Hoffman, H. (1989). "Misinformation and Memory: The Creation of New Memories." *Journal of Experimental Psychology: General, 118,* 100–104.

Loftus, E. and Kaufman, L. (1992). "Why Do Traumatic Experiences Sometimes Produce Good Memory (Flashbulbs) and Sometimes No Memory (Repression)? In E. Winograd and U. Neisser (eds.), *Affects and Accuracy in Recall: Studies of Flashbulb Memories* (pp. 212–23). New York: Cambridge University Press.

Loftus, E. and Ketcham, K. (1991). *Witness for the Defense.* New York: St. Martin's Press.

Loftus, E., Miller, D., and Burns, H. (1978). "Semantic Integration of Verbal Information into a Visual Memory." *Journal of Experimental Psychology: Human Learning and Memory, 4,* 19–31.

Loftus, E. and Yapko, M. (in press). "Psychotherapy and the Recovery of Repressed Memories." In T. Ney (ed.), *Allegations in Child Sexual Abuse Cases: Assessment and Management.* New York: Brunner/Mazel.

Loftus, E. and Zanni, G. (1975). "Eyewitness Testimony: The Influence of Wording of a Question." *Bulletin of the Psychonomic Society, 5,* 86–88.

Lynn, S., Weekes, J., and Milano, M. (1989). "Reality vs. Suggestion: Pseudomemory in Hypnotizable and Simulating Subjects." *Journal of Abnormal Psychology, 98,* 137–44.

Masson, J. (1984). *The Assault on Truth: Freud's Suppression of the Seduction Theory.* New York: Farrar, Straus and Giroux.

McConkey, K., Labelle, L., Bibb, B., and Bryant, R. (1990). "Hypnosis and Suggested Pseudomemory. The Relevance of Test Context. *Australian Journal of Psychology, 42,* 197–206.

McConkey, K. and Sheehan, P. (1980). "Inconsistency in Hypnotic Age Regression and Cue Structure as Supplied by the Hypnotist." *International Journal of Clinical and Experimental Hypnosis, 28,* 394–408.

Milgram, S. (1974). *Obedience to Authority.* New York: Harper & Row.

Mingay, D. (1986). "Hypnosis and Memory for Incidentally Learned Scenes." *British Journal of Experimental and Clinical Hypnosis, 3,* 173–83.

Moss, D. (1988). " 'Real' Dolls Too Suggestive: Do Anatomically Correct Dolls Lead to False Abuse Charges?" *American Bar Association Journal, 24* (December 1).

Nash, M. (1987). "What, If Anything, Is Regressed about Hypnotic Age Regression? A Review of the Empirical Literature." *Psychological Bulletin, 102,* 42–52.

———. (1992). "Retrieval of Childhood Memories in Psychotherapy." Paper presented at the Annual Convention of the American Psychological Association, Washington, D.C.

Nathan, D. (1992, October). "Cry Incest." *Playboy, 39,* 10, 84–88, 162–64.

Neisser, U. (1982). *Memory Observed: Remembering in Natural Contexts.* San Francisco: W.H. Freeman.

———. (1991). "A Case of Misplaced Nostalgia." *American Psychologist, 46,* 1, 34–36.

Neisser, U. and Harsch, N. (1992). "Phantom Flashbulbs: False Recollections of Hearing the News about *Challenger.*" In E. Winograd and U. Neisser (eds.), *Affect and Accuracy in Recall: Studies of Flashbulb Memories* (pp. 9–31). New York: Cambridge University Press.

Nogrady, H., McConkey, K., and Perry, C. (1985). "Enhancing Visual Memory: Trying Hypnosis, Trying Imagination, and Trying Again." *Journal of Abnormal Psychology, 2,* 194–204

Ofshe, R. (1989). "Coerced Confessions: The Logic of Seemingly Irrational Action." *Cultic Studies Journal, 6,* 1–15.

———. (1992). "Inadvertent Hypnosis During Interrogation: False Confession Due to Dissociative State, Misidentified Multiple Personality, and the Satanic Cult Hypothesis." *International Journal of Clinical and Experimental Hypnosis, XL.,* pp. 125–56.

Okerblom, J. and Sauer, M. (1992, September 13–15). "Haunting Accusations." San Diego *Union-Tribune.*

Olio, K. (1989). "Memory Retrieval in the Treatment of Adult Survivors of Sexual Abuse." *Transactional Analysis Journal, 19,* 93–94.

Olson, W. (1991). *The Litigation Explosion.* New York: NAL-Dutton.

Orne, M. (1979). "The Use and Misuse of Hypnosis in Court." *International Journal of Clinical and Experimental Hypnosis, 27,* 311–41.

Ornstein, R. (1991). *The Evolution of Consciousness.* New York: Prentice-Hall.

Peele, S. (1989). *Diseasing of America.* Lexington, MA: Lexington Books.

Pettinati, H. (ed.) (1988). *Hypnosis and Memory.* New York: Guilford.

Piaget, J. (1962). *Play, Dreams and Imitation in Childhood.* New York: Norton.

Pillemer, D. and White, S. (1989). "Childhood Events Recalled by Children and Adults." *Advances in Child Development and Behavior, Vol. 21.* New York: Academic Press.

Poole, D. and White, L. (1991). "Effects of Question Repetition on the Eyewitness Testimony of Children and Adults." *Developmental Psychology, 27,* 975–86.

Pope, H. and Hudson, J. (1992). "Is Childhood Sexual Abuse a Risk Factor for *Bulimia Nervosa*?" *American Journal of Psychiatry, 149,* 450–63.

Poston, C. and Lison, K. (1990). *Reclaiming Our Lives: Hope for Adult Survivors of Incest.* New York: Bantam.

Putnam, W. (1979). "Hypnosis and Distortions in Eyewitness Memory." *International Journal of Clinical Hypnosis, 27,* 437–48.

Raskin, D. and Esplin, P. (1991). "Assessment of Children's Statements of Sexual Abuse." In J. Doris (ed.), *The Suggestibility of Children's Recollections* (pp. 153–64). Washington, D.C.: American Psychological Association.

Rich, C. (1990). "Accuracy of Adults' Reports of Abuse in Childhood." *American Journal of Psychiatry, 147,* 1389.

Bibliography

Rubin, D. (1986). *Autobiographical Memory*. Cambridge: Cambridge University Press.

Salter, S. (1993, April 4–9). "Buried Memories, Broken Families." San Francisco *Examiner*.

Scheflin, A. and Shapiro, J. (1989). *Trance on Trial*. New York: Guilford.

Sgroi, S. (1989). "Stages of Recovery for Adult Survivors of Child Sex Abuse." In S. Sgroi (ed.), *Vulnerable Populations: Sexual Abuse Treatment for Children, Adult Survivors, Offenders and Persons with Mental Retardation (Vol. 2)*. Lexington, MA: Lexington Books.

Sears, D., Peplau, L., Freedman, J., and Taylor, S. (1988). *Social Psychology*. New York: Prentice-Hall.

Sheehan, P. and Grigg, L. (1985). "Hypnosis, Memory, and the Acceptance of an Implausible Cognitive Set." *British Journal of Clinical and Experimental Hypnosis*, 3, 5–12.

Sheehan, P., Statham, D., and Jamieson, G. (1991). "Pseudomemory Effects Over Time in the Hypnotic Setting." *Journal of Abnormal Psychology*, 100, 1, 39–44.

Smith, M. (1983). "Hypnotic Memory Enhancement of Witnesses: Does It Work?" *Psychological Bulletin*, 94, 387–407.

Snyder, M. (1984). "When Belief Creates Reality?" in L. Berkowitz (ed.), *Advances in Experimental Social Psychology*, Vol. 18, (pp. 247–305). Orlando FL: Academic Press.

Snyder, M. and Swann, W. (1978). "Hypothesis-Testing Processes in Social Interaction." *Journal of Personality and Social Psychology*, 11, 1202–12.

Spiegel, D. (1989). "Hypnosis in the Treatment of Victims of Sexual Abuse." *Psychiatric Clinics of North America*, 12, 295–305.

Spiegel, D. and Cardena, E. (1991). "Disintegrated Experience: The Dissociative Disorders Revisited." *Journal of Abnormal Psychology*, 100, 3, 366–78.

Spiegel, H. (1974). "The Grade Five Syndrome: The Highly Hypnotizable Person." *International Journal of Clinical and Experimental Hypnosis*, 22, 303–319.

————. (1980). "Hypnosis and Evidence: Help or Hindrance?" *Annals of the New York Academy of Science, 347,* 73–85.

Sundberg, N., Taplin, J., and Tyler, L. (1983). *Introduction to Clinical Psychology.* Englewood Cliffs, NJ: Prentice-Hall.

Tavris, C. (1993, January 3). "Beware the Incest-Survivor Machine." *New York Times Review of Books.*

Terr, L. (1983). "Chowchilla Revisited: The Effects of Psychic Trauma Four Years After a Schoolbus Kidnapping." *American Journal of Psychiatry, 140,* 1543–50.

————. (1988a). "Anatomically Correct Dolls: Should They Be Used as a Basis for Expert Testimony?" *Journal of the American Academy of Child and Adolescent Psychiatry, 27,* 254–57.

————. (1988b). "What Happens to Early Memories of Trauma? A Study of Twenty Children Under Age Five at the Time of Documented Traumatic Events." *Journal of the American Academy of Child and Adolescent Psychiatry, 27,* 96–104.

————. (1990). *Too Scared to Cry: Psychic Trauma in Childhood.* New York: Harper & Row.

Toglia, M. (1991). "Commentary: Memory Impairment—It Is More Common than You Think." In J. Doris (ed.), *The Suggestibility of Children's Recollections* (pp. 40–46). Washington, D.C.: American Psychological Association.

Torrey, E. (1992). *Freudian-Fraud.* New York: HarperCollins.

Trepper, T. and Barret, M. (1989). *Systemic Treatment of Incest.* New York: Brunner/Mazel.

Trott, J. (1991). "The Grade Five Syndrome." *Cornerstone, 20,* 16–18.

Underwager, R. and Wakefield, H. (1990). *The Real World of Child Interrogations.* Springfield, IL: Charles C. Thomas.

Wagstaff, G. and Mercer, K. (1993). "Does Hypnosis Facilitate Memory for Deep Processed Stimuli?" *Contemporary Hypnosis,* (Vol. 10), 2, 59–66.

Wakefield, H. and Underwager, R. (1992). "Uncovering Memories of Alleged Sexual Abuse: The Therapists Who Do It. *Issues in Child Abuse Investigations, 4,* 197–213.

Watkins, J. (1989). "Hypnotic Hypermnesia and Forensic Hypnosis: A Cross-Examination." *American Journal of Clinical Hypnosis, 32,* 71–83.

Weekes, J., Lynn, S., Green, J., and Brentar, J. (1992). "Pseudomemory in Hypnotized and Task-Motivated Subjects." *Journal of Abnormal Psychology, 101,* 356–60.

Weiner-Davis, M. (1992). *Divorce-Busting.* New York: Summit Books.

Wexler, R. (1990). *Wounded Innocents: The Real Victims of the War Against Child Abuse.* Buffalo, NY: Prometheus Books.

Whitley, G. (1992). "Abuse of Trust." *D. Magazine,* January, 36–39.

Worchel, S. and Cooper, J. (1979). *Understanding Social Psychology.* Homewood, IL: Dorsey Press.

Wright, L. (1993a, May 17). "Remembering Satan—Part I." *The New Yorker,* 60–81.

———. (1993b, May 24). "Remembering Satan—Part II." *The New Yorker,* 54–76.

Wylie, M. (1993, September/October). "The Shadow of a Doubt." *Family Therapy Networker, 17,* 5, 18–29, 70–73.

Yapko, M. (1988). *When Living Hurts: Directives for Treating Depression.* New York: Brunner/Mazel.

———. (1989). "Disturbance of Temporal Orientation as a Feature of Depression." In M. Yapko (ed.), *Brief Therapy Approaches to Treating Anxiety and Depression* (pp. 106–118). New York: Brunner/Mazel.

———. (1990). *Trancework: An Introduction to the Practice of Clinical Hypnosis* (2nd ed.). New York: Brunner/Mazel.

Yapko, M. (1993, September/October). "The Seductions of Memory." *Family Therapy Networker, 17,* 5, 30–37.

———. (1993). "Are We Uncovering Traumas or Creating Them? Hypnosis, Regression and Suggestions of Abuse." In L. Vandecreek, S. Knapp, and T. Jackson (eds.), *Innovations in Clinical Practice* (Vol. 12, pp. 519–27). Sarasota, FL: Professional Resources Press.

————. (1994a). "Suggestability and Repressed Memories of Abuse: A Survey of Psychotherapists' Beliefs." *American Journal of Clinical Hypnosis*, 36, 3, 163–71.

————. (1994b). "Memories of the Future: Regression and Suggestions of Abuse." In J. Zeig (ed.), *Ericksonian Approaches: The Essence of the Story*. New York: Brunner/Mazel.

Yuille, J. and McEwan, N. (1985). "Use of Hypnosis as an Aid to Eyewitness Memory. *Journal of Applied Psychology*, 70, 389–400.

Yuille, J. and Wells, G. (1991). "Concerns about the Application of Research Findings: The Issue of Ecological Validity." In J. Doris (ed.), *The Suggestibility of Children's Recollections* (pp. 118–28). Washington, D.C.: American Psychological Association.

Zelig, M. and Beidelman, W. (1981). "The Investigative Use of Hypnosis: A Word of Caution." *International Journal of Clinical and Experimental Hypnosis*, 29, 401–12.

INDEX

abandonment, 19, 113–14, 144–45, 169
abuse, child:
  accusations of, *see* accusations of abuse
  case histories of, 23–26, 29–31, 35–36, 39–40, 108–10, 122–23, 155–56, 187–88, 190–91, 216, 219–20
  critical evaluation of, 27–29, 37, 38, 41
  emotional impact of, 21, 28, 178–79, 183, 185
  intuitive diagnosis of, 43, 118–19, 126, 128, 165
  investigation of, 155–76, 201–2, 216–17, 218
  long-term knowledge of, 31, 90, 157
  media coverage of, 17, 19, 32–33, 36–37, 41, 42–43, 79, 89, 90, 112–13, 118, 126, 130, 137–39, 148, 149–50, 197, 221–25
  myths about, 20–22, 41
  organizations for, 203
  perpetrators of, 29, 161–62, 181, 182–83, 184, 214, 215
  as political issue, 20
  potential for, 115–16
  prevalence of, 18–19, 114–15, 221

  public opinion on, 26, 28
  reality of, 21, 22, 33, 38, 100, 221
  reports of, 115–16
  secrecy of, 31, 90, 115–16, 157, 169–70, 183, 193
  as sexual fantasy, 114–15, 136, 150–51, 154, 211
  social impact of, 36–37, 41
  "specialists" in, 20, 33, 42–43, 114, 118–19, 160, 168, 171–72, 216
  survivors of, *see* survivors, abuse
  symptoms checklist for, 20, 27, 37, 107, 113–14, 117, 127, 148–49, 154, 164–65, 211, 227
  therapy guidelines for, 206–13, 218
accusations of abuse, 129–54, 177–96
  accused vs. accuser in, 130–31, 134, 177–79
  active neutrality in, 189–90, 192
  belief in, 129–31, 134–37, 149–50, 152, 153, 156–57, 190–91, 221–27
  child–parent relationship and, 143, 144–47, 154, 171–72, 182–84, 214
  confessions and, 29, 161–62, 181, 182–83, 184, 214, 215

Index

Index

Index

Index

CPSIA information can be obtained at www.ICGtesting.com

265455BV00002B/14/P